A Free Catholic Concise Liturgy

And Other Useful Writings

Alan R. Kemp

Hermitage Desktop Press

A Free Catholic Concise Liturgy

And Other Useful Writings

Alan R. Kemp

For more information please contact the publisher:

Hermitage Desktop Press
P.O. Box 167
Vaughn, WA 98394

ISBN: 978-0692435038

Printed in the United States of America

Table of Contents

ACKNOWLEDGMENTS

I wish to gratefully acknowledge the original version of *The Liturgy of the Liberal Catholic Church,* upon which foundation this concise liturgy was based. I also wish to acknowledge Archbishop Herman Adrian Spruit, Archbishop Meri Louise Spruit, Archbishop Lowell Paul Wadle, Archbishop Richard Gundrey, Father Francis (Mahieu) Acharya, and Dom Bede Griffiths, Brother Wayne Teasdale, and Peace Pilgrim, whose legacies I gladly acknowledge. In addition, numerous other sources were consulted, making the present volume possible.

PREFACE

"Ritual is older than thought, simpler and wilder than thought."

–G.K. Chesterton

"Ritual is to the internal sciences what experiment is to the external sciences."

–Timothy Leary

"Rituals contain the rules of right behavior towards those superhuman powers on which we depend all our life. These rules are generally incomprehensible to modem man. He is no longer able to produce within himself, even in a playful manner, the state of mind of a person who truly believes in the reality of those powers."

–Amaury de Riencourt

"The beauty of the ritual action is one of its essential properties for man has not served God rightly unless he has also served him in beauty."

–C.G. Jung

"Whatever may happen to Christianity it is essential that the ancient traditions of the Mass ... be preserved, and the churches of Catholicism continue to be the arena of such Sacred Operas as the Mass, their supreme and classic type ... Its external shell of superstition may fall away ... It will become clearly visible as the Divine Drama it is, the embodied presentation of the Soul's great adventure, the symbolic Initiation ..."

–Havelock Ellis

Likewise we extend our thanks to the late Patriarch of the Catholic Apostolic Church of Antioch–Malabar Rite, Herman Adrian Spruit; late Matriarch, Meri Louise Spruit; and to Bishop Charles Hampton of the Liberal Catholic Church, American Province, without whose lives of service and prayer, this *Concise Liturgy* book would be sadly impoverished. We also thank Archbishop Richard Gundrey, the former Presiding Archbishop of the Catholic Apostolic Church of Antioch, whose innovations in liturgy have inspired so many of us.

It is expected that this book will be periodically and variously improved, corrected, revised, and expanded, as prayerful men and women are moved by the Holy Spirit.

ABOUT THE ASCENSION ALLIANCE AND COMMUNITY OF ASCENSIONISTS

The Ascension is a spiritual, historical, event. The Ascension movement is a spiritual movement "without ceiling" or affiliation with any other established ecclesiastical body.

While the Ascension movement is born of the vision of a "Free Catholicism," a fledgling "Independent Catholic" movement, the "Emerging Church," and "Jewish Renewal," it is really a much larger stirring of Spirit that beckons all persons of faith to transcend old ways that no longer work and ascend to higher levels of consciousness and spiritual living. To use a metaphor from New Testament scripture: Don't put new wine into old wineskins.

In keeping with the wisdom of spiritual reflection, we can, however, say Ascension is open to exploring new insights in conversation with and respect for ancient traditions.

If your own Spirit resonates with what you're reading, perhaps you were already part of the Ascension movement and didn't even know it. If so, read on.

CHRISTIC

We are a part the one Mystical Body of Christ. We acknowledge Jesus, the Christ, as Emanuel, God incarnated in human form, as our founder, inspiration, living head, teacher, and eternal high priest. We

1

accept the historic creeds as divinely inspired, but we also also acknowledge they were often used to exclude rather than embace all the people of God. We uphold the great commandments of both Hebrew scripture and New Testament: love God with all you heart, mind, and strength; likewise, your fellow human beings, all of whom were created in God's divine image.

VISION OF A FREE CATHOLICISM

We see a Free Catholicism as a movement of Spirit endeavoring to break loose from old ways that no longer work; reclaiming the original blessing of the primitive, universal, Church. We are a mystical movement without ceiling, walls, or affiliation with any other ecclesiastical body. We do, however, lay claim to apostolic succession, the tradition in which bishops trace their consecrations, from bishop to bishop, in an unbroken line back to the original apostles.

INDEPENDENT CATHOLIC MOVEMENT

Independent Catholic churches are Catholic groups not in communion with the Roman Catholic Church, who hold valid apostolic succession for their bishops, and are not formally affiliated with other historic churches. Most trace their apostolic succession through bishops of the Old Catholic and Oriental Orthodox churches. There are over 100 such groups in the United States today.

Although the term Old Catholic was first used in 1853 to describe those Catholics belonging to independent see at Utrecht in the Netherlands, most scholars date the "modern" Old Catholic movement to the 1870s, after the First Vatican Council declared the Roman Catholic Pope infallible when speaking "ex-cathedra" on matters of faith and morals. These churches were supported by the independent Old Catholic Archbishop of Utrecht who ordained their priests and bishops. Later, they united more formally under the name Utrecht Union of Churches.

The Oriental Orthodox churches, sometimes called "Non-Calcedonian," include the Armenian, Assyrian, Coptic, and the Syrian "Jacobite" churches, which did not ratify the declarations of the Council of Calcedon, in 451 A.D.

The Independent Catholic movement came to Great Britain in 1908 when Arnold Harris Mathew was consecrated a bishop in the Old Catholic Church, which, incorrectly believed he had a significant following in the United Kingdom, and also that there would be a wave of clergy wanting to leave the Church of England as a result of Pope Leo XIII's declaration that Anglican orders were null and void. Mathew believed that Old Catholicism would provide a home for these disaffected clergy. However, the expected mass conversions never happened. Before breaking with the Union of Utrecht, however, Mathew consecrated several persons to the episcopacy, from whom a number of new churches quickly developed, including the Liberal Catholic Church, whose first bishop was James Wedgwood, consecrated by F.S. Willoughby, who in turn had been consecrated by Mathew.

The founding bishop and leader of the Ascension organization, was consecrated by bishops of the Catholic Apostolic Church of Antioch, who trace its

3

the own apostolic succession, or lineage, through both Old Catholic and Oriental Orthodox bishops.

EMERGING CHURCH MOVEMENT

The Emerging Church Movement is a Christian movement of the late 20th and early 21st century. Participants are variously described as evangelical, post-evangelical, liberal, post-liberal, charismatic, neocharismatic and post-charismatic. Participants seek a faith that will help them live authentic lives in what they believe to be a troubled "postmodern" world. Proponents often call the movement a "conversation" to emphasize its developing and decentralized nature, its vast range of standpoints, and its commitment to dialogue.

EMBRACING JEWISH RENEWAL

We embrace the oldest of Christian traditions, acknowledging that Jesus, the Christ, was a Jew. Not only this, but a pious Jew, steeped in his faith and culture, including its mystical traditions, like a child raised on mother's milk. The term Jewish Renewal describes the teachings and practices of a group of present-day Jews that is attempting to reinvigorate Judaism with mystical, musical, and meditative practices. It often includes Judaism's prophetic and mystical traditions. It brings kabbalistic and Hasidic theory and practice into a non-Orthodox, egalitarian framework, a phenomenon sometimes referred to as neo-Hasidism. Like Hasidic Jews, Renewal Jews often add ecstatic practices to traditional worship, such as meditation, chant and dance. In augmenting traditional ritual, adherents also borrow freely and openly from the mystical traditions of other faiths, e.g. Buddhism and Sufism. The movement's most

4

prominent leader was Rabbi Zalman Schachter-Shalomi.

SACRAMENTAL

We are sacramental. We hold that the sacraments are both visible signs, or a manifestations, of divine grace, and expressions of divine power that are made available to help us in life and in our spiritual growth. We make the sacraments of Holy Eucharist (Communion), Reconciliation (Penance), Holy Unction (healing of the sick), and Holy Matrimony available to all who seek them. Baptism is freely conferred as a rite of formal initiation into Christ's mystical body. Confirmation seals the commitment to a Christian way of life. Holy Orders is an initiation available to qualified candidates called to serve God and God's people.

CONTEMPORARY

We maintain that eternal truth cloaks itself in garb appropriate to the age, and that the outward expressions of religion should keep pace with human development. We do not shrink from new knowledge. Our form of Free Catholicism Renewal embraces ancient truth, sacred scripture, purposeful prayer, traditional liturgy, but strives to creatively explore new expressions of ritual, art, community-building, and healing.

FELLOWSHIP

Our church is a spiritual fellowship of sojourners on the spiritual path. We give ourselves and others encouragement to live revealed truth. To live the truth is to become ever more the Christ, the true Self, the source of real happiness and abiding fellowship.

LOVE CENTERED

We are part of a movement of love. We accept Saint John's testimony that God is Love. For us, Christ's ministry is the law of love: "Love the Lord, thy God, with thy whole heart, thy whole mind and thy whole strength; and love thy neighbor as thyself. This is the whole of the Law and the prophets." Saint Augustine epitomized Christian ethics in the precept, "Love and do as you will."

UNIVERSAL

We maintain that the Holy Spirit acts through pure channels everywhere, regardless of age, sex, race, creed or culture. There is only one true God, however this God is known or worshipped; hence, there is eternally only one holy universal Presence, regardless of the cultural form it happens to assume in a given time and place. We revere the saints, sages, and holy ones of all ages and places.

MYSTICAL

We are a mystical movement, keeping in mind the Old Testament words, "Be still and know I AM" - God. We honor a saying attributed to Christ, "The kingdom of heaven lies within you and outside you," and acknowledge that the great advancements in

6

spiritual truth is made by those who learn to look within. If God is Love, then it is through our love that we come to a real and abiding knowledge of God. For Christians, love is spiritual knowledge par excellence.

SPIRITUAL

We seek to draw back the veil, first to discover the deeper intellectual import and then the experiential dimension which is the true meaning of spiritual symbolism in scripture, ritual, liturgy and theology.

OPEN COMMUNION

We hold that a purpose of Christian Fellowship is to perpetuate the historical sacramental tradition as instituted by Jesus Christ. We maintain that the sacraments are channels of divine grace. Therefore, we make them easily available to all. Since the Eucharist puts us in communion with the Christ, it is a channel of Grace without parallel. Therefore, at our altars all reverent persons are welcome to receive communion.

OPEN HOLY ORDERS

Holy Orders are open to all qualified candidates. While we value the principle of the "priesthood of the laity," we also we recognize the importance of valid Holy Orders and professional preparation of clergy. Our solution is to make orders available to all qualified candidates who are called and chosen. Other than demonstrating educational aptitude and prior life experience that shows academic and spiritual evidence of the potential to successfully complete a program of priestly formation at the graduate level, there are no other restrictions.

We have developed a highly decentralized program of study that offers structured guidance and mentorship for those willing to undergo rigorous study and practice that may lead to ordination as a "barefoot priest" within the context of Free Catholic Renewal. We welcome students from diverse backgrounds and spiritual traditions. The Program may either supplement other studies or serve as the primary preparation for ordained ministry. Each candidate's formation process is supervised by a Formation Committee, including a Formation Director selected by the Program, the candidate, and at least one other mentor selected by the candidate, usually a clergy member, educator, spiritual director, counselor, or other individual poised to support and help the candidate. Those who achieve ordination must be prepared to support themselves as "barefoot priests" in the world. We are not able to provide financial support.

INTRODUCTION

In the Ascension movement, we tend to think of the ancient sacraments as physical manifestations of Divine Grace. We count seven of them, although we also recognize that there may be many other "sacramentals." The seven traditional sacraments in the Catholic tradition are: Baptism, Confirmation or Chrismation, the Eucharist or Divine Liturgy, Unction, Reconciliation or Penance, Matrimony, and Holy Orders. This Free Catholic Concise Liturgy is intended to be a useful resource on the Sacraments and sacramental of the Church.

STRUCTURE OF ALL RITUAL

Initiation

Cleansing

Commemoration

Administration

Benediction

Look for these elements in every rite and in daily life.

THE SERVICES OF PRIME AND COMPLINE

(Sanctification of Time: Morning & Evening)

These are services of prayer, rather than sacramental instances. Prime is the second of seven canonical hours, usually said about 6:00 a.m., and Compline is said just before retiring. They may be conducted, therefore, by anyone, privately or publicly.

The structure of both services is one of utmost simplicity ... a quiet, reverent simplicity. They help to nurture such a spirit in those who conduct or attend such services frequently.

The purpose of both services is to lead consciousness from any sense of separateness into a consciousness of trust, oneness, and a spirit of praise.

The general order, then, is as follows:

1. Invocation
2. Confiteor and absolution
3. Psalms and scripture lessons
4. Profession of faith
5. Prayers
6. Benediction

A short devotional service may be based on Prime or Compline by omitting the Bible readings, the second and third psalms, and the office hymn.

Although the outline remains the same, variety is introduced into this framework by the variety of Bible reading allowed, the selection of prayers used, and the inclusion of various hymns and spiritual songs.

A little history of these services may help you feel your participation in a great tradition. In an earlier time, in both great abbeys and in solitary hermitages, God-loving men and women who had dedicated their lives to prayer realized a need for rhythm and order in their devotional expression. As time went on, certain "hours" were established as times of prayer frequently through the day, each one a meditation dedicated to a particular facet of the Opus Dei, the Work of God.

At the time of the Reformation, two trends influenced these numerous "prayer hours." First, a strong trend toward simplification brought about a reduction of the frequency of the prayer hours; and, second, a strong desire to include all people in the work, whether they were in monasteries or not, placed special emphasis on some service of daily prayer. These two services evolved into our present form of Prime (Morning Prayer) and Compline (Evening Prayer).

So in these services you are uniting with an ancient tradition of deep devotional prayer, as exemplified in the chanting and praises of those who had vowed their whole lives to God-attunement. You can almost see the brothers and sisters of the convents and monasteries filing silently into their choir stalls to unite hearts and voices in the adoration of God, and the renewed offering up of their lives to His divine direction.

If you are musically inclined, you would do well to experiment with chanting one of these services in its entirety; and comparing the effects on consciousness with those which arise when the service is simply spoken.

PREPARATION FOR PRIME OR COMPLINE

Optional: Vest in alb-cassock and girdle or cincture (or just alb and cincture); and in the sanctuary slippers or shoes

Light altar candles. The form included below can be modified for use by a non-priest by replacing the priest's blessings with entreaties, and by making minor changes in language.

Though in no way necessary for this service, it may aid in elevating the mood and spirit of the hour if you cense the room where you will conduct the service; just a little portion of incense will suffice.

Select and mark with ribbon or other clear marker the Bible readings and/or prayers you are going to include in the service. You may use the Epistle and Gospel of the week, or any other selection from the lectionary. If you have the Liberal Catholic Liturgy, you may wish to include some of the fine and beautiful special prayers listed on pages 425 to 432. If you do not have this liturgy, you may wish to use the Lectionaries available through Roman Catholic or Episcopal sources.

In normal, ideal practice, the person leading Prime or Compline does not stand before the altar, but rather faces the altar from chair or prayer-desk set at one side of the altar, usually the epistle or right hand side. You may find this impractical or undesirable in your private sanctuary; in such a case, experiment with reasonable alternatives. In public or community services, it is far better to abide by the traditional forms, however.

To help set the tone for this simple service, you may wish to play a few minutes of inspiring, devotional music on your stereo or instrument before beginning.

PRIME (Morning Prayer)

All stand

INVOCATION

Priest: (Optional) The priest may recite in Hebrew the Shema, the traditional Judaic call to prayer. *(For the words to the Shema, see "A Eucharistic Liturgy for Peace and Ascension," which appears later in this book).*

In the name of God the Creator (or Father-Mother), the Word made Flesh † (or Son), and the Holy Spirit.
R: Amen.

Priest: Our help is in the name of God the Creator
C: Who has made heaven and earth

Priest: At morning and at evening will we praise God
C: For our hearts rest ever in his love

THE CONFITEOR (or Confession)

Priest: Let us now prepare ourselves in consciousness by asking forgiveness for our wrong doings and admitting our human imperfections. So, at this time in an act of humbleness and truth, let us pray together sincerely admitting our wrong doings and asking God to cleanse us.

All say together

All: **I admit to God, to the saints, and to all here present that I failed to love God and my neighbor as I ought to have, committing wrongs in thought, word, and deed, by what I have done and by what I have not done. I** acknowledge my failings and that I have missed the mark many times. I now seek God's forgiveness and ask blessed Mary, the angels, the saints, and you my brothers and sisters, to pray for me to the Lord our God.

Priest: May almighty God have mercy on us, forgive us for our wrong doings, and bring us all, in peace, to eternal spiritual life.

God the Creator (or Father-Mother), † Word made Flesh (or Son), and Holy Spirit, bless, preserve and sanctify you; the Lord in his loving kindness look down upon you and be gracious unto you; the Lord † free you from the burden of your wrong doings and grant you the grace and comfort of the Holy Spirit.
R: Amen.

THE FIRST PSALM *(1 Chronicles 23:30)*

With a small group, it may not be appropriate to say or sing the Psalm selection antiphonally. A simple reading of this or another suitable Psalm would be appropriate

Antiphon

(Right side) **You shall stand every morning to thank and praise the Lord**
(Left side) **at morning and likewise in the evening**

1.	*(Right side)* **O come, let us sing to the Lord**
	(Left side) **let us heartily rejoice in the strength of our salvation**

2.	*(Right side)* Let us come before his presence with thanksgiving
(Left side) and show ourselves glad in him with psalm

3.	*(Right side)* The sea is his and he made it
(Left side) and his hands prepared the dry land

4.	*(Right side)* He is the Lord our God
(Left side) and we are the people of his pasture and the sheep of his hand

(Right side) Glory be to God, the Creator (or Father-Mother), and to the † Word made Flesh (or Son)
(Left side) and to the Holy Spirit

(Right side) As it was in the beginning, is now and ever shall be
(Left side) world without end. Amen.

THE READING(S)

All stand or are seated and the epistle of the day is read by the priest, ministrant, or other appointed reader/lector.

At the conclusion of the reading

Reader:	This is the word of the Lord.
R:	**Thanks be to God**

After the epistle, the following psalm (or another) is sung or read.

THE SECOND PSALM *(Job 38)*

Antiphon

(Right side) **The morning stars sang together:**
(Left side) **and all the children of God shouted for joy**

1. *(Right side)* **My voice shall you hear in the morning, O Lord**
(Left side) **I will direct my prayer to you and look up**

2. *(Right side)* **I will sing of your power**
(Left side) **and praise your loving kindness between times in the morning**

3. *(Right side)* **In the evening and morning will I call**
(Left side) **and he will hear my voice**

4. *(Right side)* **The tenderness of the Lord is new every morning**
(Left side) **great, O Lord, is your faithfulness**

(Right side) **Glory be to God, the Creator (or Father-Mother), and to the Word made Flesh † (or Son)**
(Left side) **and to the Holy Spirit**

(Right side) **As it was in the beginning, is now and ever shall be**
(Left side) **world without end. Amen.**

GOSPEL READING

All: **Alleluia, Alleluia, Alleluia** *(Except during Lent, in which case an appropriate substitute is used)*

The people stand or sit as the gospel selection is read

When the Gospel is announced all say

All: **Glory to you, Lord**

When the Gospel reading is concluded

Reader: This is the Gospel of the Lord
All: **Glory be to you, Lord, Jesus Christ**

PROFESSION OF FAITH

It is customary that the profession of faith be one of the creeds, however, some Independent Catholic, Old Catholic, some churches within the worldwide Anglican communion, and many celebrants within our liberal tradition, prefer alternative affirmations, several of which are included among the professions of faith which are located at the back of this book. If one of these is selected, do so knowing that this diverges from Roman Catholic/Orthodox custom, wherein the recitation of the creed by the officiant establishes his/her credentials by proclaiming adherence to orthodoxy

The people are seated. The collection is taken, if any, after which the priest turns to the people saying

COLLECTS

The priest recites the collect for the day and other collects, if any. The number of collects used is traditionally set at one, three, or seven. The following two collects could serve as appropriate additions to the collect for the day if three collects are chosen

Priest: O God, our Creator, who is almighty and everlasting, and who sustains us and the entire universe; we ask that you use your power to protect and sustain us today. Grant us the strength to overcome error and selfishness, that everything we do may be influenced by your grace, to seek truth and do that which is right.
R: Amen.

O Christ, we dedicate this new day to you, praying that your spirit, which dwells in us, will inspire everything we do. Teach us to see your life in all people and guide us in the path that leads to understanding, peace and goodwill.
R: Amen.

THIRD PSALM *(Psalms 30:5)*

Antiphon

> *(Right side)* **Heaviness may endure for a night**
> *(Left side)* **but joy comes in the morning**

1. *(Right side)* **The just shall be as the light of the morning**
(Left side) **even a morning without clouds**

2. *(Right side)* **As the tender grass springs from the earth**
(Left side) **as clear shining after the rain**

3. *(Right side)* **The righteous shall be clearer than the noonday**
(Left side) **they will shine forth, and be as the morning**

4. *(Right side)* **Their light shall break forth as the dawn**
(Left side) **Their righteousness shall go before them and the glory of the Lord shall be their reward**

(Right side) **Glory be to God, the Creator (or Father-Mother), and to the † Word made Flesh (or Son)**
(Left side) **and to the Holy Spirit**

(Right side) **As it was in the beginning, is now and ever shall be**
(Left side) **world without end. Amen.**

CONCLUDING PRAYER

Priest: Be with us, Lord, throughout this day, that in everything we begin, continue, and end, we express your inspiration. **R: Amen.**

Priest: Breath on us, O Spirit of God

C: **With your strength we can do anything**
Priest: May our hearts be filled with your love
C: **With your strength we can do anything**

Priest: Glory be to God, our Creator (or Father-Mother), and to the Word made Flesh † (or Son), and to the Holy Spirit.
C: **With your strength we can do anything**

BENEDICTION

Priest: Unto God's gracious love and protection we commit ourselves; may God † bless us and keep us; be with us and be gracious to us; may God shine the light of his grace upon us and give us his peace, today and evermore. **R: Amen.**

COMPLINE (EVENING PRAYER)

(All stand)

INVOCATION

Priest: (Optional) The priest may recite in Hebrew the, traditional Judaic call to prayer.

In the name of God the Creator (or Father-Mother), the Word made Flesh † (or Son), and the Holy Spirit.
R: Amen.

Priest: O God, open thou our lips
C: and from our mouths shall pour forth your praise

Priest: Our help is in the name of the Lord
C: who has made heaven and earth

Priest: At morning and at evening will we praise him
C: for our hearts rest ever in his love

THE CONFITEOR (or Confession)

Priest: Let   us   now   prepare   ourselves   in consciousness by asking forgiveness for our wrong doings and admitting our human imperfections. So, at this time in an act of humbleness and truth, let us pray together sincerely admitting our wrong doings and asking God to cleanse us.

All say together

All: I admit to God, to the saints, and to all here present that I failed to love God and my neighbor as I ought to have, committing wrongs in thought, word, and deed, by what I have done and by what I have not done. I acknowledge my failings and that I have missed the mark many times. I now seek God's forgiveness and ask blessed Mary, the angels, the saints, and you my brothers and sisters, to pray for me to the Lord our God.

Priest: May almighty God have mercy on us, forgive us for our wrong doings, and bring us all, in peace, to eternal spiritual life.

God the Creator (or Father-Mother), † Word made Flesh (or Son), and Holy Spirit, bless, preserve and sanctify you; the Lord in his loving kindness look down upon you and be gracious unto you; the Lord † free you from the burden of your wrong doings and grant you the grace and comfort of the Holy Spirit.
R: Amen.

FIRST PSALM *(Psalms 18:28)*

With a small group, it may not be appropriate to say or sing the Psalm selection antiphonally. A simple reading of this or another suitable Psalm would be appropriate

Antiphon

(Right side) You are my lamp, O Lord
(Left side) The Lord will lighten my darkness

1.   *(Right side)* Behold nightfall comes
   (Left side) and darkness covers the earth

2.   *(Right side)* But your candle, O Lord, shines upon my head
   (Left side) and by your light I walk through   the darkness

3.   *(Right side)* You have brought us out of darkness and out of the shadow of death
   (Left side) and broken our bonds asunder

4.   *(Right side)* Yea, the darkness is not darkness with you, the night is as clear as the day
   (Left side) the darkness and the light to you   are both alike

   (Right side) Glory be to God, the Creator (or Father-Mother), and to the † Word made Flesh (or Son)
   (Left side) and to the Holy Spirit

   (Right side) As it was in the beginning, is now and ever shall be
   (Left side) World without end. Amen.

FIRST READING

All stand or are seated and the epistle of the day is read by the priest, ministrant, or other appointed reader/lector

After the epistle, the following psalm is sung or read

SECOND PSALM *(1 Peter 2:9)*

Antiphon

(Right side) **He has called us out of darkness**
(Left side) **Into his marvelous light**

1. *(Right side)* **Who is there that walks in darkness**
    (Left side) **and has no light?**

2. *(Right side)* **Let them trust in the Lord**
    (Left side) **and stay upon our God**

3. *(Right side)* **To the godly there arises light   in the darkness**
    (Left side) **he is merciful, loving and righteous**

4. *(Right side)* **I am the light, says the Lord**
    (Left side) **he who follows me shall not walk in darkness, but shall have the light of life**

    (Right side) **Glory be to God, the Creator (or Father-Mother), and to the † Word made Flesh (or Son)**
    (Left side) **and to the Holy Spirit**

(Right side) **As it was in the beginning, is now and ever shall be**
(Left side) **world without end. Amen.**

GOSPEL READING

All: **Alleluia, Alleluia, Alleluia** *(Except during Lent, in which case an appropriate substitute is used)*

The people stand or sit as the gospel selection is read

When the Gospel is announced all say

All: **Glory to you, Lord**

When the Gospel reading is concluded

Reader: This is the Gospel of the Lord
All: **Glory be to you, Lord, Jesus Christ**

PROFESSION OF FAITH

It is customary that the profession of faith be one of the creeds, however, some Independent Catholic, Old Catholic, some churches within the world wide Anglican communion, and many celebrants within our liberal tradition, prefer alternative affirmations, several of which are included among the professions of faith located near the end of this book. If one of these is selected, do so knowing that this diverges from Roman Catholic/Orthodox custom, wherein the recitation of the creed by the officiant establishes his/her credentials by proclaiming adherence to orthodoxy

The people are seated. The collection is taken, after which the priest turns to the people saying

COLLECTS

The priest recites the collect for the day and other collects, if any. The number of collects used is traditionally set at one, three, or seven. The following two collects could serve as appropriate additions to the collect for the day if three collects are chosen

Priest: O God, our Creator, who is almighty and everlasting, and who sustains us and the entire universe; we ask that you use your power to protect and sustain us tonight. Grant us the strength to overcome error and selfishness, that everything we do may be influenced by your grace, to seek truth and do that which is right. Send forth your spiritual power so that our bodies will be kept safe from physical danger and our souls from all evil influences. **R: Amen.**

O Christ, teach us to see your life in all people and guide us in the path that leads to understanding, peace and goodwill. **R: Amen.**

NUNC DIMITIS *(Luke 2:28-32)*

The people may sit while the psalm is sung or said

Antiphon

> *(Right side)* **I will lay me down in peace and take my rest.**
> *(Left side)* **For it is you, Lord, only who lets me dwell in safety**

1. *(Right side)* Lord, now let your servant depart in peace
    (Left side) according to your word

2. *(Right side)* For my my eyes have seen
    (Left side) your salvation

3. *(Right side)* Which you have prepared
    (Left side) before the face of all people

4. *(Right side)* To be a light to lighten the gentiles
    (Left side) and to the glory of your people Israel

    (Right side) Glory be to God, the Creator (or Father-Mother), and to the † Word made Flesh (or Son)
    (Left side) and to the Holy Spirit

    (Right side) As it was in the beginning, is now and ever shall be
    (Left side) world without end. Amen.

CONCLUDING PRAYER

Priest: Be with us in our homes, O God, and let your holy angels dwell therein, to preserve us in peace; and let your blessing † rest ever upon us.
R: Amen.

Priest: Look, O God, upon this your family.
C: Into your hands I entrust my spirit
Priest: Hide us under the shadow of your wings
C: Into your hands I entrust my spirit

28

Priest: Glory be to God our Creator (or Father-Mother), and to the † Word made Flesh (or Son), and to the Holy Spirit.

C: Into your hands I entrust my spirit

BENEDICTION

Priest: Unto God's gracious love and protection we commit ourselves; may God † bless us and keep us; be with us and be gracious to us; may God shine the light of his grace upon us and give us his peace, today and evermore.
R: Amen.

AN INTRODUCTION TO THE EUCHARISTIC LITURGY OR MASS

The liturgy contained on the following pages is part of a tradition that goes back to the very beginnings of the Christian faith. In the Eastern Orthodox tradition the celebration of the Eucharist is most often referred to as "the Divine Liturgy." In the Western Catholic tradition the rite, which celebrates the Eucharist, literally translates as "blessing." This liturgy is more commonly referred to as the "mass." In the early days of the church when Christians gathered, a blessing or prayer was said over the wine and bread, the wine and bread, which scripture and the traditions of the church teach us become the Body and Blood of Christ.

The Eucharistic liturgy has evolved since those early days. The most common rite used in the Eastern Orthodox churches is named after St. John Chrysostom. While Chrysostom died in 407 (Attwater, 1983) the liturgy bearing his name first appeared some three centuries later (Davies, 1986). In the West a variety of masses were used in different places at different times, and there was no real uniformity until a standard, known as the "Tridentine Mass," was published in the sixteenth century, during the reign of Pope Pius V. Said in Latin throughout the world in Roman Catholic churches, it reigned supreme in the West until the Second Vatican Council.

The Ascension Alliance is an independent Catholic (universal) jurisdiction, which traces its heritage, or "apostolic succession," to the ancient churches in both the West and East. Its Western lineage is traced through the Liberal Catholic Church and the Dutch Old Catholic Church. Our Eastern roots are traced to the Syrian Orthodox Church at Antioch through the Indian branch, which is centered in the Malabar region of southern India.

When the Liberal Catholic Church adopted its liturgy it retained the form of the Tridentine Mass, translated it into the vernacular, and purged it of some of its condemnatory language, in an effort to make it more in keeping with the deep love and spirituality of the faith. According to Eric Taylor, the mass adopted by the Liberal Catholic Church, "Retained the full Tridentine mass, with its stately ritual undiminished but purified of all that was unworthy of Christian worship and incompatible with the teaching of Christ." A related liturgy was developed by Archbishop Lowell Paul Wadle, an esoterically minded primate. The Ascension Alliance is an open communtion. Its liturgy is intended as a guide, not a requirement. Affiliated communities are encouraged to develop their own creative liturgies. However, we have included a number of contemporary liturgies to serve as examples. Included are liturgies based on: the Taizé Eucharistic Liturgy, the New Zealand Prayer Book, and a beautiful liturgy developed by the Trappist community at Kurisumala, India, which harmonizes its native Indian culture with Christian Eucharistic worship. The Ascension Alliance is an open communion. The Eucharistic liturgies contained on the following pages, what we are referring to as Eucharistic Celebrations for Peace and Ascension, are an attempt to integrate the best of these rich and beautiful liturgies in a way that respects the Eucharistic tradition of the Christian Church.

THE LITURGICAL SEASONS

The liturgical year is divided into several seasons. The year begins with the first Sunday in Advent, the time of preparation for Christmas. The feasts celebrating the birth of Christ marks the onset of the Christmas season, which lasts until the first Sunday after the Epiphany. The period of time preceding the commemoration of the Passion of our Lord, the other major solemnity of the Church, marks the next major liturgical season. It begins on Ash Wednesday, the first day of Lent, which occurs on the Wednesday of the seventh week before Easter. Holy week begins with Passion Sunday, or Palm Sunday, which occurs on Sunday of the week immediately preceding Easter. The Easter season continues until Pentecost, which is celebrated seven weeks after Easter.

Other times of the year are now referred to as "Ordinary Time." There are two periods of Ordinary Time. The first period in Ordinary Time begins with the first Sunday after the Epiphany and ends with Ash Wednesday, the first day of the Lenten season. Because the time of Easter changes each year, the number of weeks in the first period of Ordinary Time ranges from four to nine. To assist the user, readings for nine Sundays is included in this concise liturgy. The second period of Ordinary Time begins after Pentecost and continues until the onset of the Advent season. There are a total of either thirty-three or thirty-four Sundays in Ordinary Time. The last Sunday in Ordinary Time is celebrated as the Feast of Christ the King. Because other feasts and holy days, which may fall upon a scheduled Sunday in Ordinary Time, take precedence, not all Sundays in Ordinary Time are necessarily celebrated.

Many churches in the "independent Movement" have followed, more-or-less closely, the liturgical calendar adopted by the Liberal Catholic Church. This is only fitting since we trace a major part of our heritage to this church. The Liberal Catholic liturgical calendar cycles the readings on an annual basis. For many years now, the Roman Catholic Church, the Anglican Communion, and other mainline bodies have adopted a three-year cycle, so as to include as many of the important parts of the Old and New Testament as possible. This New Catholic Concise Liturgy has opted to use this more complete three-year cycle of readings. So, the readings included here will be fairly consistent with the modern lectionaries adopted by the Roman and Anglican communions. They are identified in this concise liturgy as being for years A, B , or C.

Because of the variability in when movable feasts, and other special feasts, are celebrated there is a fairly wide divergence in the number of Sundays in Ordinary Time. If the number of weeks in Ordinary Time is thirty-four for the year, the number of the week after Pentecost is the number which follows the last Sunday before Ash Wednesday. If the number of weeks in Ordinary Time is thirty-three for the year, the number of the week which would otherwise follow Pentecost is omitted. Because of this complicated formula, it is important for users of this liturgy to consult with current liturgical calendars to ensure that the proper feast is celebrated. The information provided on the following pages will, however, give the reader a fairly good idea about when these are celebrated.

MOVABLE FEASTS

Advent Sunday   Nearest to 30 Nov, whether before or after

Septuagesima   Nine weeks before Easter

Sexagesima   Eight weeks before Easter

Quinquagesima   Seven weeks before Easter

Ash Wednesday   Wednesday preceding the first Sunday in Lent

Quadragesima   Six weeks before Easter

Refresh Sunday   Fourth Sunday in Lent or three weeks before Easter

Passion Sunday   Fifth Sunday in Lent or two weeks before Easter

Palm Sunday   One week before Easter

Maundy Thursday   Thursday preceding Easter

Good Friday   Friday preceding Easter

Holy Saturday   Saturday preceding Easter

Easter Sunday   First Sunday after the full moon which happens upon or next after the twenty-first day of March; if the full moon happens upon a Sunday, Easter day is the Sunday after.

Ascension day   Forty days after Easter

Pentecost   Seven weeks after Easter

Trinity Sunday   First Sunday after Pentecost or Whitsunday

Corpus Christi   Thursday next after Trinity
                          Sunday (celebrated on the
                          Sunday after Trinity Sunday)

A TABLE OF FEASTS AND HOLY DAYS

Date/Class/Vestment/Color

Immaculate Conception	Dec 8	White
Nativity of Our Lord	Dec 25 A	White
New Year's Day	Jan 1 B	White
The Epiphany	Jan 6 A	White
Baptism of Our Lord	Jan 13 A	White
Presentation in the Temple	Feb 2 B	White
The First Day of Lent	Movable D	Violet
Annunciation of Our Lady	Mar 25 A	White
Maundy or Holy Thursday	Movable A	White
Good Friday	Movable A	Violet
Holy Saturday	Movable B	Violet
Easter Day	Movable A	White
Ascension Day	Movable A	White
Corpus Christi	Movable A	White
Saint Alban, Martyr	June 22 C	Red
Saint John the Baptist	June 24 B	White
Saints Peter and Paul	June 29 B	Red
The Visitation of Our Lady	July 2 B	White
The Transfiguration	Aug 6 A	White
Assumption Of Our Lady	Aug 15 A	White
Nativity Of Our Lady	Sep 8 A	White
Triumph of the Cross	Sep 14 A	White
Saints Cosmas & Damian	Sep 26 C	Red
Michael and All Angels	Sep 29 A	White
Saint Francis, Confessor	Oct 4 C	White
All Saints' Day	Nov 1 A	White
All Souls' Day	Nov 2 B	Violet
Patron Saint	A	White or Red

Dedication of a Church	A	White
National Thanksgiving	B	White
Dedication St. John Nov 9	B	Red
Sundays in Advent		

First	A	Blue or Violet
Second	C	Blue or Violet
Third	B	Blue or Violet or Rose
Fourth	C	Blue or Violet

Sundays after Christmas

First	C	White
Second	C	White

Sundays after the Epiphany

First	C	White
Second	C	Green
Third	C	Green
Fourth	C	Green
Fifth	C	Green
Sixth	C	Green

Septuagesima	B	Red
Sexagesima	B	Red
Quinquagesima	A	Red
Sundays in Lent		

The First	B	Violet
Second	C	Violet
Third	C	Violet
Fourth	B	Rose *or* Violet
Fifth	C	Violet
Sixth (Palm Sunday)	A	Red

Easter Sunday	A	White

Other Sundays of Easter

Second	B	White
Third	C	White
Fourth	C	White
Fifth	C	White
Sixth	C	White
Seventh	C	White
Ascension Day	A	White
Pentecost or Whitsunday	A	Red
Trinity Sunday	A	White
Baptism of Lord	B	White
Christ the King	B	White
Sundays in Ordinary Time	D	Green*

Feasts commemorating martyrs, Red; feasts commemorating saints, White

THE PRECEDENCE OF FEASTS & HOLY DAYS

1.   Whenever two holy days fall upon the same day, the collect, readings and gospel used shall be those of the day which holds the higher rank (A being highest), but the collect of the other shall be recited after the collect of the day.

2.   Whenever two holy days of equal rank fall upon the same day, the celebrant shall decide which day he will celebrate; but the collect of the day not celebrated shall be recited after the collect of the day preferred.

3.   Class A festivals are celebrated for eight days; the eighth day is called the 'octave', the intermediate days within the octave'. A Sunday falling within the octave of such a festival is Class A, and (with the exception noted in rule 4) the collect, readings and gospel of the festival shall be used, but the collect of the Sunday shall be recited after the collect of the day. If the first day of a festival with an octave falls on a Sunday and is celebrated on that day the festival shall not be celebrated on the following Sunday, only the collect of the festival being said after the collect of the day.

4.   Whenever a feast or holy day of whatever class falls within the octave of a festival, the collect, epistle and gospel of the feast or holy day itself shall be used, but the collect of the festival shall be said after the collect of the day.

5.   The dedication festival of a church has an octave and takes precedence of all but the greatest feasts of the year.

6.   The festival of the patron saint of any church or country is for that church or country a feast of the rank of Class A and has an octave.

READINGS FOR SUNDAYS AND SELECTED OTHER HOLY DAYS

* YEAR A *

First Sunday of Advent

First Reading: Isaiah 2:1-5
Psalm: Psalms 122:1-2, 3-4, 4-5, 6-7, 8-9
Second Reading: Romans 13:11-14
Gospel: Matthew 24:37-44

Second Sunday of Advent

First Reading: Isaiah 11:1-10
Psalm: Psalms 72:1-2, 7-8, 12-13, 17
Second Reading: Romans 15:4-9
Gospel: Matthew 3:1-12

Third Sunday of Advent

First Reading: Isaiah 35:1-6, 10
Psalm: Psalms 146:6-7, 8-9, 9-10
Second Reading: James 5:7-10

Gospel: Matthew 11:2-11

Fourth Sunday of Advent

First Reading: Isaiah 7:10-14
Psalm: Psalms 24:1-2, 3-4, 5-6
Second Reading: Romans 1:1-7
Gospel: Matthew 1:18-24

Christmas Eve Readings for Vigil Mass for Christmas

First Reading: Isaiah 62:1-5
Psalm: Psalms 89:4-5, 16-17, 27, 29
Second Reading: Acts 13:16-17, 22-25
Gospel: Matthew 1:1-25

Readings for Midnight Mass for Christmas

First Reading: Isaiah 9:1-6
Psalm: Psalms 96:1-2, 2-3, 11-12, 13
Second Reading: Titus 2:11-14
Gospel: Luke 2:1-14

Christmas Readings for Mass at Dawn

First Reading: Isaiah 62:11-12
Psalm: Psalms 97:1, 6, 11-12
Second Reading: Titus 3:4-7
Gospel: Luke 2:15-20

Readings for Mass during the day

First Reading: Isaiah 52:7-10
Psalm: Psalms 98:1, 2-3, 3-4, 5-6
Second Reading: Hebrews 1:1-6
Gospel: John 1:1-18 or 1:1-5, 9-14

First Sunday After Christmas Feast of the Holy Family

First Reading: Sirach 3:2-6, 12-14
Psalm: Psalms 128:1-2, 3, 4-5
Second Reading: Colossians 3:12-21
Gospel: Matthew 2:13-15, 19-23

Second Sunday after Christmas

First Reading: Sirach 24:1-4, 8-12
Psalm: Psalms 147:12-13, 14-15, 19-20
Second Reading: Ephesians 1:3-6, 15-18
Gospel: John 1:1-18 or 1:1-5, 9-14

Epiphany of the Lord

First Reading: Isaiah 60:1-6
Psalm: Psalms 72:1-2, 7-8, 10-11, 12-13
Second Reading: Ephesians 3:2-3, 5-6
Gospel: Matthew 2:1-12]

Baptism of the Lord [1st Sunday After the Epiphany - Perpetually replaces the First Sunday in Ordinary Time]

First Reading: Isaiah 42:1-4, 6-7
Psalm: Psalms 29:1-2, 3-4, 3, 9-10
Second Reading: Acts 10:34-38
Gospel: Matthew 3:13-17]

Second Sunday in Ordinary Time

First Reading: Isaiah 49:3, 5-6
Psalm: Psalms 40:2, 4, 7-8, 8-9, 10
Second Reading: First Corinthians 1:1-3
Gospel: John 1:29-34

Third Sunday in Ordinary Time

First Reading: Isaiah 8:23--9:3
Psalm: Psalms 27:1, 4, 13-14
Second Reading: 1 Corinthians 1:10-13, 17
Gospel: Matthew 4:12-23 or 4:12-17

Fourth Sunday in Ordinary Time

First Reading: Zephaniah 2:3; 3:12-13
Psalm: Psalms 146:6-7, 8-9, 9-10
Second Reading: First Corinthians 1:26-31
Gospel: Matthew 5:1-12

Fifth Sunday in Ordinary Time

First Reading: Isaiah 58:7-10
Psalm: Psalms 112:4-5, 6-7, 8-9
Second Reading: First Corinthians 2:1-5
Gospel: Matthew 5:13-16

Sixth Sunday in Ordinary Time

First Reading: Sirach 15:15-20
Psalm: Psalms 119:1-2, 4-5, 17-18, 33-34
Second Reading: First Corinthians 2:6-10
Gospel: Matthew 5:17-37 or 5:20-22, 27-28, 33-34, 37

Seventh Sunday in Ordinary Time

First Reading: Leviticus 19:1-2, 17-18
Psalm: Psalms 103:1-2, 3-4, 8, 10, 12-13
Second Reading: First Corinthians 3:16-23
Gospel: Matthew 5:38-48

Eighth Sunday in Ordinary Time

First Reading: Isaiah 49:14-15
Psalm: Psalms 62:2-3, 6-7, 8-9
Second Reading: First Corinthians 4:1-5
Gospel: Matthew 6:24-34

Ninth Sunday in Ordinary Time

First Reading: Deuteronomy 11:18, 26-28
Psalm: Psalms 31:2-3, 3-4, 17, 25
Second Reading: Romans 3:21-25, 28
Gospel: Matthew 7:21-27

Ash Wednesday

First Reading: Joel 2:12-18
Psalm: Psalms 51:3-4, 5-6, 12-13, 14, 17
Second Reading: 2 Corinthians 5:20--6:2
Gospel: Matthew 6:1-6, 16-18

First Sunday of Lent

First Reading: Genesis 2:7-9, 3:1-7
Psalm: Psalms 51:3-4, 5-6, 12-13, 14, 17
Second Reading: Romans 5:12-19
        or 5:12, 17-19
Gospel: Matthew 4:1-11

Second Sunday of Lent

First Reading: Genesis 12:1-4
Psalm: Psalms 33:4-5, 18-19, 20, 22
Second Reading: Second Timothy 1:8-10
Gospel: Matthew 17:1-9

Third Sunday of Lent

First Reading: Exodus 17:3-7
Psalm: Psalms 95:1-2, 6-7, 8-9
Second Reading: Romans 5:1-2, 5-8
Gospel: John 4:5-42 or 4:5-15, 19-26, 39, 40-42

Fourth Sunday of Lent

First Reading: First Samuel 16:1, 6-7, 10-13
Psalm: Psalms 23:1-3, 3-4, 5, 6
Second Reading: Ephesians 5:8-14
Gospel: John 9:1-41 or 9:1, 6-9, 13-17, 34-38

Fifth Sunday of Lent

First Reading: Ezekiel 37:12-14
Psalm: Psalms 130:1-2, 3-4, 5-6, 7-8
Second Reading: Romans 8:8-11
Gospel: John 11:1-45 or 11:3-7, 17, 20-27, 33-45

Passion (Palm) Sunday

Readings for the Entrance
The Procession
Gospel: Matthew 21:1-11
Psalm 24
Psalm 47
or
The Solemn Entrance
Gospel: Matthew 21:1-11 or

The Simple Entrance

Readings for Mass
First Reading: Isaiah 50:4-7
Psalm: Psalms 22:8-9, 17-18, 19-20, 23-24
Second Reading: Philippians 2:6-11
Gospel: Matthew 26:14--27:66 or 27:11-54

Holy Thursday

Chrism Mass
First Reading: Isaiah
61:1-3, 6, 8-9
Psalm: Psalms 89:21-
22, 25, 27
Second Reading:
Revelation 1:5-8
Gospel: Luke 4:16-21

**Evening Mass of the
Lord's Supper**

First Reading: Exodus
12:1-8, 11-14
Psalm: Psalms 116:12-
13, 15-16, 17-18
Second Reading: First
Corinthians 11:23-26
Gospel: John 13:1-15

**Good Friday - No
Daily Mass**

Celebration of the
Lord's Passion

First Reading: Isaiah
52:13--53:12
Psalm: Psalms 31:2, 6,
12-13, 15-16, 17, 25
Second Reading:
Hebrews 4:14-16; 5:7-
9
Gospel: John 18:1--
19:42

Holy Saturday

**Readings for Vigil
Mass for Easter
Sunday**

First Reading: Genesis
1:1--2:2 or 1:1, 26-31
Psalm: 104:1-2, 5-6,
10, 12, 13-14, 24, 35
or Psalms 33:4-5, 6-7,
12-13, 20-22
Second Reading:
Genesis 22:1-18 or
22:1-2, 9, 10-13, 15-18
Responsorial Psalm:
Psalms 16:5, 8, 9-10,
11
Third Reading: Exodus
14:15--15:1
Psalm: Exodus 15:1-2,
3-4, 5-6, 17-18
Fourth Reading: Isaiah
54:5-14
Psalm: Psalms 30:2, 4,
5-6, 11-12, 13
Fifth Reading: Isaiah
55:1-11
Psalm: Isaiah 12:2-3,
4, 5-6
Sixth Reading: Baruch
3:9-15, 32--4:4
Psalm: Psalms 19:8, 9,
10, 11
Seventh Reading:
Ezekiel 36:16-28
Psalm: Psalms 42:3, 5;

43:3, 4,
or Isaiah 12:2-3, 4, 5-
6,
or Psalms 51:12-13,
14-15, 18-19
Epistle: Romans 6:3-
11
Psalm: Psalms 118:1-
2, 16, 17, 22-23
Gospel: Matthew 28:1-
10

Easter Sunday

First Reading: Acts
10:34, 37-43
Psalm: Psalms 118:1-
2, 16-17, 22-23
Second Reading:
Colossians 3:1-4,
or First Corinthians
5:6-8
Gospel: John 20:1-9

Second Sunday of Easter

First Reading: Acts
2:42-47
Psalm: Psalms 118:2-
4, 13-15, 22-24
Second Reading: First
Peter 1:3-9
Gospel: John 20:19-31

Third Sunday of Easter

First Reading: Acts
2:14, 22-28
Psalm: Psalms 16:1-2,
5, 7-8, 9-10, 11
Second Reading: First
Peter 1:17-21
Gospel: Luke 24:13-35

Fourth Sunday of Easter

First Reading: Acts
2:14, 36-41
Psalm: Psalms 23:1-3,
3-4, 5, 6
Second Reading: First
Peter 2:20-25
Gospel: John 10:1-10

Fifth Sunday of Easter

First Reading: Acts
6:1-7
Psalm: Psalms 33:1-2,
4-5, 18-19
Second Reading: First
Peter 2:4-9
Gospel: John 14:1-12

Sixth Sunday of Easter

First Reading: Acts 8:5-8, 14-17
Psalm: Psalms 66:1-3, 4-5, 6-7, 16, 20
Second Reading: First Peter 3:15-18
Gospel: John 14:15-21

The Ascension (40 Days After Easter) [In some dioceses celebrated on 7th Sunday in Easter]

First Reading: Acts 1:1-11
Psalm: Psalms 47:2-3, 6-7, 8-9
Second Reading: Ephesians 1:17-23
Gospel: Mark 16:15-20

Seventh Sunday of Easter

First Reading: Acts 1:12-14
Psalm: Psalms 27:1, 4, 7-8
Second Reading: First Peter 4:13-16
Gospel: John 17:1-11

Pentecost or Whitsunday

First Reading: Acts 2:1-11
Psalm: Psalms 104:1, 24, 29-30, 31, 34
Second Reading: 1 Corinthians 12:3-7, 12-13
Gospel: John 20:19-23

Trinity Sunday

First Reading: Exodus 34:4-6, 8-9
Psalm: Daniel 3:52, 53, 54, 55, 56
Second Reading: 2 Corinthians 13:11-13
Gospel: John 3:16-18

[In the U.S. - Corpus Christi

First Reading: Deuteronomy 8:2-3, 14-16
Psalm: Psalms 147:12-13, 14-15, 19-20
Second Reading: 1 Corinthians 10:16-17
Gospel: John 6:51-58]

Tenth Sunday in Ordinary Time

First Reading: Hosea 6:3-6
Psalm: Psalms 50:1, 8, 12-13, 14-15
Second Reading: Romans 4:18-25
Gospel: Matthew 9:9-13

Eleventh Sunday in Ordinary Time

First Reading: Exodus 19:2-6
Psalm: Psalms 100:1-2, 3, 5
Second Reading: Romans 5:6-11
Gospel: Matthew 9:36--10:8

Twelfth Sunday in Ordinary Time

First Reading: Jeremiah 20:10-13
Psalm: Psalms 69:8-10, 14, 17, 33-35
Second Reading: Romans 5:12-15
Gospel: Matthew 10:26-33

Thirteenth Sunday in Ordinary Time

First Reading: Second Kings 4:8-11, 14-16
Psalm: Psalms 89:2-3, 16-17, 18-19
Second Reading: Romans 6:3-4, 8-11
Gospel: Matthew 10:37-42

Fourteenth Sunday in Ordinary Time

First Reading: Zechariah 9:9-10
Psalm: Psalms 145:1-2, 8-9, 10-11, 13-14
Second Reading: Romans 8:9, 11-13
Gospel: Matthew 11:25-30

Fifteenth Sunday in Ordinary Time

First Reading: Isaiah 55:10-11
Psalm: Psalms 65:10, 11, 12-13, 14
Second Reading: Romans 8:18-23
Gospel: Matthew 13:1-23 or 13:1-9

Sixteenth Sunday in Ordinary Time

First Reading: Wisdom 12:13, 16-19
Psalm: Psalms 86:5-6, 9-10, 15-16
Second Reading: Romans 8:26-27
Gospel: Matthew 13:24-43 or 13:24-30

Seventeenth Sunday in Ordinary Time

First Reading: First Kings 3:5, 7-12
Psalm: 119:57, 72, 76-77, 127-128, 129-130
Second Reading: Romans 8:28-30
Gospel: Matthew 13:44-52 or 13:44-46

Eighteenth Sunday in Ordinary Time

First Reading: Isaiah 55:1-3
Psalm: Psalms 145:8-9, 15-16, 17-18
Second Reading: Romans 8:35, 37-39
Gospel: Matthew 14:13-21

Nineteenth Sunday in Ordinary Time

First Reading: First Kings 19:9, 11-13
Psalm: Psalms 85:9, 10, 11-12, 13-14
Second Reading: Romans 9:1-5
Gospel: Matthew 14:22-33

Twentieth Sunday in Ordinary Time

First Reading: Is 56 1:6-7
Psalm: Psalm 67
Second Reading: Rom 11:13-15, 29-32
Gospel: Mt 15:21-26

Assumption of the Virgin Mary into Heaven

First Reading: Revelation 11:19; 12:1-6, 10
Psalm: Psalms 45:10, 11, 12, 16
Second Reading: First Corinthians 15:20-26
Gospel: Luke 1:39-56

Twenty-first Sunday in Ordinary Time

First Reading: Isaiah 22:15, 19-23
Psalm: Psalms 138:1-2, 2-3, 6, 8
Second Reading: Romans 11:33-36
Gospel: Matthew 16:13-20

Twenty-second Sunday Ordinary Time

First Reading: Jeremiah 20:7-9
Psalm: Psalms 63:2, 3-4, 5-6, 8-9
Second Reading: Romans 12:1-2
Gospel: Matthew 16:21-27

Twenty-third Sunday in Ordinary Time

First Reading: Ezekiel 33:7-9
Psalm: Psalms 95:1-2, 6-7, 8-9
Second Reading: Romans 13:8-10
Gospel: Matthew 18:15-20

Twenty-fourth Sunday Ordinary Time

First Reading: Sirach 27:30--28:7
Psalm: Psalms 103:1-2, 3-4, 9-10, 11-12
Second Reading: Romans 14:7-9
Gospel: Matthew 18:21-35

Twenty-fifth Sunday in Ordinary Time

First Reading: Isaiah 55:6-9
Psalm: Psalms 145:2-3, 8-9, 17-18
Second Reading: Philippians 1:20-24, 27
Gospel: Matthew 20:1-16

Twenty-sixth Sunday in Ordinary Time

First Reading: Ezekiel 18:25-28
Psalm: Psalms 125:4-5, 6-7, 8-9
Second Reading: Philippians 2:1-11 or 2:1-5

Gospel: Matthew
21:28-32

Twenty-seventh Sunday in Ordinary Time

First Reading: Isaiah
5:1-7
Psalm: Psalms 80:9,
12, 13-14, 15-16, 19-
20
Second Reading:
Philippians 4:6-9
Gospel: Matthew
21:33-43

Twenty-eighth Sunday Ordinary Time

First Reading: Isaiah
25:6-10
Psalm: Psalms 23:1-3,
3-4, 5, 6
Second Reading:
Philippians 4:12-14,
19-20
Gospel: Matthew 22:1-
14 or 22:1-10

Twenty-ninth Sunday in Ordinary Time

First Reading: Isaiah
45:1, 4-6
Psalm: Psalms 96:1, 3,
4-5, 7-8, 9-10
Second Reading: First

Thessalonians 1:1-5
Gospel: Matthew
22:15-21

Thirtieth Sunday in Ordinary Time

First Reading: Exodus
22:20-26
Psalm: Psalms 18:2-3,
3-4, 47, 51
Second Reading: First
Thessalonians 1:5-10
Gospel: Matthew
22:34-40

Thirty-first Sunday in Ordinary Time

First Reading: Malachi
1:14--2:2, 8-10
Psalm: Psalms 131:1,
2, 3
Second Reading: First
Thessalonians 2:7-9,
13
Gospel: Matthew 23:1-
12

Thirty-second Sunday in Ordinary Time

First Reading: Wisdom
6:12-16
Psalm: Psalms 63:2, 3-
4, 5-6, 7-8
Second Reading: First
Thessalonians 4:13-17

or 4:13-14
Gospel: Matthew 25:1-13

Thirty-third Sunday in Ordinary Time

First Reading: Pvb 31:10-13, 19-20, 30-31
Psalm: Psalms 128:1-2, 3, 4-5
Second Reading: First Thessalonians 5:1-6
Gospel: Matthew 25:14-30 or 25:14-15, 19-20

Last Sunday in Ordinary Time Christ the King

First Reading: Ezekiel 34:11-12, 15-17
Responsorial Psalm: Psalms 23:1-2, 2-3, 5, 6
Second Reading: 1 Corinthians 15:20-26, 28
Gospel: Matthew 25:31-46

* YEAR B *

First Sunday of Advent

First Reading: Isaiah 63:16-17, 19
Psalm: Psalms 80:2-3, 15-16, 18-19
Second Reading: First Corinthians 1:3-9
Gospel: Mark 13:33-37

Second Sunday of Advent

First Reading: Isaiah 40:1-5, 9-11
Psalm: Psalms 85:9-10, 11-12, 13-14
Second Reading: Second Peter 3:8-14
Gospel: Mark 1:1-8

Third Sunday of Advent

First Reading: Isaiah 61:1-2, 10-11
Psalm: Luke 1:46-48, 49-50, 53-54
Second Reading: First Thessalonians 5:16-24
Gospel: John 1:6-8, 19-28

Fourth Sunday of Advent

First Reading: Second Samuel 7:1-5, 8-11, 16
Psalm: Psalms 89:2-3, 4-5, 27, 29
Second Reading: Romans 16:25-27
Gospel: Luke 1:26-38

Christmas Eve

Readings for Vigil Mass for Christmas
First Reading: Isaiah 62:1-5
Psalm: Psalms 89:4-5, 16-17, 27, 29
Second Reading: Acts 13:16-17, 22-25
Gospel: Matthew 1:1-25

Readings for Midnight Mass for Christmas

First Reading: Isaiah 9:1-6
Psalm: Psalms 96:1-2, 2-3, 11-12, 13
Second Reading: Titus 2:11-14
Gospel: Luke 2:1-14

Christmas

Readings for Mass at Dawn
First Reading: Isaiah 62:11-12
Psalm: Psalms 97:1, 6, 11-12
Second Reading: Titus 3:4-7
Gospel: Luke 2:15-20

Readings for Mass during the day
First Reading: Isaiah 52:7-10
Psalm: Psalms 98:1, 2-3, 3-4, 5-6
Second Reading: Hebrews 1:1-6
Gospel: John 1:1-18 or 1:1-5, 9-14

Feast of the Holy Family

Readings for Mass
First Reading: Sirach 3:2-6, 12-14
Psalm: Psalms 128:1-2, 3, 4-5
Second Reading: Colossians 3:12-21
Gospel: Luke 2:22-40 or 2:22, 39-40

54

Second Sunday of Christmas

First Reading: Sirach 24:1-4, 8-12
Psalm: Psalms 147:12-13, 14-15, 19-20
Second Reading: Ephesians 1:3-6, 15-18
Gospel: John 1:1-18 or 1:1-5, 9-14

[In the U.S. - Epiphany of the Lord

Readings for Mass
First Reading: Isaiah 60:1-6
Psalm: Psalms 72:1-2, 7-8, 10-11, 12-13
Second Reading: Ephesians 3:2-3, 5-6
Gospel: Matthew 2:1-12]

[Outside U.S. - Baptism of the Lord

First Reading: Isaiah 42:1-4, 6-7
Psalm: Psalms 29:1-2, 3-4, 3, 9-10
Second Reading: Acts 10:34-38
Gospel: Mark 1:7-11]

Second Sunday in Ordinary Time

First Reading: First Samuel 3:3-10, 19
Psalm: Psalms 40:2, 4, 7-8, 8-9, 10
Second Reading: 1 Corinthians 6:13-15, 17-20
Gospel: John 1:35-42

Third Sunday in Ordinary Time

First Reading: Jonah 3:1-5, 10
Psalm: Psalms 25:4-5, 6-7, 8-9
Second Reading: First Corinthians 7:29-31
Gospel: Mark 1:14-20

Fourth Sunday in Ordinary Time

First Reading: Deuteronomy 18:15-20
Psalm: Psalms 95:1-2, 6-7, 7-9
Second Reading: 1 Corinthians 7:32-35
Gospel: Mark 1:21-28

Fifth Sunday in Ordinary Time

First Reading: Job 7:1-4, 6-7
Psalm: Psalms 147:1-2, 3-4, 5-6
Second Reading: 1 Corinthians 9:16-19, 22-23
Gospel: Mark 1:29-39

Sixth Sunday in Ordinary Time

First Reading: Leviticus 13:1-2, 44-46
Psalm: Psalms 32:1-2, 5, 11
Second Reading: 1 Corinthians 10:31--11:1
Gospel: Mark 1:40-45

Seventh Sunday in Ordinary Time

First Reading: Isaiah 43:18-19, 21-22, 24-25
Psalm: Psalms 41:2-3, 4-5, 13-14
Second Reading: 2 Corinthians 1:18-22
Gospel: Mark 2:1-12

Eighth Sunday in Ordinary Time

First Reading: Hosea 2:15-17, 21-22
Psalm: Psalms 103:1-2, 3-4, 8, 10, 12-13
Second Reading: Second Corinthians 3:1-6
Gospel: Mark 2:18-22

Ninth Sunday in Ordinary Time

First Reading: Deuteronomy 5:12-15
Psalm: Psalms 81:3-4, 5-6, 6-8, 10-11
Second Reading: Second Corinthians 4:6-11
Gospel: Mark 2:23--3:6 or 2:23-28

Ash Wednesday

First Reading: Joel 2:12-18
Psalm: Psalms 51:3-4, 5-6, 12-13, 14, 17
Second Reading: 2 Corinthians 5:20--6:2
Gospel: Matthew 6:1-6, 16-18

First Sunday of Lent

First Reading: Genesis 9:8-15
Psalm: Psalms 25:4-5, 6-7, 8-9
Second Reading: First Peter 3:18-22
Gospel: Mark 1:12-15

Second Sunday of Lent

First Reading: Genesis 22:1-2, 9, 10-13, 15-18
Psalm: Psalms 116:10, 15, 16-17, 18-19
Second Reading: Romans 8:31-34
Gospel: Mark 9:2-10

Third Sunday of Lent

First Reading: Exodus 20:1-17 or 20:1-3, 7-8, 12-17
Psalm: Psalms 19:8, 9, 10, 11
Second Reading: 1 Corinthians 1:22-25
Gospel: John 2:13-25

Fourth Sunday of Lent

First Reading: 2 Chronicles 36:14-17, 19-23
Psalm: Psalms 137:1-2, 3, 4-5, 6
Second Reading: Ephesians 2:4-10
Gospel: John 3:14-21

Fifth Sunday of Lent

First Reading: Jeremiah 31:31-34
Psalm: Psalms 51:3-4, 12-13, 14-15
Second Reading: Hebrews 5:7-9
Gospel: John 12:20-33

Passion (Palm) Sunday

Readings for the Entrance
The Procession
Gospel: Mark 11:1-10, or John 12:12-16
Psalm 24
Psalm 47 or

The Solemn Entrance
Gospel: Mark 11:1-10, or John 12:12-16
or

The Simple Entrance

Readings for Mass

First Reading: Isaiah 50:4-7
Psalm: Psalms 22:8-9, 17-18, 19-20, 23-24
Second Reading:

Philippians 2:6-11
Gospel: Mark 14:1--
15:47 or 15:1-39

Holy Thursday

Chrism Mass
First Reading: Isaiah
61:1-3, 6, 8-9
Psalm: Psalms 89:21-
22, 25, 27
Second Reading:
Revelation 1:5-8
Gospel: Luke 4:16-21

Evening Mass of the
Lord's Supper
First Reading: Exodus
12:1-8, 11-14
Psalm: Psalms 116:12-
13, 15-16, 17-18
Second Reading: 1
Corinthians 11:23-26
Gospel: John 13:1-15

Good Friday - No Daily Mass

Celebration of the
Lord's Passion
First Reading: Isaiah
52:13--53:12
Psalm: Psalms 31:2, 6,
12-13, 15-16, 17, 25
Second Reading:
Hebrews 4:14-16; 5:7-
9
Gospel: John 18:1--
19:42

Holy Saturday - No Daily Mass

Readings for Vigil Mass for Easter Sunday

First Reading: Genesis
1:1--2:2 or 1:1, 26-31
Psalms 104:1-2, 5-6,
10, 12, 13-14, 24, 35,
or Psalms 33:4-5, 6-7,
12-13, 20-22
Second Reading:
Genesis 22:1-18 or
22:1-2, 9, 10-13, 15-18
Psalms 16:5, 8, 9-10,
11
Third Reading: Exodus
14:15--15:1
Psalm: Exodus 15:1-2,
3-4, 5-6, 17-18
Fourth Reading: Isaiah
54:5-14
Psalm: Psalms 30:2, 4,
5-6, 11-12, 13
Fifth Reading: Isaiah
55:1-11
Psalm: Isaiah 12:2-3,
4, 5-6
Sixth Reading: Baruch
3:9-15, 32--4:4
Psalm: Psalms 19:8, 9,
10, 11
Seventh Reading:
Ezekiel 36:16-28
Psalm: Psalms 42:3, 5;

43:3, 4, or Isaiah 12:2-3, 4, 5-6, or Psalms 51:12-13, 14-15, 18-19
Epistle: Romans 6:3-11
Psalm: Psalms 118:1-2, 16, 17, 22-23
Gospel: Mark 16:1-8

Easter Sunday

First Reading: Acts 10:34, 37-43
Psalm: Psalms 118:1-2, 16-17, 22-23
Second Reading: Colossians 3:1-4, or 1 Corinthians 5:6-8
Gospel: John 20:1-9

Second Sunday of Easter

First Reading: Acts 4:32-35
Psalm: Psalms 118:2-4, 13-15, 22-24
Second Reading: First John 5:1-6
Gospel: John 20:19-31

Third Sunday of Easter

First Reading: Acts 3:13-15, 17-19
Psalm: Psalms 4:2, 4, 7-8, 9
Second Reading: First

John 2:1-5
Gospel: Luke 24:35-48

Fourth Sunday of Easter

First Reading: Acts 4:8-12
Psalm: Psalms 118:1, 8-9, 21-23, 26, 21, 29
Second Reading: First John 3:1-2
Gospel: John 10:11-18

Fifth Sunday of Easter

First Reading: Acts 9:26-31
Psalm: Psalms 22:26-27, 28, 30, 31-32
Second Reading: First John 3:18-24
Gospel: John 15:1-8

Sixth Sunday of Easter

First Reading: Acts 10:25-26, 34-35, 44-48
Psalm: Psalms 98:1, 2-3, 3-4
Second Reading: First John 4:7-10
Gospel: John 15:9-17

The Ascension (40 Days After Easter) [In some dioceses celebrated on 7th Sunday in Easter]

First Reading: Acts 1:1-11
Psalm: Psalms 47:2-3, 6-7, 8-9
Second Reading: Ephesians 1:17-23
Gospel: Mark 16:15-20

Seventh Sunday of Easter

First Reading: Acts 1:15-17, 20-26
Psalm: Psalms 103:1-2, 11-12, 19-20
Second Reading: First John 4:11-16
Gospel: John 17:11-19

Pentecost or Whitsunday

First Reading: Acts 2:1-11
Psalm: Psalms 104:1, 24, 29-30, 31, 34
Second Reading: 1 Corinthians 12:3-7, 12-13
Gospel: John 20:19-23

Trinity Sunday

First Reading: Deuteronomy 4:32-34, 39-40
Psalm: Psalms 33:4-5, 6, 9, 18-19, 20, 22
Second Reading: Romans 8:14-17
Gospel: Matthew 28:16-20

[In the U.S. - Corpus Christi

First Reading: Exodus 24:3-8
Psalm: Psalms 116:12-13, 15-16, 17-18
Second Reading: Hebrews 9:11-15
Gospel: Mark 14:12-16, 22-26]

Tenth Sunday in Ordinary Time

First Reading: Gen 3:9-15
Psalm: Psalms 130
Second Reading: 2 Corinthians 4:13 - 5:1
Gospel: Mark 3:20-35

Eleventh Sunday in Ordinary Time

First Reading: Ezekiel 17:22-24
Psalm: Psalms 92

Second Reading: 2
Corinthians 5:6-10
Gospel: Mark 4:26-34

**Twelfth Sunday in
Ordinary Time**

First Reading: Job
38:1, 8-11
Psalm: Psalms 107:23-
24, 25-26, 28-29, 30-
31
Second Reading: 2
Corinthians 5:14-17
Gospel: Mark 4:35-41

**Thirteenth Sunday in
Ordinary Time**

First Reading: Wisdom
1:13-15, 2:23-24
Psalm: Psalms 30:2, 4,
5-6, 11, 12, 13
Second Reading: 2
Corinthians 8:7, 9, 13-
15
Gospel: Mark 5:21-43
or 5:21-24, 35-43

**Fourteenth Sunday in
Ordinary Time**

First Reading: Ezekiel
2:2-5
Psalm: Psalms 123:1-
2, 2, 3-4
Second Reading: 2
Corinthians 12:7-10
Gospel: Mark 6:1-6

**Fifteenth Sunday in
Ordinary Time**

First Reading: Amos
7:12-15
Psalm: Psalms 85:9-
10, 11-12, 13-14
Second Reading:
Ephesians 1:3-14 or
1:3-10
Gospel: Mark 6:7-13

**Sixteenth Sunday in
Ordinary Time**

First Reading:
Jeremiah 23:1-16
Psalm: Psalms 23:1-3,
3-4, 5, 6
Second Reading:
Ephesians 2:13-18
Gospel: Mark 6:30-34

**Seventeenth Sunday
in Ordinary Time**

First Reading: Second
Kings 4:42-44
Psalm: Psalms 145:10-
11, 15-16, 17-18
Second Reading:
Ephesians 4:1-6
Gospel: John 6:1-15

Eighteenth Sunday in Ordinary Time

First Reading: Exodus 16:2-4, 12-15
Psalm: Psalms 78
Second Reading: Ephesians 4:17, 20-24
Gospel: John 6:24-35

Nineteenth Sunday in Ordinary Time

First Reading: First Kings 19:4-8
Psalm: Psalms 34:2-3, 4-5, 6-7, 8-9
Second Reading: Ephesians 4:30--5:2
Gospel: John 6:41-51

Twentieth Sunday in Ordinary Time

First Reading: Proverbs 9:1-6
Psalm: Psalms 34:2-3, 10-11, 12-13, 14-15
Second Reading: Ephesians 5:15-20
Gospel: John 6:51-58

Twenty-first Sunday in Ordinary Time

First Reading: Joshua 24:1-2, 15-17, 18
Psalm: Psalms 34:2-3, 16-17, 18-19, 20-21, 22-23
Second Reading: Ephesians 5:21-32
Gospel: John 6:60-69

22nd Sunday in Ordinary Time

First Reading: Deuteronomy 4:1-2, 6-8
Psalm: Psalms 15:2-3, 3-4, 4-5
Second Reading: James 1:17-18, 21-22, 27
Gospel: Mark 7:1-8, 14-15, 21-23

Twenty-third Sunday in Ordinary Time

First Reading: Isaiah 35:4-7
Psalm: Psalms 146:7, 8-9, 9-10
Second Reading: James 2:1-5
Gospel: Mark 7:31-37

24th Sunday in Ordinary Time

First Reading: Isaiah 50:4-9
Psalm: Psalms 116:1-2, 3-4, 5-6, 8-9
Second Reading: James 2:14-18
Gospel: Mark 8:27-35

Twenty-fifth Sunday in Ordinary Time

First Reading: Wisdom 2:17-20
Psalm: Psalms 54:3-4, 5, 6-8
Second Reading: James 3:16--4:3
Gospel: Mark 9:30-37

Twenty-sixth Sunday in Ordinary Time

First Reading: Numbers 11:25-29
Psalm: Psalms 19:8, 10, 12-13, 14
Second Reading: James 5:1-6
Gospel: Mark 9:38-43, 45, 47-48

27th Sunday in Ordinary Time

First Reading: Genesis 2:18-24
Psalm: Psalms 128:1-2, 3, 4-5, 6
Second Reading: Hebrews 2:9-11
Gospel: Mark 10:2-16 or 10:2-12

28th Sunday in Ordinary Time

First Reading: Wisdom 7:7-11
Psalm: Psalms 90:12-13, 14-15, 16-17
Second Reading: Hebrews 4:12-13
Gospel: Mark 10:17-30 or 10:17-27

Twenty-ninth Sunday in Ordinary Time

First Reading: Isaiah 53:10-11
Psalm: Psalms 33:4-5, 18-19, 20, 22
Second Reading: Hebrews 4:14-16
Gospel: Mark 10:35-45 or 10:42-45

Thirtieth Sunday in Ordinary Time

First Reading: Jeremiah 31:7-9
Psalm: Psalms 126:1-2, 2-3, 4-5, 6
Second Reading: Hebrews 5:1-6

Gospel: Mark 10:46-52

Thirty-first Sunday in Ordinary Time

First Reading: Deuteronomy 6:2-6
Psalm: Psalms 18:2-3, 3-4, 47, 57
Second Reading: Hebrews 7:23-28
Gospel: Mark 12:28-34

Thirty-second Sunday in Ordinary Time

First Reading: First Kings 17:10-16
Psalm: Psalms 146:7, 8-9, 9-10
Second Reading: Hebrews 9:24-28
Gospel: Mark 12:38-44 or 12:41-44

Thirty-third Sunday in Ordinary Time

First Reading: Daniel 12:1-3
Psalm: Psalms 16:5, 8, 9-10, 11
Second Reading: Hebrews 10:11-14, 18
Gospel: Mark 13:24-32

Last Sunday in Ordinary Time Christ the King

First Reading: Daniel 7:13-14
Psalm: Psalms 93:1, 1-2, 5
Second Reading: Revelation 1:5-8
Gospel: John 18:33-37

* YEAR C *

First Sunday of Advent

First Reading: Jeremiah 33:14-16
Psalm: Psalms 25:4-5, 8-9, 10, 14 Second Reading: First Thessalonians 3:12--4:2
Gospel: Luke 21:25-28, 34-36

Second Sunday of Advent

First Reading: Baruch 5:1-9
Psalm: Psalms 126:1-2, 2-3, 4-5, 6
Second Reading: Philippians 1:4-6, 8-11
Gospel: Luke 3:1-6

Third Sunday of Advent

First Reading:
Zephaniah 3:14-18
Psalm: Isaiah 12:2-3,
4, 5-6
Second Reading:
Philippians 4:4-7
Gospel: Luke 3:10-18

Fourth Sunday of Advent

First Reading: Micah
5:1-4
Psalm: Psalms 80:2-3,
15-16, 18-19
Second Reading:
Hebrews 10:5-10
Gospel: Luke 1:39-45

Christmas Eve

Readings for Vigil
Mass for Christmas
First Reading: Isaiah
62:1-5
Psalm: Psalms 89:4-5,
16-17, 27, 29
Second Reading: Acts
13:16-17, 22-25
Gospel: Matthew 1:1-25

Readings for Midnight Mass

First Reading: Isaiah
9:1-6
Psalm: Psalms 96:1-2,
2-3, 11-12, 13

Second Reading: Titus
2:11-14
Gospel: Luke 2:1-14

Christmas

Readings for Mass at
Dawn
First Reading: Isaiah
62:11-12
Psalm: Psalms 97:1, 6,
11-12
Second Reading: Titus
3:4-7
Gospel: Luke 2:15-20

Readings for Mass during the day

First Reading: Isaiah
52:7-10
Psalm: Psalms 98:1, 2-3, 3-4, 5-6
Second Reading:
Hebrews 1:1-6
Gospel: John 1:1-18 or
1:1-5, 9-14

Feast of he Holy Family

First Reading: Sirach
3:2-6, 12-14
Psalm: Psalms 128:1-2, 3, 4-5
Second Reading:
Colossians 3:12-21
Gospel: Luke 2:41-52

Second Sunday of

Christmas

First Reading: Sirach 24:1-4, 8-12
Psalm: Psalms 147:12-13, 14-15, 19-20
Second Reading: Ephesians 1:3-6, 15-18
Gospel: John 1:1-18 or 1:1-5, 9-14

[In the U.S. - Epiphany

First Reading: Isaiah 60:1-6
Psalm: Psalms 72:1-2, 7-8, 10-11, 12-13
Second Reading: Ephesians 3:2-3, 5-6
Gospel: Matthew 2:1-12]

[Outside U.S. - Baptism of the Lord

First Reading: Isaiah 42:1-4, 6-7
Psalm: Psalms 29:1-2, 3-4, 3, 9-10
Second Reading: Acts 10:34-38
Gospel: Luke 3:15-16, 21-22]

Second Sunday in Ordinary Time

First Reading: Isaiah 62:1-5
Psalm: Psalms 96:1-2, 2-3, 7-8, 9-10
Second Reading: First Corinthians 12:4-11
Gospel: John 2:1-12

Third Sunday in Ordinary Time

First Reading: Nehemiah 8:2-4, 5-6, 8-10
Psalm: Psalms 19:8, 9, 10, 15
Second Reading: 1 Corinthians 12:12-30 or 12:12-14, 27
Gospel: Luke 1:1-4, 4:14-21

Fourth Sunday in Ordinary Time

First Reading: Jeremiah 1:4-5, 17-19
Psalm: Psalms 71:1-2, 3-4, 5-6, 15-17
Second Reading: 1 Corinthians 12:31--13:13 or 13:4-13
Gospel: Luke 4:21-30

Fifth Sunday in Ordinary Time

First Reading: Isaiah 6:1-2, 3-8
Psalm: Psalms 138:1-2, 2-3, 4-5, 7-8
Second Reading: First Corinthians 15:1-11 or 15:3-8, 11
Gospel: Luke 5:1-11

Sixth Sunday in Ordinary Time

First Reading: Jeremiah 17:5-8
Psalm: Psalms 1:1-2, 3, 4, 6
Second Reading: 1 Corinthians 15:12, 16-20
Gospel: Luke 6:17, 20-26

Seventh Sunday in Ordinary Time

First Reading: 1 Samuel 26:2,7-9, 12-13, 22-23
Psalm: Psalms 103:1-2, 3-4, 8, 10, 12-13
Second Reading: 1 Corinthians 15:45-49
Gospel: Luke 6:27-38

Eighth Sunday in Ordinary Time

First Reading: Sirach 27:4-7
Psalm: Psalms 92:2-3, 13-14, 15-16
Second Reading: 1 Corinthians 15:54-58
Gospel: Luke 6:39-45

Ninth Sunday in Ordinary Time

First Reading: First Kings 8:41-43
Psalm: Psalms 117:1, 2
Second Reading: Galatians 1:1-2, 6-10
Gospel: Luke 7:1-10

Ash Wednesday

First Reading: Joel 2:12-18
Psalm: Psalms 51:3-4, 5-6, 12-13, 14, 17
Second Reading: 2 Corinthians 5:20--6:2
Gospel: Matthew 6:1-6, 16-18

First Sunday of Lent

First Reading: Deuteronomy 26:4-10
Psalm: Psalms 91:1-2, 10-11, 12-13, 14-15
Second Reading: Romans 10:8-13

Gospel: Luke 4:1-13

Second Sunday of Lent

First Reading: Genesis 15:5-12, 17-18
Psalm: Psalms 27:1, 7-8, 8-9, 13-14
Second Reading: Philippians 3:17--4:1 or 3:20--4:1
Gospel: Luke 9:28-36

Third Sunday of Lent

First Reading: Exodus 3:1-8, 13-15
Psalm: Psalms 103:1-2, 3-4, 6-7, 8, 11
Second Reading: 1 Corinthians 10:1-6, 10-12
Gospel: Luke 13:1-9

Fourth Sunday of Lent

First Reading: Joshua 5:9, 10-12
Psalm: Psalms 34:2-3, 4-5, 6-7
Second Reading: Second Corinthians 5:17-21
Gospel: Luke 15:1-3, 11-32

Fifth Sunday of Lent

First Reading: Isaiah 43:16-21
Psalm: Psalms 126:1-2, 2-3, 4-5, 6
Second Reading: Philippians 3:8-14
Gospel: John 8:1-11

Passion (Palm) Sunday

Readings for the Entrance
The Procession
Gospel: Luke 19:28-40
Psalm 24
Psalm 47
The Solemn Entrance
Gospel: Luke 19:28-40
or

The Simple Entrance

Readings for Mass
First Reading: Isaiah 50:4-7
Psalm: Psalms 22:8-9, 17-18, 19-20, 23-24
Second Reading: Philippians 2:6-11
Gospel: Luke 22:14--23:56 or 23:1-49

Holy Thursday

Chrism Mass
First Reading: Isaiah 61:1-3, 6, 8-9
Psalm: Psalms 89:21-22, 25, 27
Second Reading: Revelation 1:5-8
Gospel: Luke 4:16-21

Evening Mass of the Lord's Supper
First Reading: Exodus 12:1-8, 11-14
Psalm: Psalms 116:12-13, 15-16, 17-18
Second Reading: First Corinthians 11:23-26
Gospel: John 13:1-15

Good Friday - No Daily Mass

Celebration of the Lord's Passion
First Reading: Isaiah 52:13--53:12
Psalm: Psalms 31:2, 6, 12-13, 15-16, 17, 25
Second Reading: Hebrews 4:14-16; 5:7-9
Gospel: John 18:1--19:42

Holy Saturday - No Daily Mass

Readings for Vigil Mass for Easter Sunday

First Reading: Genesis 1:1--2:2 or 1:1, 26-31
Psalms 104:1-2, 5-6, 10, 12, 13-14, 24, 35, or Psalms 33:4-5, 6-7, 12-13, 20-22
Second Reading: Genesis 22:1-18 or 22:1-2, 9, 10-13, 15-18
Psalm: Psalms 16:5, 8, 9-10, 11
Third Reading: Exodus 14:15--15:1
Psalm: Exodus 15:1-2, 3-4, 5-6, 17-18
Fourth Reading: Isaiah 54:5-14
Psalm: Psalms 30:2, 4, 5-6, 11-12, 13
Fifth Reading: Isaiah 55:1-11
Psalm: Isaiah 12:2-3, 4, 5-6
Sixth Reading: Baruch 3:9-15, 32--4:4
Psalm: Psalms 19:8, 9, 10, 11
Seventh Reading: Ezekiel 36:16-28
Psalm: Psalms 42:3, 5;

43:3, 4, or Isaiah 12:2-3, 4, 5-6, or Psalms 51:12-13, 14-15, 18-19
Epistle: Romans 6:3-11
Psalm: Psalms 118:1-2, 16, 17, 22-23
Gospel: Luke 24:1-12

Easter Sunday

First Reading: Acts 10:34, 37-43
Psalm: Psalms 118:1-2, 16-17, 22-23
Second Reading: Colossians 3:1-4, or First Corinthians 5:6-8
Gospel: John 20:1-9

Second Sunday of Easter

First Reading: Acts 5:12-16
Psalm: Psalms 118:2-4, 13-15, 22-24
Second Reading: Rev 1:9-11, 12-13, 17-19
Gospel: John 20:19-31

Third Sunday of Easter

First Reading: Acts 5:27-32, 40-41
Psalm: Psalms 30:2, 4, 5-6, 11-12, 13
Second Reading:

Revelation 5:11-14
Gospel: John 21:1-19 or 21:1-14

Fourth Sunday of Easter

First Reading: Acts 13:14, 43-52
Psalm: Psalms 100:1-2, 3, 5
Second Reading: Revelation 7:9, 14-17
Gospel: John 10:27-30

Fifth Sunday of Easter

First Reading: Acts 14:21-27
Psalm: Psalms 145:8-9, 10-11, 12-13
Second Reading: Revelation 21:1-5
Gospel: John 13:31-33, 34-35

Sixth Sunday of Easter

First Reading: Acts 15:1-2, 22-29
Psalm: Psalms 67:2-3, 5, 6, 8
Second Reading: Rev 21:10-14, 22-23
Gospel: John 14:23-29

The Ascension (40 Days After Easter) [In some dioceses celebrated on 7th Sunday in Easter]

First Reading: Acts 1:1-11
Psalm: Psalms 47:2-3, 6-7, 8-9
Second Reading: Ephesians 1:17-23
Gospel: Mark 16:15-20

Seventh Sunday of Easter

First Reading: Acts 7:55-60
Psalm: Psalms 97:1-2, 6-7, 9
Second Reading: Rev 22:12-14, 16-17, 20
Gospel: John 17:20-26

Pentecost or Whitsunday

First Reading: Acts 2:1-11
Psalm: Psalms 104:1, 24, 29-30, 31, 34
Second Reading: 1 Corinthians 12:3-7, 12-13
Gospel: John 20:19-23

Trinity Sunday

First Reading: Proverbs 8:22-31
Psalm: Psalms 8:4-5, 6-7, 8-9
Second Reading: Romans 5:1-5
Gospel: John 16:12-15

[In the U.S. - Corpus Christi

First Reading: Genesis 14:18-20
Psalm: Psalms 110:1, 2, 3, 4
Second Reading: First Corinthians 11:23-26
Gospel: Luke 9:11-17]

Tenth Sunday in Ordinary Time

First Reading: First Kings 17:17-24
Psalm: Psalms 30:2, 4, 5-6, 11, 12, 13
Second Reading: Galatians 1:11-19
Gospel: Luke 7:11-17

Eleventh Sunday in Ordinary Time

First Reading: Second Samuel 12:7-10, 13
Psalm: Psalms 32:1-2, 5, 7, 11
Second Reading:

Galatians 2:16, 19-21
Gospel: Luke 7:36--
8:3 or 7:36-50

**Twelfth Sunday in
Ordinary Time**

First Reading:
Zechariah 12:10-11
Psalm: Psalms 62:2, 3-
4, 5-6, 8-9
Second Reading:
Galatians 3:26-29
Gospel: Luke 9:18-24

**Thirteenth Sunday in
Ordinary Time**

First Reading: First
Kings 19:16-21
Psalm: Psalms 16:1-2,
5, 7-8, 9-10, 11
Second Reading:
Galatians 5:1, 13-18
Gospel: Luke 9:51-62

**Fourteenth Sunday in
Ordinary Time**

First Reading: Isaiah
66:10-14
Psalm: Psalms 66:1-3,
4-5, 6-7, 16, 20
Second Reading:
Galatians 6:14-18
Gospel: Luke 10:1-12,
17-20 or 10:1-9
Fifteenth Sunday in

Ordinary Time

First Reading:
Deuteronomy 30:10-14
Psalm: Psalms 69:14,
17, 30-31, 33-34, 36,
37
Second Reading:
Colossians 1:15-20
Gospel: Luke 10:25-37

**Sixteenth Sunday in
Ordinary Time**

First Reading: Genesis
18:1-10
Responsorial Psalm:
Psalms 15:2-3, 3-4, 5
Second Reading:
Colossians 1:24-28
Gospel: Luke 10:38-42

**Seventeenth Sunday
in Ordinary Time**

First Reading: Genesis
18:20-32
Psalm: Psalms 138:1-
2, 2-3, 6-7, 7-8
Second Reading:
Colossians 2:12-14
Gospel: Luke 11:1-13

Eighteenth Sunday in Ordinary Time

First Reading:
Ecclesiastes 1:2; 2:21-23
Responsorial Psalm:
Psalms 95:1-2, 6-7, 8-9
Second Reading:
Colossians 3:1-5, 9-11
Gospel: Luke 12:13-21

Nineteenth Sunday in Ordinary Time

First Reading: Wisdom 18:6-9
Psalm: Psalms 33:1, 12, 18-19, 20-22
Second Reading:
Hebrews 11:1-2, 8-19
or 11:1-2, 8-12
Gospel: Luke 12:32-48
or 12:35-40

Twentieth Sunday in Ordinary Time

First Reading:
Jeremiah 38:4-6, 8-10
Psalm: Psalms 40:2, 3, 4, 18
Second Reading:
Hebrews 12:1-4
Gospel: Luke 12:49-53

Twenty-first Sunday in Ordinary Time

First Reading: Isaiah 66:18-21
Psalm: Psalms 117:1, 2
Second Reading:
Hebrews 12:5-7, 11-13
Gospel: Luke 13:22-30

22nd Sunday in Ordinary Time

First Reading: Sirach 3:17-18, 20, 28-29
Psalm: Psalms 68:4-5, 6-7, 10-11
Second Reading:
Hebrews 12:18-19, 22-24
Gospel: Luke 14:1, 7-14

Twenty-third Sunday in Ordinary Time

First Reading: Wisdom 9:13-18
Psalm: Psalms 90:3-4, 5-6, 12-13, 14-17
Second Reading:
Philemon 1:9-10, 12-17
Gospel: Luke 14:25-33

24th Sunday in Ordinary Time

First Reading: Exodus 32:7-11, 13-14
Psalm: Psalms 51:3-4, 12-13, 17, 19
Second Reading: First Timothy 1:12-17
Gospel: Luke 15:1-32 or 15:1-10

Twenty-fifth Sunday in Ordinary Time

First Reading: Amos 8:4-7
Psalm: Psalms 113:1-2, 4-6, 7-8
Second Reading: First Timothy 2:1-8
Gospel: Luke 16:1-13 or 16:10-13

Twenty-sixth Sunday in Ordinary Time

First Reading: Amos 6:1, 4-7
Psalm: Psalms 146:7, 8-9, 9-10
Second Reading: First Timothy 6:11-16
Gospel: Luke 16:19-31

27th Sunday in Ordinary Time

First Reading: Habakkuk 1:2-3, 2:2-4
Psalm: Psalms 95:1-2, 6-7, 8-9
Second Reading: 2 Timothy 1:6-8, 13-14
Gospel: Luke 17:5-10

28th Sunday in Ordinary Time

First Reading: Second Kings 5:14-17
Responsorial Psalm: Psalms 98:1, 2-3, 3-4
Second Reading: Second Timothy 2:8-13
Gospel: Luke 17:11-19

Twenty-ninth Sunday in Ordinary Time

First Reading: Exodus 17:8-13
Psalm: Psalms 121:1-2, 3-4, 5-6, 7-8
Second Reading: 2 Timothy 3:14--4:2
Gospel: Luke 18:1-8

Thirtieth Sunday in Ordinary Time

First Reading: Sirach 35:12-14, 16-18
Psalm: Psalms 34:2-3, 17-18, 19, 23
Second Reading: Second Timothy 4:6-8, 16-18
Gospel: Luke 18:9-14

Thirty-first Sunday in Ordinary Time

First Reading: Wisdom 11:22--12:1
Psalm: Psalms 145:1-2, 8-9, 10-11, 13, 14
Second Reading: 2 Thessalonians 1:11--2:2
Gospel: Luke 19:1-10

Thirty-second Sunday in Ordinary Time

First Reading: Second Maccabees 7:1-2, 9-14
Psalm: Psalms 17:1, 5-6, 8, 15
Second Reading: 2 Thessalonians 2:16--3:5
Gospel: Luke 20:27-38 or 20:27, 34-38

Thirty-third Sunday in Ordinary Time

First Reading: Malachi 3:19-20
Psalm: Psalms 98:5-6, 7-8, 9
Second Reading: 2 Thessalonians 3:7-12
Gospel: Luke 21:5-19

Last Sunday in Ordinary Time Christ the King

First Reading: Second Samuel 5:1-3
Psalm: Psalms 122:1-2, 3-4, 4-5
Second Reading: Colossians 1:12-20
Gospel: Luke 23:35-43

SPECIAL DAYS OF REMEMBRANCE

Feb 2 - Presentation of the Lord

First Reading: Malachi 3:1-4
Psalm: Psalms 24:7, 8, 9, 10
Second Reading: Hebrews 2:14-18
Gospel: Luke 2:22-40 or 2:22-32

Mar 19 - St. Joseph, Husband of Mary

First Reading: Second Samuel 7:4-5, 12-14, 16
Psalm: Psalms 89:2-3, 4-5, 27, 29
Second Reading: Romans 4:13, 16-18, 22
Gospel: Matthew 1:16, 18-21, 24, or Luke 2:41-51

Mar 25 - The Annunciation of the Lord

First Reading: Isaiah 7:10-14
Psalm: Psalms 40:7-8, 8-9, 10, 11
Second Reading: Hebrews 10:4-10
Gospel: Luke 1:26-38

Apr 29 - Saint Catherine of Siena

First Reading: Acts 13:13-25 or First John 1:5--2:2
Psalm: Psalms 89:2-3, 21-22, 25, 27
Gospel: John 13:16-20

May 31 - The Visitation of Mary

First Reading: Zephaniah 3:14-18, or Romans 12:9-16
Psalm: Isaiah 12:2-3, 4, 5-6
Gospel: Luke 1:39-56

Jun 24 - Birth of St. John the Baptist

First Reading: Isaiah 49:1-6
Psalm: Psalms 139:1-3, 13-14, 14-15
Second Reading: Acts 13:22-26
Gospel: Luke 1:57-66, 80

June 29 - The Holy Apostles (Peter and Paul)

First Reading: Acts
12:1-11
Psalm: Psalms 34:2-3,
4-5, 6-7, 8-9
Second Reading: 2
Timothy 4:6-8, 17-18
Gospel: Matthew
16:13-19

Jul 22 - St. Mary Magdalene

First Reading: Song of
Songs 3:1-4,
    or Second
Corinthians 5:14-17
Psalm: Psalms 63:2, 3-
4, 5-6, 8-9
Gospel: John 20:1-2,
11-18

Aug 6 - Transfiguration of the Lord

First Reading: Daniel
7:9-10, 13-14
Psalm: Psalms 97:1-2,
5-6, 9
Second Reading:
Second Peter 1:16-19
Gospel: Mark 9:2-10

Aug 15 - Assumption Virgin Mary

First Reading:
Revelation 11:19;
12:1-6, 10

Psalm: Psalms 45:10,
11, 12, 16
Second Reading: First
Corinthians 15:20-26
Gospel: Luke 1:39-56

Sep 8 - Nativity of the Virgin Mary

First Reading: Micah
5:1-4,
or Romans 8:28-30
Psalm: Psalms 13:6, 6
Gospel: Matthew 1:1-
16, 18-23
or 1:18-23

Sep 14 - Triumph of the Cross

First Reading:
Numbers 21:4-9
Psalm: Psalms 78:1-2,
34-35, 36-37, 38
Second Reading:
Philippians 2:6-11
Gospel: John 3:13-17

Sep 26 - Sts. Cosmas & Damian

First Reading:
Proverbs 21:1-6, 10-13
Psalm: Psalms 119:1,
27, 30, 34, 35, 44
Gospel: Luke 8:19-21

Sep 29 - Michael, Gabriel, and Raphael (Archangels and all Angels)

First Reading: Daniel 7:9-10, 13-14,
or Revelation 12:7-12
Pm: Psalms 138:1-2, 2-3, 4-5
Gospel: John 1:47-51

Oct 4 - Saint Francis of Assisi

First Reading: Jonah 1:1--2:1, 11
Psalm: Psalms 2:2, 3, 4, 5, 8
Gospel: Luke 10:25-37
or Galatians 6:14-18

Nov 1 - All Saints

First Reading: Revelation 7:2-4, 9-14
Psalm: Psalms 24:1-2, 3-4, 5-6
Second Reading: First John 3:1-3
Gospel: Matthew 5:1-12

Nov 2 - All Souls Day (Feast of the Faithful Departed in Christ)

First Reading: (Optional) Wisdom 3:1-9
or 3:1-6, 9, or
Isaiah 25:6, 7-9
Psalm: Psalms 27:1, 4, 7, 8, 9, 13-14,
or Ps 103:8, 10, 13-14, 15-16, 17-18
Second Reading: (Optional) Romans 6:3-9
or 6:3-4, 8-9,
or First Corinthians 15:20-24, 25-28
Gospel: (Optional) Matthew 25:31-46,
or John 11:17-27 or 11:21-27

Dec 14 - St. John of the Cross

First Reading: 1 Corinthians 2:1-10
or Zephaniah 3:1-2, 9-13
Psalm: Psalms 34:2-3, 6-7, 17-18, 19, 23
Gospel: Matthew 21:28

A EUCHARISTIC LITURGY FOR PEACE AND ASCENSION

(This Mass was developed by Archbishop Alan Kemp. It is the liturgy which has been celebrated by Ascension Mission and Ascension Mission Ministries since approximately 1997.)

Under certain circumstances a candle lighting component may be appropriately added to the celebration of the Holy Eucharist. Here are two options

LIGHTING THE CANDLES

> *(The Mass candles are lit either in private before the beginning of Mass or as a preparatory rite. If done as a preparatory rite the following prayers are said:)*

O God, who made the light shine forth from the darkness (Isa 60:1), make it shine in our midst;

Be gracious to us and bless us and make your face to shine upon us (Ps 67:1)

O Christ, the true light (Jn 1:9), enlighten us;

Make us children of the light (Eph 5:8) and of the day, and heirs of your everlasting kingdom;

O Holy Spirit, open our eyes to the

comprehension of truth (Eph 1:13);
And, guide us (Jn 14:26), Holy Spirit, on
our path.

All: Amen

LUCERNARION *(Taizé candle lighting)*

According to rubrics published by the Taizé Community, this short liturgy of the light may be said between the Introduction and the Psalm during certain evening services

The candles are lit while this song is being sung

Joyous light of Glory,
of the heavenly immortal and blessed Father,
Jesus Christ!

The sun is setting,
and we look to the evening light;
we sing to the Father, the Son and the Holy Spirit of God!

Thou art worthy of being for ever sung with pure voices,
Son of God, Giver of Life,
the universe proclaims thy glory!

INTROIT LITURGY

OPENING SONG (INTROIT OR ENTRANCE ANTIPHON)

(Stand for song. The ministers enter the sanctuary.)

(The opening song may be a psalm, a hymn that is sung from a hymnal, or an appropriate recording, which is played.)

(People may be seated at conclusion of the song)

BLESSING WITH HOLY WATER (ASPERGES)

> *(Receiving the aspergill, the celebrant touches it to his forehead.)*

Priest Cleanse me with hyssop, and I will be clean; wash me, and I will be whiter than snow (Psalms 51:7).

> *(Sprinkling the altar in the middle; then chancel to the left and the right, and continuing. Turning to the people and sprinkling them with the same triple motion)*

Informal greeting

INVOCATION

All make the sign of the cross as the chief celebrant makes the following invocation:)

Priest In the name of God, who is Creator, ✝ Word Made Flesh, and the Holy Spirit.

R   Amen.

Priest *(Additional option: In recognition that Jesus was a pious Jew, the traditional Hebrew call to prayer may be chanted. This both affirms the three identities within the One Nature of God and honors our Jewish heritage.)*

Sh'ma Israel, Adonai Elohaynu, Adonai Y'hud. O hear, O Israel, the Lord our God, the Lord is One.

INTRODUCTORY DIALOG

(Informal welcoming remarks and announcements)

Priest The Lord be with you.
Cn   **And also with you.**

(The following may be said or sung by priest)

Almighty God, to whom all hearts are open, all desires known, and from whom no secret are hidden; cleanse the thoughts of our hearts by the inspiration of your Holy Spirit, so that we may truly love you and worthily praise your holy name; we ask this through Christ our Lord.

R.   **Amen.**

THE CONFITEOR (OR CONFESSION)

*(At the option of the celebrant, the Confiteor **or** the Kyrie may be omitted since they both serve essentially the same function)*

Priest Let us now prepare ourselves in consciousness by asking forgiveness for our wrong doings and admitting our human imperfections. So, at this time in an act of humbleness and truth, let us pray together sincerely admitting our wrong doings and asking God to cleanse us.

(All say together:)

All **I admit to God, to the saints, and to all here present that I have failed to love God and my neighbor as I ought to have, committing wrongs in thought, word, and deed, by what I have done and by what I have not done. I acknowledge my failings and that I have missed the mark many times. I now seek God's forgiveness and ask blessed Mary, the angels, the saints, and you my brothers and sisters, to pray for me to the Lord our God.**

Priest May almighty God have mercy on us, forgive us for our wrong doings, and bring us all, in peace, to eternal spiritual life.

THE KYRIE

(The people sit or kneel and sing with the priest either to the accompaniment of a recorded Kyrie or the simple Kyrie included below, which may be said or chanted.)

Priest Kyrie eleison (Lord, have mercy)
Cn   Kyrie eleison

Priest Christie eleison (Christ, have mercy)
Cn   Christie eleison

THE ABSOLUTION

(Turning to the altar, the priest says or sings:)

Priest O God, open thou our lips.
Cn   And from our mouths shall pour forth Your praise.

Priest Transform our failings and shortcomings, we ask You, O God, so we might enter your spiritual domain, the Holy of Holies, with pure minds and hearts. We ask this in the name of the Christ.
All   Amen.

Priest Let each of us acknowledge the wrongs we have committed, and humbling yourself before God, let us remember that it is God's will to forgive us for our wrong doings and have mercy on us through Jesus Christ.

(Pause for reflection)

To all who thus repent, I declare absolution of your wrong doings ✝ in the name of God, who is Creator, Word Made Flesh, and Holy Spirit.

R: **Amen.**

CENSING

(This is optional, especially if the asperses and/or confiteor are included in the rite. If used, the priest blesses the incense in the customary manner and then censes the altar, sanctuary area, and the people. It may be desirable to have music during the censing.)

(If the Lucernarion is used, the priest and people say the following:)

Priest An angel came and stood at the altar. He was given much incense to offer, with the prayers of all God's people (Rev 8:3).

All An angel came and stood at the altar.

Priest The smoke of the incense ... went up before God (Rev 8:4).

All With the prayers of all God's people.

Priest Glory be to God the Creator, and to the † Son, and to the Holy Spirit.

All An angel came and stood at the altar.

THE COLLECTS (prayer before liturgy of the word)

(There should be 1, 3, or 7 collects. The priest recites the collect for the day and other collect(s), if any, and then the following, if 3 or 7 collects are chosen.)

Priest O Holy Spirit, sanctifier of the faithful, visit us, we pray, and give us Your inspiration; enlighten our minds more and more with the light; establish within our hearts a love of the truth; increase in us true religion; nourish us with all goodness; and in Your great love keep us, O blessed Spirit, Whom with the Creator and the Son, we worship and glorify as one. **R. Amen.**

LITURGY OF THE WORD

FIRST READING *(The people are seated)*

(After the Reading)

Reader This is the Word of the Lord
Cn   Thanks be to God

RESPONSORIAL PSALM

SECOND READING

(After the Reading)

Reader This is the Word of the Lord
Cn   Thanks be to God

THE GOSPEL

All   Alleluia ... Alleluia ... Alleluia ... *(All rise. This may be said, sung as a community, or a recorded rendition may be played).*

Deacon (or Priest): A reading from the holy gospel according to N.

All   Glory to You, Lord.

Priest This is the Gospel of the Lord
          (Upon conclusion of the Gospel)
All   Praise to you, Lord Jesus Christ.

THE HOMILY OR SERMON

(If there is to be a homily or sermon, it follows here, preceded by the following invocation:

Priest In the Name of God, the Creator, † and of the Son, and of the Holy Spirit.).
All   R. Amen.

PROFESSION OF FAITH *(Optional. If used, see back pages)*

PRAYERS OF THE PEOPLE

Priest O God of all, Source and Establisher and Preserver of the eternal path we pray that peace and tranquillity will descend on the whole world and on us who offer Your eternal sacrifice. It was this sacrifice that has restored the cosmic order and reestablished our spiritual paths. May all of us grow in the eternal life which You give to us. We pray to the Lord.

Cn   Lord, hear our prayer.

Deacon   We pray for our leaders. [Individual leaders mentioned, as well as all bishops, priests, and ministers of the Church. May also include all spiritual leaders of good faith everywhere.] We pray to the Lord.

Cn   Lord, hear our prayer.

Deacon   We pray for the unity of the Churches and the peace and serenity of all communities of love and service. O Christ, you were the servant of the people and of the whole world, and the Son of Mary, who offered herself to Your Father as the Lord's servant, prompt us to be servant-Churches in the world today. We pray to the Lord.

Cn   Lord, hear our prayer.

Deacon   Lord, You are the Resurrection and the Life who raise the dead and lead them to dwell in Your Father's house. Bless all the living and the dead and all those in need, especially those who asked prayers from us. We pray to the Lord.

Cn   Lord, hear our prayer.

Deacon   We pray that justice with love will reign all over the world, that harmony be restored among all nations and races, and be preserved in this our country, its neighbors, and in the whole of creation. We pray to the Lord.

Cn   Lord, hear our prayer.

Deacon   We pray for our planet – for the air, for the rains, the dews, and the fruits of the earth, for the seasons of growth and of harvesting. We pray for all living beings, that all who control the oceans and the earth, and space may respect nature and share its treasures with the millions who are in want. We pray to the Lord.

Cn Lord, hear our prayer.

Deacon We pray for our land, that You may give to her leaders a spirit of dedication and service, for building up our people into an integrated and deeply united and prosperous nation. We pray to the Lord.

Cn Lord, hear our prayer.
(free prayers)

A MOMENT OF SILENCE & PRIVATE PRAYER

Priest Let us take a moment in silence to center ourselves and offer our own silent prayers, communing privately and secretly in the holy place that is within.

Priest And so it is, Amen.

LITURGY OF THE EUCHARIST

OFFERTORY

(The people are seated. The collection is taken up and/or written prayers gathered.)

(The priest offers the offering of the host at eye level, facing the altar.)
(The gifts are brought forward and placed on the altar by the people)
(Singing of the doxology)

DOXOLOGY

Priest Praise God from whom all blessings flow; Praise Him all creatures here below; Praise him above ye heavenly hosts; Praise Father, Son, and Holy Ghost. Amen.

PRIEST'S PRAYER OF THANKSGIVING

*(Either version 1 or 2 of the following is used for both bread and wine. The traditional Hebrew blessing, version 2, may be used here if **not** integrated into the anemnesis.)*

Priest 1.   Accept, O God, maker and giver of all good things, this bread which we offer You, as a symbol of Your bounty, and as a token of our sacrifice of praise and thanksgiving.   May it become to us, that most precious gift, the Body of Your Son, Jesus Christ, which gives life to Your children, both living and departed. *(Priest elevates the offering of bread.)*

or

2.   Baruch   ata   Adonai, Elohaynu melech ha-olom, ha-motzi   lechem   min   ha'arets – Blessed be you, O Lord our God, Who brings forth bread from the earth.

Cn   Amen.

(The priest elevates the offering of bread)
(Either version 1 or 2 of the following is used for both bread and wine.

The traditional Hebrew blessing, version 2, may be used here if ***not*** *integrated into the anemnesis.)*

1.   As we now mix water with this wine in token of the union of the divine and human natures in Christ, Jesus, let us be mindful that we rest in Christ, He in us, just as He also abides with God, the Father.

or

2.   Baruch ata Adonai, Elohaynu melech ha-olom, boray peri ha'gafen – Blessed be you, O Lord our God, Who brings forth the fruit of the vine.

(The priest pours the wine and a little water into the chalice, saying:)

Priest May this chalice of joy and gladness which we offer to You with thankful hearts become to us the Blood of Your Son, Jesus Christ, which takes away the sin of this world. *(Priest elevates the offering of wine.)*

Cn Amen.

LAVABO

Priest *(Psalm 26: 6-7).* I wash my hands in innocence, and go around your altar, O Lord, singing aloud a song of thanksgiving, and telling all your wondrous deeds.

We praise You, O God, for the Glory of Your Gifts resound throughout the universe. Glory be to God our Creator, and to the † Son, and to the Holy Spirit.

Cn **As it was in the beginning, is now, and ever shall be, world without end. Amen.**

ORATE FRATRES (Exhortation)

(Turning toward the people, the priest says:)

Priest Brothers and sisters, please pray that our prayers and this sacrifice will be acceptable to God, Who is Creator of us all.

Cn **May the Lord our God receive these humble but sincerely offered gifts.**

SECRET PRAYER

(Turning towards the altar the priest says:)

Priest You are the source of all life and goodness; through your eternal Word you have created all things from the beginning and formed us in your own image.

We ask that You receive, O God, this † Oblation, and we pray that reverently receiving these holy mysteries we will be filled with Your Grace.

Priest The Lord be with you.
Cn   And also with you.

SURSUM CORDA

Priest Lift up your hearts.
Cn   We lift them up to the Lord.

Priest Let us give thanks to the Lord our God.
Cn   It is just and right to do so.

PREFACE

Priest It is not only right to do this but it is both our great joy and our responsibility that we should at all times and in all places give thanks to God.

(Here follows the proper Preface)

Priest Therefore, with the faithful who rest in him, with angels and archangels, the saints, sages, mystics, and all the company of heaven, we proclaim your great and glorious name, forever praising you and saying:

SANCTUS AND BENEDICTUS QUI VENIT

(The people sit or kneel and sing:)

All   **Holy, Holy, Holy, Lord God of Hosts, Heaven and earth are full of Your Glory; Hosanna in the highest.**

Blessed is he that comes in the Name of the Lord; Hosanna in the Highest.

ANAPHORA/EPICLESIS

(Form 1) *(Special rubrics are available)*

Priest We now center our attention on this bread and fruit of the vine. May the pure, perfect, and Holy Light of the Christ, that lives within us, now consecrate these gifts, changing them into our spiritual food and drink, by the action of the Holy Spirit. In and through these gifts, may they become for us earthly manifestations of God, to consume into our bodies, so that our bodies may become ever more perfect conduits for God's power, that we might be unified with God in Christ, and that we, in turn, might live this earthly life by letting our own light shine so that others may see that light, so that we ourselves become evermore living sacraments, embodying the Christ consciousness, seeding others with the strengthening Bread of God's Word, and healing others with the life giving Wine of God's Love.

LAST SUPPER & WORDS OF INSTITUTION

Priest And now we remember Jesus and what He did, Who, in the night in which He was betrayed, took bread into His holy and innocent hands, and with His eyes lifted up towards heaven, He gave thanks to You, Almighty God, our Father, and He blessed It.

(If not previously used in the prayer of thanksgiving over the gifts, the following traditional Hebrew blessing may be said at the option of the celebrant: Baruch ata Adonai, Elohaynu melech ha-olom, ha-motzi lechem min ha'arets – Blessed be you, O Lord our God, Who brings forth bread from the earth).

He broke It, and gave It to His disciples saying: "All of you, take and eat of this for

This is my Body

which was broken for you. Do this in remembrance of me."

(The Host is elevated)

100

Priest In like manner, after He had supped, He took the cup, and when He had given thanks He blessed it.

(If not previously used in the prayer of thanksgiving over the gifts, the following traditional Hebrew blessing may be said at the option of the celebrant: Baruch ata Adonai, Elohaynu melech ha-olom, boray peri ha'gafen – Blessed be you, O Lord our God, Who brings forth the fruit of the vine.)

and He gave It to His disciples saying: All of you, drink of this, for

This is my Blood

Of the New and Everlasting Covenant, which is shed for you and for many for the remission of sins. Do this as often as you drink it in remembrance of me.

GREAT OBLATION AND PRAYERS

(Based upon practices of the Eastern church, this optional crossing of the arms may be included. When used, the priest lifts the paten with host and chalice, and crossing his arms with them says the prayer which follows. Regardless if arms are crossed the prayer is always said.)

Priest Wherefore, O God, our Creator, we offer to You these, the most precious Gifts which You Yourself have bestowed upon us, this pure Host of life everlasting and the Chalice of eternal salvation, and we pray that you will bid Your holy angels to bear our Oblation to your spiritual realm, there to be offered by Christ, Who, as the Eternal High Priest, forever offers Himself as sacrifice for all humankind.

Priest and People Together

We open ourselves to your Grace, we offer ourselves, our souls, and our bodies for a Holy and living sacrament of

the power of God. We know that through your Grace, O God, our lives will die many times to old habits and to negative thinking, and to actions that do not serve us any more. Let us be continually resurrected into new life as the Christ is reborn in us again and again. We pray that all those who are participating in this Holy Communion with us now may be awakened to this spiritual grace and heavenly benediction, and that we may come to recognize our oneness with the Christ so that we may express more deeply the Christ dwelling in us. As this happens to us here today, we know that the consciousness of all life on earth is being brought more closely to a state of peace.

Priest *(Chanted.)* Through Him, with Him, in Him, in the unity of the Holy Spirit. **R: Amen.**

THE LORD'S PRAYER

(When the Lord's Prayer is sung, substitute the words debt and debtor for trespass and trespasser, in concert with the music available).

Priest And now standing and holding hands, let us sing the Lord's Prayer, the prayer which Christ, Jesus, taught us to pray.

All **Sing or say the Lord's Prayer:**

**Our Father which art in heaven
Hallowed be thy name
Thy kingdom come
Thy will be done
On earth as it is in heaven
Give us this day our daily bread
And forgive our debts
As we forgive our debtors
And lead us not into temptation
But deliver us from evil**

**(For thine is the kingdom, and
  the power, and the glory
Forever, Amen.)**

THE PEACE

Priest Let us exchange a sign of the Peace. [Formal alternative: O Christ, who said to Your apostles, "Peace I leave with you, My peace I give to you;" regard not our sins, but the faith of Your Church and grant Her that peace and unity which are agreeable to Your holy will; You, who lives and reigns God, forever and ever.

Cn   Amen.]

(The priest exchanges the sign of peace with the deacon or other ministers, and bids that all exchange the sign of peace with each other.)

THE CONFRACTION (Breaking Bread)

COMMUNION

Priest Holy things for the Holy.

(The priest elevates the chalice and host. After this he/she communicates, then administers to the clergy and servers. If communion is administered by intinction he/she says:)

May the Body and Blood ✝ of Christ bring you to everlasting spiritual life.

If administered in both species separately the minister(s) say(s):

The Body of Christ
The Blood of Christ
or
The Body and Blood of our lord, Jesus Christ, which were given up for you

(After the communicants have received both the Body and Blood of Christ they return to their seats and either kneel or sit.)

ABLUTIONS

(The remaining portions of the Body of Christ that will be reserved are removed. Any fragments or crumbs placed in the chalice. The priest cleans the chalice with unconsecrated wine, then his/her fingers with wine and water. Finally, whatever remains in the chalice is consumed.)

CONCLUDING PRAYERS/BLESSING

(The following prayer may be omitted)

Priest Let us all pray together by giving thanks and rededicating our lives to spiritual principles.

(Choice 1)

Priest and People say together: **Almighty, and Everliving God, we now truly give thanks for these Holy Mysteries, for this spiritual food and drink, for this opportunity for Holy Communion with You, the Indwelling Spirit, which is our true heritage. We give thanks because we know that we are truly incorporated into the**

Mystical Body of Christ, and that our human selves are washed clean, renewed, transformed in mind, and healed in body. We know that from this holy experience, we are better prepared to serve all humankind, to love more deeply, to forgive more surely. We pray that peace will reign in the hearts of all the people of the earth.

We rededicate our lives to awakening the spirit within us, practicing in our lives spiritual principles, walking with the Holy Spirit of God, embodying the Christ in our every word and deed. We give thanks for this truth. And so it is, Amen.

BLESSING

Priest The Lord be with you.
Cn   And also with you.

Priest May Christ our Lord give us the grace to continue our lives in the spirit of this sacrifice, overcoming evil with good, falsehood with truth, and hatred with love. By seeing our good works, may others also come to glorify God.

Cn   **Amen.**

Priest In the name of God, the Creator, † Son, and the Holy Spirit, the peace of God, which passes all understanding, keep your hearts and your minds in Christ Jesus (Phil 4:7).

Cn   **Amen.**

Priest The mass is never ended. Its presence is always with us. So, let us go forth in peace to love God and our fellow human beings.

INTRODUCTION TO A
EUCHARISTIC POOJA

This liturgy is derived from the *Bharatiya Pooja*, which is a Eucharistic liturgy of the monks of Kurisumala Ashram, a monastery located near the town of Vagamon, in the Malabar region of southern India. While the monks are Trappists (Cistertian Order of the Strict Observance), their praxis, their dharma if you will, attepts to integrate Catholic worship with the Hindu-Indian culture in which it is practiced. The *Bharatiya Pooja* is the liturgy they use on days other than Sundays or major feasts, when the Syro-Malankara rite is used. It is the liturgy of their daily lives, and is most dear to their hearts.

The *Bharatiya Pooja* was developed by and under the direction of the ashram's previous abbot, Father Francis Mahieu, the Acharya, who died in January, 2002. He and Dom Bede Griffiths, of blessed memory, co-founded the ashram. They are luminary figures, so the liturgy was probably quite safe so long as Father Francis lived. There was concern, however, that with Father Francis' passing the *Bharatiya Pooja* might fall into disuse, or even be formally suppressed, because it lacked the support of the Church's hierarchy.

We edited the *Bharatiya Pooja* for North American use, renaming it *A Malabar Rite Eucharistic Pooja*. We are making it available, in part, because we wish to see the spirit of the *Bharatiya Pooja* preserved, protected, and used, even

110

if only by a limited readership. Explanations have been added, rubrics made more clear, and minor editing done to make it more suitable to the needs of a non-Indian readership. We have added an explicit absolution, used the Western wording of the Lord's Prayer, and substituted a more familiar version of the institution narrative. The original typewritten text has been "word processed" by computer, cleaned up, and made more attractive, while preserving the integrity of the original. The lengthy introduction is omitted. While it represents excellent scholarship and provides fascinating background we felt it was too lengthy for a booklet of this scope. Despite whatever flaws and defects it may have, we hope you will find the present edition to be a helpful and inspiring resource. If it assists one soul in coming closer to God it will be justified.

A EUCHARISTIC POOJA

*Derived from the Bharatiya Pooja Developed by
The Trappist Monks
of Kurisumala Ashram, India*

*[Symbols: Pr = presider/priest; Cn = Congregation;
Dn = Deacon]*

PREPARATORY LITURGY

*While a hymn is sung, the celebrants, dressed for the
liturgy enter the church in procession to the low altar
(about 18 inches high),[1] carrying water, a small lit
lamp, incense, flowers. The people stand. The cross is
in a prominent place and the Bible is on the low altar,
with the talam (the large brass tray on which are set
the paten and the cup). The sacred lamp, the
nilavilakku, a tall oil lamp, sits unlit on the floor in
front of the low altar. It is venerated with flowers, the
decorations often taking the form of a cross.*

Hymn

> Graciously open the door of eternity
> that the world may see Your brightness.
> You are the fullness of brightness.
> We remain in darkness.
> Be pleased to remove Your veil.
> Let us, Your people, see Your truth.

ATMASAJJIKARANAM (SPIRITUAL PREPARATION)

When they have reached the altar, looking towards the east, the celebrants stand prayerfully with folded hands for some time.

They make a profound bow to the altar and remain in silence. The celebrant(s) touches hands to lips then to altar. Then:

Pr   Aum! Shanti, Shanti, Shantih.

       O Lord of all,True Embodiment of Being, Knowledge, and Bliss

All   Bless us, that we may offer this holy sacrifice with pure minds and sincere hearts.

SPRINKLING OF WATER (Asperges)

A priest sprinkles holy water around the altar.

       O! Sacchidananda, may this altar, which brings You down to us become Your dwelling place. May it be made pure like the altar on high!

Sprinkling holy water on the people while walking down and the nave:

Pr   May we, who offer this sacrifice, be blessed by the holy water of Your grace!

Cn   May we be perfected by the boons and gifts of Your Holy spirit.

LIGHTING THE LAMP

Holding up the small lit lamp towards the East, as if he were receiving it from there, the celebrant prays:

Pr   O Lord Christ, Mediator between the Eternal Creator and us creatures, Heavenly Everburning Source of Love, we offer You our hearts.

While the priest lights the lamp

Cn   O eternal light, source of revelation, illumine us

While the following hymn is sung, the celebrant lights the tall nilavilakku lamp and venerates it by extending both palms over the flame, bringing them to the eyes. Each one of the assembly does the same from their places in the congregation. After this all sit down.

Hymn

Perfect, Eternal, True Light,
Jesus, You are my refuge.
Over a world full of darkness
Heavenly Light spreads its rays.
Jesus, You are my refuge.

VANDANA KIRTHANA (Canticle of Praise and Adoration)

Pr   Aum! Adoration to You, Creator, Word, and Holy Spirit.
Adoration to the Splendor of the Eternal Sacchidananda
Adoration to You, God of Truth and Love.

114

Cn **Aum. Lord of the Universe! Ever-Conscious-One! Lord of the Universe! Adoration to You!**
Aum. Most Adorable One. Self-Far-and-Near, ...
Adoration to You always! (3 times)

Silent adoration

SPIRITUAL CLEANSING – Confiteor

> *A moment of silence to contemplate errors made since the last celebration of the Eucharist or Reconciliation. At the end of this time the priest touches the altar with both hands and brings them to his eyes as a sign of purification.*

Pr Let us pray that the Lord will look favorably upon this sacrifice. May the intercession of the Blessed Virgin, our Mother, and of the Apostle Thomas plead for us.

Cn **Let us remember the prophets, apostles, martyrs, sages and mystics who have attained pure bliss. May their protection be with us at this altar!**

Pr O Merciful Lord of all, we stand in awe of you. You are health to the sick, strength to the weak, and the forgiver of all. We seek refuge in Your mercy. Heal us, and help us celebrate this service with pure minds and hearts.

Cn **May the Lord be merciful, forgive our errors, and give us Grace.**

Pr   O God, forgive us for our wrong doings, and bring us all, in peace, to eternal spiritual life.

May God bless, preserve and sanctify you; the Lord in his loving kindness look down upon you and be gracious unto you.

In the Name of the Creator, Word, and Holy Spirit, the Lord ✝ absolve you and free you from the burdens of your wrong doings and grant you the grace and comfort of the Holy Spirit.

R: **Amen.**

Pr   Beloved, in accordance with the teaching of Christ our Lord, let us offer peace to one another before we offer the sacrifice.

As a sign of mutual love, all offer peace to one another. The Indian form of placing one's hands between the hands of the other is most appropriate.

Pr   O Lord of all, You are the Liberator and the way

Cn   **You opened the path of love to us. You have cleansed the stains on our souls and made them beautiful again, as the flowers of the field. We thank You for Your Grace and the many gifts You have showered on us.**

LITURGY OF THE WORD
AND UPASANA (MEDITATION)

Pr   O Lord of all, You reveal, Yourself in different ways to us creatures who live in expectation of Your vision. Enlighten our minds that we may hear and understand the eternal truths you Speak to us.

Cn   May we be prophets of the Eternal Word, the inspiration of the sages.

The readers/lectors bow to the priest asking his blessing before reading the word of God, while he extends his right hand towards them, saying:

Pr   May Christ our Lord strengthen and inspire you who read the Scriptures.

The readers/lectors read the holy words.

After each reading there should be a few moments for reflection and meditation.

Hymn before the Gospel, during which the gospel reader (a priest or deacon – if a deacon reads he receives a blessing from priest) incenses the Bible, then venerates it by applying both hands first to the book, then to his eyes.

All   O Lord Christ, Satguru of the whole world! lead us from the unreal to the real, from darkness to the light, and from death to immortality.

Blessing the people with the Bible in the form of a cross

Pr   The peace of Christ be with you.

Cn   Now and for ever.

Pr   The Gospel of our Lord Jesus Christ
      according to the apostle ... the evangelist ...

*The priest or deacon reads the Gospel. After reading
he venerates the Bible by touching it with the palms of
his hands; then he brings them to his eyes. After an
appropriate period of reflection there is a homily,
followed by a moment of silence.*

MANASA POOJA (Inner Offering – Offertory)

Hymn

O Jesus, God, praise to You always!
O Jesus, God, glory to You always!
O Jesus, God, praise to You always!
Hymns of praise to God, always!

*During this hymn the celebrant sprinkles water
around the offerings, a sign of purification and
sanctification. He can also sip some water as a sign
of inner cleansing.*

Pr   Let us offer ourselves and these gifts to a
      merciful and loving God.

*The priest raises the bread and the wine while the
following hymn is sung.*

118

Hymn

An offering of light on the tray of the sky.
An offering of flowers on the tray of the earth.
An offering of love on the tray of life
An offering of life on the tray of Golgotha.
Here on this altar, the hill of Golgotha and the
wooden Cross. The land of Tyaga and the
place of Yoga. The cup of the blood, The cup
of the blood. The offering of the life of life.
An offering of light on the tray of the sky
An offering of flowers on the tray of the earth.
An offering of love on the tray of life
An offering of life on the tray of Golgotha.

Pr   Father-Mother God,
**All   Graciously accept these gifts as a memorial
of Your self-gift to us, consummated by the
passion, death and resurrection of your
divine son, and as a symbol of our own
offering.**

VENERATION OF THE OFFERINGS
(Doxology)

*The priest and people together venerate the offerings
of bread and wine on the talam:*

Aum.   Adoration to the Lord, Eternal God.
Aum.   Adoration to the Lord, Being,
          Knowledge and Bliss.
Aum.   Adoration to the Lord, Path of
          Truth.
Aum.   Adoration to the Lord, Life Eternal.
Aum.   Adoration to the Lord, Son of the
          Virgin.

Aum.	Adoration to the Lord, Fullness of the Godhead.
Aum.	Adoration to the Lord, True Man.
Aum.	Adoration to the Lord, True Embodiment of Sacrifice.

The priest incensing the offerings on the talam circlewise, prays

Pr   May this altar be sanctified by the fragrance of Your holiness, like the first sacrificial altar, source of the origins and order of the whole creation, like the tent of meeting with the ark of the covenant covered by the cloud.

May it be sanctified like Golgotha when the rocks split and the tombs opened, when the eternal sacrifice was consumated.

UDGITA-AVAHANAM (Anaphora)

Creation and Salvation History

Pr   In commemoration of the economy of salvation, let us sing in praise of the everlasting mercy of God, who out of His eternal love for us revealed Himself and opened to us the path of liberation.

Hymn

O Fullness of Eternal Being,
O Fullness of Incomparable Wisdom,
O Fullness of Ineffable Beauty,
To You we bow, give us Your Grace.
O Fullness of Eternal Being.

Silent Adoration

Pr   Father-Mother God, without beginning or end, imperishable, you called the universe into existence and You preserve it through your love, that you might give it a share in your life, everlastingly. your glory pervades the whole creation. Every atom, every sphere of life is filled with your presence.

Cn   Eternal source of all, we praise your glory, we adore your awesome power.

Pr   The whole universe praises your Great Glory, who in the beginning started the work of creation, when there was only a formless void shrouded in darkness. But with your Spirit hovering over the abyss, and by your powerful Word, you called the universe into existence, out of nothingness into being, and you created the light out of darkness.

Cn   We praise you, silent and hidden, invisible One, the formless, who gave name and form to all creatures.

We offer our thanksgiving to you who created us in your image and likeness.[31] You gave us eternal life and, like a parent, you took us under your providence, and blessed us by giving us the gift of reason to grasp the truth, and the will to love what is good.

True embodiment of Being, Knowledge and Bliss, you are our father and mother. You

alone are our salvation. It is you who give us peace.

Pr   Because humankind disobeyed you, who are goodness itself, we lost eternal life and the dharma declined, ignorance surrounded us with spiritual darkness. Nevertheless, in the indescribable tenderness of your love, you remembered us and you promised us salvation. Through the prophets and teachers of dharma, you revealed the message of salvation. Those who sought the truth with a pure mind became witnesses to the mysteries of salvation through their spiritual and moral charisms.

Cn   **O Light of the nations, your wisdom is inscrutable and Your universal providence wonderful.**

Pr   When the fullness of time came, remembering the covenants you made with our fathers Noah, with Abraham and Moses, you the invisible one became visible. You the eternal Son became a man, born of a virgin. By your example and precepts, you taught us the way to liberation and revealed the Kingdom of Heaven by signs and wonders. By your passion, death and resurrection, you redeemed us for ever. You united us as the new people of God, to be rooted in faith and love. You sent your Holy Spirit that we might realize your presence in our hearts.

Cn   **Lord Jesus the Christ, eternal praise to you for your inexpressible self-gift to us. May**

the mystery of salvation be perfected in us who live in expectation of the vision of your form in the universe.

Pr You instituted the one sacrifice and sacrament to be offered until you return, and you appointed us your ministers, to offer this sacrifice in a community. Therefore, in accordance with your teachings, in your Church assembled here, we commemorate and accomplish your saving mystery.

EPICLETIC HYMN

Extending the hands above the holy offerings:

Pr Giver of devotion! Essential wisdom!
Cn **Embodiment of love and Lord of beauty!**
Bestower of peace!
Giver of salvation and all boons!
Holy Spirit, come down, my Lord!
Adoration to you!

A moment of silent adoration

INSTITUTION NARRATIVE

Priest: And now we remember Jesus and what He did, Who, in the night in which He was betrayed, took bread into His holy and innocent hands, and with His eyes lifted up towards heaven, He gave thanks to You, Almighty God and He blessed It.

The following traditional Hebrew blessing may be said at the option of the celebrant:

Baruch ata Adonai, Elohaynu melech ha-olom, ha-motzi lechem min ha'arets –
Blessed be you, O Lord our God, Who brings forth bread from the earth

He broke It, and gave It to His disciples saying: "All of you, take and eat of this for

This is my Body

which was broken for you. Do this in remembrance of me."

The Host is elevated

Priest: In like manner, after He had supped, He took the cup, and when He had given thanks He blessed it.

The following traditional Hebrew blessing may be said at the option of the celebrant: Baruch ata Adonai, Elohaynu melech ha-olom, boray peri ha'gafen – Blessed be you, O Lord our God, Who brings forth the fruit of the vine

and He gave It to His disciples saying: All of you, drink of this, for

This is my Blood

Of the New and Everlasting Covenant, which is shed for you and for many for the remission of sins. Do this as often as you drink it in remembrance of me.

ANUSMARANA (Anamnesis)

Raising the hands and looking upwards

Pr   Eternal Father-Mother, having received this example from holy tradition, we commemorate and celebrate the passion, death and resurrection of Your Divine Son until His glorious return.

AVAHANAM (Epiclesis)

Pr   *Fluttering his right hand*

Dn   How awesome is this

over the bread and the

moment, when the Holy and

left over the chalice, he

Life-giving Spirit is

prays silently

moved to descend from the
heights of heaven above,
Have mercy on me, Lord!
and hovers over this
Send Your Holy Spirit upon
Eucharist here set before
me and upon this offering,
us, and rests on it and
that He may descend on it
hallows it. We tremble

and make it the life-
giving body, who, by His
hovering, perfects all the
mysteries of the Church.

with awe and wonder.
With joined hands, let us
bow our heads in
supplication to the Lord.

Cn   **May peace and good hope be with us all.**

Pr   Hear us, O Lord! Hear us, O Lord! Hear us, O Lord, and be gracious to all!

Cn   **Lord, have mercy on us.**

Waving his hand three times over the bread and making the sign of the cross three times, he prays:

Pr   May the Holy Spirit, coming down and abiding here, make this bread the life-giving body, the very body of our God and Savior Jesus Christ.

Cn   **Amen.**

Waving his right hand over the chalice and making the sign of the cross three times, he prays:

Pr   And make this chalice into the blood of the New Covenant, the redeeming blood, the very blood of our God and Savior Jesus Christ.

Cn   **Amen.**

Raising the hands

Pr   May these Mysteries of which we partake make us partakers of Your joy, Lord, and we will offer praise and thanksgiving to You, and Your Uniquely Beloved Son and Your Holy Spirit, now and always and for ever.

Cn   Amen.

ARTHANA (Intercessions)

Pr   O Lord of all, Source and Establisher and Preserver of eternal dharma we pray that peace and tranquillity may descend on the whole world and on us who offer Your eternal sacrifice. It was this sacrifice that restored the cosmic order and reestablished dharma. May all men grow in the eternal life which You give them.

Cn   Lord, hear our prayer.

Dn   We pray for our leaders. [Individual leaders mentioned, as well as all bishops, priests, and ministers of the Church. May also include all spiritual leaders everywhere.]

Cn   Lord, hear our prayer.

                               Dn
We pray for the unity of the Churches and the peace and serenity of all communities of love and service. You were the servant of the people and of the whole world, and the Son of Mary, who offered herself to Your Father as the Lord's servant, prompt us to be servant-Churches in the world today.

Cn   Lord, hear our prayer.

Dn   Lord, You are the Resurrection and the Life who raise the dead and lead them to dwell in Your Father's house. Bless all the living and the dead and all those in need, especially those who asked prayers from us.

Cn   Lord, hear our prayer.

Dn   We pray that justice with love may reign all over the world and harmony be restored among all nations and races, and preserved in this our country, its neighbors, and in the whole of creation.

Cn   Lord, hear our prayer.

Dn   We pray for our planet – for the air, for the rains and the dews and the fruits of the earth, for the seasons of growth and of harvesting; we pray for all living beings, that all who control the oceans and the earth, and space may respect nature and share its treasures with the millions who are in want.

Cn   Lord, hear our prayer.

Dn   We pray for our land, that You may give to her leaders a spirit of dedication and service, for building up our people into an integrated and deeply united and prosperous nation.

Cn   Lord, hear our prayer.

PRASANNA POWA (Oblation and Elevation)

Pr   Father-Mother God, we worship You and we thank You for having made us to come near the body and blood of Your Divine Son through Your Holy Spirit.

128

Raising the talam with both hands: Triple arati, or Trivitharati with light, incense and flowers.

All   **This is the divine food that comes down from heaven. This is the divine presence that gives the immortal nectar[54] to the soul. May this sacred presence take possession of us and may we be one with the Lord.**

The priest places the talam with the consecrated bread and wine on the altar for a moment of silent adoration for all.

NIDHANAM (Communion)

Hymn

You are the Celestial Food dwelling in Heaven.
The Immortal Nectar that has come down upon earth.
The Salvation of the World,
The Inexhaustible Spiritual Treasure of Mankind
You are the Power of Life, the Light of the World,
The Supreme Lord of the Universe,
The Most Revered King of Kings.
You are the Great Soul and Good Master
The Remission of sins,
The Holy Place of pilgrlms.
You are the Almighty, Knowledge and Bliss,
The Friend of the poor
The Ocean of Love.
You are the Lord of my soul.

The priest breaks the bread of life and signs it with the precious blood.

Pr   May the Body of our Lord and His Precious Blood be mingled together and perfected for ever.

The particle of His Body is dropped in the chalice with His Blood

May it be unto the pardon of our sins and for the hope of eternal life.

Fraction Hymn

O Gracious and Merciful Lord, give us Your grace.
Lord Jesus, we bow to Your feet, we Your devotees.
Give us Your grace.
O Gracious and Merciful Lord, give us Your grace.
Loving Lord, give us Your grace,
a simple glance full of mercy.
O Gracious and Merciful Lord, give us Your grace.

Pr   O Christ, son of the Living God
All   May we be bearers of immortality. Lord of plenty, dwell within us. You are our refuge, You are the sole goal of our life.

Pr   Brethren, behold the heavenly banquet that is prepared for us by Christ our Lord.
Cn   Lord, we are unworthy; graciously make us worthy to receive You.

Pr   O Lord of all, You have said: Ask and you shall receive, seek and you shall find, knock and it shall be opened to you receive our petitions and grant us the abundance of Your blessings.

Let us say the prayer taught by Christ our Lord, and beg our loving Father-Mother to give us the life-giving bread.

All   Our Father which art in heaven, hallowed be thy name. Thy kingdom come, thy will be done on earth as it is in heaven. Give us this day our daily bread, and forgive our trespasses as we forgive those who trespass against us. Lead us not into temptation, but deliver us from evil. For thine is the kingdom, and the power, and the glory forever. Amen.

COMMUNION

Distributed under both species, while appropriate hymns are sung.

While the priest washes the sacred vessels:

Pr   O Lord of all, our Creator and Lord,

Cn   May Your Spirit dwell in us who have received Your body and blood. May we who have received the food of peace become worthy of the eternal banquet. O Lord of all, Eternal Fullness, and Center of Light, we offer You thanks for Your

boundless kindness. You have made us who are weak, worthy to enjoy the sweetness of Your words and to share in the divine mysteries. Eternal praise to You for Your gifts beyond measure.

Hymn of Praise

Cn   Holy, Holy, Holy are You, Myriads of heavenly beings sing. Gathered together even on earth we praise Your glories always.

UDVASANA
(BLESSING AND LEAVE TAKING)

Pr   Beloved, let us bear witness to Christ in our various spheres of life.

Cn   **Bless us and send us into Your harvest.**

Pr   May Christ our Lord give us the grace to continue our lives in the spirit of this sacrifice which we have offered, overcoming evil with good, falsehood with truth, and hatered with love, let us be witnesses to Christ in the actions of our lives. May our hope in Christ strengthen us in our sorrows and by our mutual love may the world come to know us as disciples of Christ. By seeing our good works, may others also come to glorify God.

Raising his hand over the congregation in blessing:

Pr   May the grace of the Lord Jesus who became incarnate in the world, the love of God, and the fellowship of the Holy Spirit be with us all!

132

Cn   **Now and for ever.**

Pr   Aum! Adoration to the Self-existent.
       Aum! Adoration to the God-man.
       Aum! Adoration to the Holy Spirit.

All   **Aum! Peace, peace, peace.**
      or
      Aum! Shanti, shanti, shantih!

A EUCHARISTIC LITURGY FROM INDIA

*Based Upon one Developed
by Dom Bede Griffiths, OSB*

The celebrant introduces the Mass and greets the community

Invocation

Priest: Fullness there, fullness here, from fullness fullness proceeds.
           Once fullness has proceeded from fullness, fullness remains.

PURIFICATION RITE

The celebrant washes his hands and sprinkles some water on the people saying

Priest: As our body is made clean by this water, may our soul be made spotless by your grace.

The celebrant invites all to review their life. Then all pray

All: **Praise to the refuge of all**
        Praise to the most merciful
        Praise to him who is eternal purity
        Praise to the spotless one
        Praise to the destroyer of sin
        Praise to the protector of the just
        Praise to the remover of ignorance.

The celebrant, holding the right hand up, facing the people, pronounces the following formula of absolution

Priest:　　May the God of peace who brought from the dead our Lord Jesus, the great shepherd of the sheep, by the blood of the eternal covenant, cleanse you from all your wrong doings and strengthen you with everything good, that you may do his will, working in you that which is pleasing in his sight, through Jesus Christ to whom be glory for ever and ever. Amen.

All exchange a sign of the peace

The lighting of the lamp: Celebrant lights the big lamp with the arati lamp

All:　　**Praise to the divine light**
　　　　Praise to the true light
　　　　Praise to the light of life
　　　　Praise to the light of the world
　　　　Praise to the light of the self
　　　　Praise to the inner light.

Priest:　　Eternal light, shining beyond the heaven's radiant sun, illuminating all regions, above, below and across, true light enlightening every one coming into the world, dispel the darkness of our hearts and enlighten us with the splendor of your glory.

All:　　**Your word is a lamp for our steps a light on our path.**

The celebrant touches the flame with the tips of his fingers and then brings his fingers to his eyes. All turn to the light and perform the same gesture

LITURGY OF THE WORD

Homage is paid to the books with light and incense

During the readings, the people remain with open hands and the palms turned upwards resting on their knees

The celebrant blesses the scripture readers with the following blessing

Priest: May he who quickens the intellect and kindles the heart strengthen you with his power to proclaim the saving word.

The Bible is read. Followed by a short silent meditation

The celebrant or bishop blesses the gospeller saying

Priest: May the Lord be in (your/my) heart and on (your/my) lips that through my heart the love of God may shine forth and through my lips his spiritual power be manifest.

The Gospel is read

Homily if any

Silent reflection

LITURGY OF THE EUCHARIST

The celebrant invites the community to formulate their intentions. He concludes the prayer of the faithful

The celebrant takes the dish of eight flowers as he says

Priest: Father, send down your Spirit upon these offerings,
the symbols of our self-gift to you.
May we be pleasing in your sight.
May we be united with the sacrifice of your Son.

The celebrant places the eight flowers on the tray with the bread and wine in the eight directions, saying each time one of the following attributes of Jesus Christ

Priest: Jesus, the Lord
Jesus, the Son of God
Jesus, the Son of Mary
Jesus, the God-man
Jesus, the true person
Jesus, the anointed one
Jesus, the true teacher
Jesus, the savior.

The celebrant making an offering with light and incense over the offerings, continues

Priest: To whom with you and the Holy Spirit be honor and glory now and forever. Amen.

EUCHARISTIC PRAYER

Priest: May your Holy Spirit, O God, enlighten our minds and open our lips, that we may sing the WONDERS of your love!

All: Help us, Spirit Divine, to proclaim God's mercy!

Priest: Let us praise and thank the Lord, our God, whose majesty pervades the universe

All: Great is his name and worthy of praise!

Priest: Let us celebrate the glory of the Lord whose splendor shines in the depths of our hearts.

All: Glory to him in whom we have our being!

Priest: O supreme Lord of the Universe, You fill and sustain everything around us. You are the Ancient of Days who turned, with the touch of your hand, chaos into order, darkness into light. Deep and wonderful, the mysteries of your creation. You formed us in your own image, entrusted the earth to our care, and called us to share in your own being, your own knowledge, your own bliss.

All: Praise to the one who is Being, knowledge, bliss!
Praise to the eternal reality!
Praise to the fullness of all perfections!

Priest: Father most kind and merciful, you want all to reach the shores of salvation. You reveal yourself to all who search for you with a sincere heart. You are the Power almighty adored in Presence hidden in nature, the Light that shines bright in the hearts of all who seek you, through knowledge and love, sacrifice and detachment. You chose for yourself a people and made with them a lasting covenant. Despite their infidelity, you were true to your promise, and taught them to long for the day of the Savior, the day of peace and salvation for all.

All: **Praise to the expectation of the Nations! Praise to the promised one of Israel! Praise to him who comes in the name of the Lord!**

Priest: O God invisible, at the favorable time you were pleased to become visible to us. Your Word, your only begotten Son, took on our human condition and was born of the Virgin Mary. As Supreme Teacher and Master, he imparted the words of eternal life to the poor and humble of heart. He went about doing good. When his hour had come, of his own accord he laid down his life as a sacrifice for our sin. Raised from the dead by you, Father, he became for us the source of life, and sent the Holy Spirit to fill the world with joy and peace. Now we pray you, Father, send this same Spirit to fill these gifts of bread and wine with his divine power, and to make present among us the great mystery of our salvation.

All: **Come, O Spirit Supreme. Come, O Spirit all-holy.**

Come, O Spirit who fill the universe.

Priest: Lord, answer me
            Lord, answer me
            Lord, answer me

Epiclesis

[Priest: May the Holy spirit descend upon this
            bread and make it the life giving body,
            saving body, the body of our God Lord
            Jesus Christ. May this wine in this chalice
            be transformed into the blood of our Lord
            and God, Jesus Christ (a very ancient
            epiclesis).

                    or

Priest: And we pray that you send your Holy
            Spirit upon the offering of your holy
            mysteries so that they may be filled with
            the Holy Spirit, unto the strengthening of
            the faith in truth (ancient Latin and Coptic
            epiclesis).

                    or

Priest: We implore you, the merciful God to send
            forth your Holy spirit upon this offering,
            to make the bread the body of Christ, and
            the wine the blood of Christ. For whatever
            the Holy Spirit touches is hallowed and
            changed (epiclesis of St. Cyril of
            Jerusalem, c. 385 A.D.)].

Words of Institution

Priest: And now we remember Jesus and what He
            did, Who, in the night in which He was
            betrayed, took bread into His holy and
            innocent hands, and with His eyes lifted
            up towards heaven, He gave thanks to
            You, Almighty God, our Father, and He
            blessed It.

            He broke It, and gave It to His disciples
            saying: "All of you, take and eat of this
            for

This is my Body

            which was broken for you. Do this in
            remembrance of me."

The Host is elevated

Priest: In like manner, after He had supped, He
            took the cup, and when He had given
            thanks He blessed it, and He gave It to His
            disciples saying: All of you, drink of this,
            for

This is my Blood

            Of the New and Everlasting Covenant,
            which is shed for you and for many for the
            remission of sins. Do this as often as you
            drink it in remembrance of me.

The chalice is elevated

Priest: And so, Father, in gratitude we celebrate the memorial of the obedient death of your Son, of his glorious resurrection from the dead, the triumphant ascension into heaven, and his outpouring of the Spirit in whom the Church is born. While we offer you his unique and holy sacrifice we await his return in glory. When he comes he will gather up the fruits of redemption, hold them together in his fullness and place them at your feet

All: **We announce your death and proclaim your resurrection, Lord Jesus; gather all your people into your kingdom when you come in glory.**

Priest: Merciful Father, bring together all your people together through the Holy Spirit in one mystical body of Jesus Christ. Help us live in fellowship. Let us remember and bless the names of the patriarchs of all the historic sees, our own matriarch, Archbishop Richard, and all the bishops, priests, deacons, and all other ministers that their ministries will always be inspired by the Christ within. Also, bless all our brethren who are not present at this Eucharist.

Bless all the efforts of all those who labor to build a world, where the poor and hungry will have their fill, where all peoples will live in harmony, where justice and peace, unity and love will reign. Grant to all the departed a share in your bliss. Welcome them in your

142

Kingdom, where, Mary, the Virgin Mother of God, the Apostles and Martyrs, the Saints of all lands and ages, unceasingly pray for us and help us share in the riches of your Son, our Lord Jesus Christ. Loving Father, send down your Spirit, the fullness of your bliss, fill with Joy and peace all of us who share in the Body and Blood of Christ, that we may be one in him, and manifest our unity in loving service. May he be the pledge of our resurrection and lead us in hope to the shore of eternal life with all the Just in the Kingdom of Heaven.

In the oneness of the Supreme Spirit, through Christ who unites all things in his fullness, we and the whole creation give to you, God of all, Father of all, honor and glory, thanks and praise, worship and adoration, now and in every age, for ever and ever.

All: **Amen. You are the fullness of Reality, one without a second, Being, Knowledge, Bliss.**

COMMUNION RITE

*The celebrant says a few words of introduction to the communion rite. Then this
prayer*

Priest: This is the Bread that came down from Heaven; whoever eats this Bread will never die. This is the cup of immortal nectar; whoever drinks of this cup will live forever. For the Lord says, "He will have eternal Life, and I will raise him up on the last day." Do you believe this?

All: **Yes, Lord, we believe, for you have the words of eternal Life.**

Then the celebrant invites the people to recite or sing the 'Lord's Prayer.' All recite with folded hands

All: **Our Father which art in heaven hallowed be thy name, thy kingdom come, thy will be done, on earth as it is in heaven. Give us this day our daily bread, and forgive our debts as we forgive our debtors. And lead us not into temptation, but deliver us from evil ... (For thine is the kingdom, and the power, and the glory, forever. Amen.)**

The celebrant breaks the bread for communion saying

Priest: The cup of blessing which we bless is the communion with the blood of Christ. The bread which we break is the communion with the body of Christ.

Because there is one bread, we who are many are one body, for we all partake of the one bread.

Then the celebrant invites the congregation to partake of the sacred meal, saying

My feast is ready, says the Lord; brothers and sisters, let us Joyfully   share   in his banquet.

After all have received communion, a short pause is observed, followed by chanting [optional]

This leads to complete silence

Prayer

CONCLUDING RITE

The celebrant addresses a few parting words, inspiring the community with a sense of mission. Then he imparts the solemn blessing, saying

Priest: May God, beyond all name and form, share with you his glory beyond measure, and make you enter into the mystery of his presence.

All: Amen.

Priest: May God who became manifest in Jesus Christ enlighten your minds, strengthen your wills and fill your hearts with love.

All: Amen.

Priest: May God, the indweller in the cave of your hearts, animate you with his life.

All: **Amen.**

Priest: And may the grace of our Lord Jesus Christ, and the love of God, and the fellowship of the Holy Spirit be with you all.

All: **Amen.**

Concluding hymn

THE CREEDS AND OTHER PROFESSIONS OF FAITH

CHOICE 1:
The Nicene Creed

All: We believe in one God, the Father, the Almighty, maker of heaven and earth, of all that is seen and unseen.

We believe in one Lord, Jesus Christ, the only Son of God, eternally begotten of the Father, God from God, Light from Light, true God from true God, begotten, not made, one in being with the Father. Through him all things were made. For us men and our salvation he came down from heaven: by the power of the Holy Spirit he was born of the Virgin Mary, and became man.

For our sake he was crucified under Pontius Pilate, he suffered, died, and was buried. On the third day he rose again in fulfillment of the Scriptures; he ascended into heaven and is seated at the right hand of the Father. He will come again in glory to judge the living and the dead, and his kingdom will have no end.

We believe in the Holy Spirit, the Lord, giver of life, who proceeds from the Father. With the Father and Son he is worshipped and glorified. He has spoken through the Prophets.

We believe in one Holy, Catholic, and Apostolic Church. We acknowledge one baptism for the forgiveness of sins. We look for the resurrection of the dead, and the life of the world to come. Amen.

CHOICE 2:
The Apostle's Creed

All: We believe in God, the Father almighty, creator of heaven and earth.

We believe in Jesus Christ, his only Son, our Lord. He was conceived by the power of the Holy Spirit and born of the Virgin Mary. He suffered under Pontius Pilate, was crucified, died, and was buried. He descended to the dead. On the third day he rose again. He ascended into heaven, and is seated at the right hand of the Father. He will come again to judge the living and the dead.

We believe in the Holy Spirit, the holy catholic Church, the communion of saints, the forgiveness of sins, the resurrection of the body, and the life everlasting.

AMEN.

CHOICE 3:
Creed as Adapted by
Fr. Edward Schillebeekx, O.P.

All: We believe in God, the Father: the omnipotence of love. He is the Creator of heaven and earth; this whole universe, with all its mysteries; this earth on which we live, and the stars to which we travel.

He knows us from eternity, he never forgets that we are made of the dust of the earth and that one day we shall return again to it as dust.

We believe in Jesus Christ, the only-beloved Son of God. For love of all of us, he has willed to share our history, our existence with us in a human way. He has dwelt as a man among us, a light in the darkness. But the darkness did not overcome him. We nailed him to the cross. And he died and was buried. But he trusted in God's final word, and is risen, once and for all; he said that he would prepare a place for us, in his Father's house, where he now dwells.

We believe in the Holy Spirit, who is the Lord and gives life. And for the prophets among us, he is language, power and fire. We believe that together we are all on a journey, pilgrims, called and gathered together, to be God's holy people, for We confess freedom from evil, the task of bringing justice and the courage to love.

We believe in eternal life, in love that is stronger than death, in a new heaven and a new earth. And we believe that we may hope for a life with God and with one another for all eternity: Glory for God and peace for men.

CHOICE 4:
New Zealand Affirmation of Faith

You, O God, are supreme and holy. You create our world and give us life. Your purpose overarches everything we do. You have always been with us. You are God.

You, O God, are infinitely generous, good beyond all measure. You came to us before we came to you. You have revealed and proved your love for us in Jesus Christ, who lived and died and rose again. You are with us now. You are God.

You, O God, are Holy Spirit. You empower us to be your gospel in the world. You reconcile and heal; you overcome death.

You are our God. We worship you.

CHOICE 5:
A Revised Act of Faith Based Upon that of the Liberal Catholic Church

We believe that God is love and power and truth and light; that perfect justice rules the world; that all his children shall one day reach his feet, however far they stray. We hold the fatherhood of God, the fellowship of humankind; we know that we do serve him best when best we serve our fellow human being. So shall his blessing rest upon us † and peace for evermore. Amen.

CHOICE 6:
Statement of Spiritual Principles
by Archbishop Richard Gundrey

All: We affirm the inseparable oneness of God and all humankind, the realization of which comes through spiritual intuition, and the implications of which are that we can aspire to reproduce divine perfection in our bodies, emotions, thoughts, and external affairs.

We affirm the freedom of each person in matters of belief.

We affirm that the Good is supreme, universal, and eternal.

We affirm that the kingdom of heaven is within us and outside us, that we are one with God, and that we should love one another and return good even where apparent negativity exists.

We affirm that the sick are healed through prayer, and we endeavor to manifest perfection because the kingdom of heaven within us is perfect already.

We affirm that our mental states are carried forward into the manifest world and become our experience through the creative law of cause and effect.

We affirm that the Divine Nature expressing Itself through us manifests as Health, Supply, Wisdom, Love, Life,

Truth, Power, Peace, Beauty, and Joy.

We affirm that the entire cosmos is the body of God, spiritual in essence, governed by God, through laws, which are spiritual in reality, even when material in appearance. And so it is, Amen.

CHOICE 7:
Alternative Creed
of Archbishop Herman Adrian Spruit

P: Where the Spirit of the Lord is, there is One True Church, Apostolic and Universal, whose Holy Faith let us now reverently and sincerely declare:

All We believe in one God, maker and ruler of all things, Father of all humankind, the source of all goodness, love, beauty, and truth.

We believe in Jesus Christ, God manifest in the flesh, our example, teacher, redeemer, and liberator.

We believe in the Holy Spirit, the Holy Saint Sophia, God present with us for guidance, comfort, purification, and strength.

We believe in the forgiveness of sins, our forgiveness of others being the measure of God's forgiveness of ours. We believe in the life of prayer and love, grace for every need, and in a generous response to our Christian obligations as a measure of our sincerity. We believe in the word of God as a sufficient rule both of faith and practice.

We believe in the final triumph of righteousness and in a dynamic quality of life, beginning on Earth and continuing through eternities. Amen.

Note: Presented to Archbishop Herman Adrian Spruit, the ordaining bishop, as a gift and legacy by the Autumn, 1979, Cathedral class of ordinands to the priesthood.

HOLY BAPTISM

Baptism is a sacrament by which the recipient is solemnly knitted to membership of Christ's holy church and grafted into His mystical body.

The exorcism is intended to deaden the germs of evil in infants, or to effect a preliminary purification in those more advanced in years.

The first anointing is, as indicated, for the strengthening and safeguarding of the candidate and is followed immediately by the baptism in the name of the Trinity and then by the second anointing with holy chrism, still further to strengthen him.

Where there is doubt about the validity or completeness of a former baptism, the sacrament is readminstered conditionally.

The pouring of the water symbolizes both the washing away of sin and the down pouring of power from on high. The font is usually placed near the entrance of the church to show that by baptism we gain admission to the church of God.

So far as is convenient, holy baptism should be administered publicly in the presence of a congregation.

FORM TO BE USED FOR INFANTS

Instructions to parents

The head of the child should be uncovered and the dress so arranged that the oil of catechumens can be applied on the neck or breast before and at the nape of the neck behind. It is customary that the 'white vesture' shall be a white silk handkerchief, presented by the godparents. This is to be blessed by the priest and is retained by the child in memory of his baptism.

For each child to be baptized there should be a godfather and godmother, who say the words of presentation respectively, according to whether the child be male or female.

All stand

THE INVOCATION

Priest: **In the name of the Father and of the † Son and of the Holy Spirit.**

R. Amen.

The people are seated

THE PRESENTATION

The child Is presented as follows

Sponsor. Reverend Father (or Mother), we present to you this child, praying that you will receive him/her into the fellowship of Christ's church.

P.   Brethren, Christ, in his great loving kindness, has ordained that his mystic bride, our holy mother the church, shall guide and protect her children at every stage from the cradle to the grave. To this end is the sacrament of holy baptism ordained, that in his name the church may give welcome and blessing to children who have newly come into this world of pilgrimage, and that the soul may dwell in a body purified from the taint of evil, sanctified and set apart for the service of almighty God.

Addressing the sponsors and congregation

Therefore, brethren of Christ's Catholic church, I pray you will join with me in this our holy rite, whereby this child shall be made a partaker of these heavenly gifts and become a member of his mystical body.

Hear the words of the gospel written by Saint Mark, beginning with the tenth chapter, thirteenth verse.

They brought young children to Christ, that he should touch them; and his disciples rebuked those that brought them. But when Jesus saw it, he was much displeased and said unto them: Suffer the little children to come unto me and forbid them not; for of such is the kingdom of God. Amen, I say unto you, whosoever shall not receive the kingdom of God as a little child, he shall not enter therein. And he took them up in his arms, put his hands upon them and blessed them.

The priest places his right hand on the head of the

child, and says

P: Let us pray.

O God, omnipotent and omnipresent, whose power works in every living creature, who alone are the source of all life and goodness, deign to shed upon this your servant, who has been called to the rudiments of the faith, a ray of your light; drive out from him all blindness of heart, break all the chains of iniquity wherewith he has been bound; open to him, O Lord, the gate of your glory, that being replenished with the spirit of your wisdom and strengthened by your mighty power, he may be free from the taint of evil desire and steadfastly advancing in holiness may joyfully serve thee in the course you hast appointed for him; through Christ our Lord. R. Amen.

THE EXORCISM

P.   In the name which is above every name, in the power of the ✝ Father and of the ✝ Son and of the Holy ✝ Ghost, I exorcise all influences and seeds of evil; I lay upon them the spell of Christ's holy church, that they trouble not this servant of God;

He again places his hand on the head of the child

For he who is the Lord of love and compassion has deigned to call this child to his holy grace and blessing and to the font of baptism.

The priest then proceeds as follows Ephphasa: that is, Be you opened

Here the priest makes the sign of the cross over the brow, the throat, and the heart of the child.

Let your mind and your heart be opened to the most holy Spirit of the living God, that your whole nature may be dedicated for ever to his service; so may you have power to receive the heavenly precepts and to be such in your conduct that you may be a pure temple of the living God.

He stretches out his right hand towards the child, and says

O God, with your ever-abiding power, watch over this your chosen servant, whom we dedicate to your service, that, using well the beginnings of your glory and heedfully observing your holy laws, he/she may be found worthy to attain to the fullness of the new birth; through Christ our Lord. R. Amen.

The priest places the end of his stole upon the child's shoulder, and says

Come into the temple of God, that you may have part with Christ unto life eternal.

THE FIRST ANOINTING

The priest takes upon his right thumb a little of the oil of catechumens. At the first two crosses the priest touches respectively the child's breast or throat and the nape of his neck, malting a small cross at each with the oil; he then, without touching the body, makes two crosses respectively before and behind the child, reaching to the entire length of the body.

P.   In the name of Christ our Lord, I ✝ anoint thee with oil for your safeguarding; may his holy angel ✝ go before thee, and ✝ follow after thee; may he be with thee in your downsitting and your uprising and keep thee in all your ways.

The Apostle's Creed is recited

All: We believe in God, the Father almighty, creator of heaven and earth.

We believe in Jesus Christ, his only Son, our Lord. He was conceived by the power of the Holy Spirit and born of the Virgin Mary. He suffered under Pontius Pilate, was crucified, died, and was buried. He descended to the dead. On the third day he rose again. He ascended into heaven, and is seated at the right hand of the Father. He will come again to judge the living and the dead.

We believe in the Holy Spirit, the holy catholic Church, the communion of saints, the forgiveness of sins, the resurrection of the body, and the life everlasting.

AMEN.

THE BAPTISM

While the godparents hold the child over the font, the priest pours some of the consecrated baptismal water over the head and forehead of the child thrice. At the same time he pronounces the words

N., I baptize you in the name of the ✝ Father and of the ✝ Son and of the Holy ✝ Ghost. Amen.

THE ANOINTING WITH CHRISM

The priest takes upon his thumb some of the sacred chrism and, anointing the child on the top of the head in the form of a cross, says:

With Christ's holy chrism do I ✝ anoint you, that his strength may prevent you in your going out and your coming in and may guide you into life everlasting.

The priest then says:
Be you closed.

Here the priest makes the sign of the cross over the brow, the throat, the heart and the navel of the child

THE RECEPTION

With his thumb, still moist with chrism, the priest makes a cross upon the child's brow; at the last clause he lays his hand upon the infant's head.

P. I receive this child into the fellowship of Christ's holy church and do ✞ sign him with the sign of the cross, in token that hereafter he/she shall not be ashamed to confess the faith of Christ our Lord, to acknowledge him when he shall come, and diligently fight under his banner against sin and selfishness, and that he/she shall continue as Christ's faithful soldier and servant throughout the ages of ages. **R.** Amen.

A white silk handkerchief is brought and the priest, having blessed it, places it upon the shoulders of the child, saying

Receive from holy church this white vesture as a pattern of the spotless purity and brightness of him whose service you have entered today and for a token of your fellowship with Christ and his holy angels, that your life may be filled with his peace.

The Lord's Prayer is recited here, if the baptism takes place outside a mass

Delivering a lighted candle to the child, the priest says

Take this burning light, enkindled from the fire of God's holy altar, for a sign of the ever-burning light of your spirit. God grant that hereafter his love shall so shine through your heart that you may continually enlighten the lives of the fellow-men.

The priest places his hand on the head of the child, saying

N., go in peace and may the Lord be with you. R. Amen.

THE CHARGE TO SPONSORS

P.   You who have brought this child here to be baptized, seeing that now he/she is regenerate of water and the Holy Spirit and grafted into the mystical body of Christ's church, remember that there lies upon you a duty not lightly to be cast aside. It is your duty to see to it that as soon as he/she is old enough to understand, he/she is taught God's holy will and commandment, as it was spoken by our Lord himself when he said: 'You shall love the Lord your God with all your heart and with all your soul and with all your mind and with all your strength. This is the first and great commandment; and the second is like unto it: 'You shall love your neighbor as yourself. On these two commandments hang all the law and the prophets.'

Also he/she shall be taught the doctrine of the holy Catholic church, into which he has [this day] been admitted and shall be brought in due course before the bishop to be confirmed.

FORM TO BE USED FOR CHILDREN

This form is to be used for children of four or five and upwards, who are able in some measure to understand the service.

All stand

THE INVOCATION

Priest. In the name of the Father and of the ✝ Son and of the Holy Spirit. R. Amen.

The people are seated

THE PRESENTATION

The child is presented as follows

Sponsor. Reverend Father, we present to you this child, praying that you will receive him/her into the fellowship of Christ's church.

P. Brethren, Christ, in his great loving kindness, has ordained that his mystic bride, our holy mother the church, shall guide and protect her children at every stage from the cradle to the grave. To this end has the sacrament of holy baptism been ordained, that in his name the church may give welcome and blessing to him/her who is come into this world of pilgrimage, and that the soul may dwell in a body purified from the taint of evil, sanctified and set apart for the service of almighty God.

Turning to the people

Therefore, brethren of Christ's catholic church, I pray you to join with me in this our holy rite, whereby this child shall be made partaker of these heavenly gifts and a member of his mystical body.

Hear the words of the gospel written by Saint Mark, in the tenth chapter, at the thirteenth verse.

They brought young children to Christ, that he should touch them; and his disciples rebuked those that brought them. But when Jesus saw it, he was much displeased and said to them: 'Suffer the little children to come unto me and forbid them not; for of such is the kingdom of God. Amen, I say unto you, whosoever shall not receive the kingdom of God as a little child, he shall not enter therein.' And he took them up in his arms, put his hands upon them and blessed them.

The priest places his right hand on the head of the child and says

P.   Let us pray.

O God, omnipotent and omnipresent, whose power works in every living creature, who alone are the source of all life and goodness, deign to shed upon this your servant, who has been called to the rudiments of the faith, a ray of your light: drive out from him/her all blindness of heart, break all the chains of iniquity wherewith he has been bound; open to him, O Lord, the gate of your glory, that, being replenished with the spirit of your wisdom and strengthened by your mighty power, may be free from the taint of evil desire and, steadfastly advancing in holiness, may joyfully serve you in the course you have appointed for him/her; through Christ our Lord. R. Amen.] The portion in brackets may be omitted.

THE EXORCISM

P.   In the name which is above every name, in the power of the ✝ Father and of the ✝ Son and of the Holy ✝ Ghost, be so purified that you may be rightly prepared to receive the first sacrament of Christ's holy church; (the priest places his hand on the head of the child) for he who is the Lord of love and compassion has deigned to call you to his holy grace and blessing and to the font of baptism.

He stretches out his right hand towards the child, and says:

Do, O Lord, with your ever-abiding power, watch over this your chosen servant, whom we dedicate to your service, that, using well the beginnings of your glory and heedfully observing your holy laws, he/she may be found worthy to attain to the fullness of new birth; through Christ our Lord. R. Amen.

The priest places the end of his stole upon the child's shoulder and says: Come into the temple of God, that you may have part with Christ unto life eternal.

THE FIRST ANOINTING

The priest now takes upon his right thumb a little of the oil of catechumens. At the first two crosses the priest touches respectively the child's breast or throat and the nape of his neck, making a small cross at each with the oil; he then, without touching the body, makes two crosses, respectively before and behind the child, reaching to the entire length of the body.

P. **In the name of Christ our Lord, I anoint you with oil for your safeguarding; may his holy angel ✟ go before thee and ✟ follow after thee; may he be with you in your downsitting and your uprising and keep you in all your ways.**

The Apostle's Creed is recited

All: **We believe in God, the Father almighty, creator of heaven and earth.**

We believe in Jesus Christ, his only Son, our Lord. He was conceived by the power of the Holy Spirit and born of the Virgin Mary. He suffered under Pontius Pilate, was crucified, died, and was buried. He descended to the dead. On the third day he rose again. He ascended into heaven, and is seated at the right hand of the Father. He will come again to judge the living and the dead.

We believe in the Holy Spirit, the holy catholic Church, the communion of saints, the forgiveness of sins, the resurrection of the body, and the life everlasting.

AMEN.

THE BAPTISM

While the child leans, or is held, over the font, the priest pours some of the consecrated baptismal water over the head and forehead of the child thrice. At the same time he pronounces the words

N., I baptize thee in the name of the ✝ Father and of the ✝ Son and of the Holy ✝ Ghost. Amen.

If the baptism be sub conditione the following is the formula

N., if you are not already baptized, then do I baptize you in the name of the ✝ Father and of the ✝ Son and of the Holy ✝ Ghost Amen.

THE ANOINTING WITH CHRISM

The priest takes upon his thumb some of the sacred chrism and, anointing the child an the top of the head in the form of a cross, says

With Christ's holy chrism do I ✝ anoint thee, that his strength may prevent you in your going out and your coming in and may guide you into life everlasting.

THE RECEPTION

With his thumb, still moist with chrism, the priest makes a cross upon the child's brow; at the last clause he lays his hand upon the child's head

P.   I receive you into the fellowship of Christ's holy church and do ✝ sign thee with the sign of the cross in token that hereafter you shall not be ashamed to confess the faith of Christ our Lord, to acknowledge him when he shall come and to diligently fight under his banner against sin and selfishness and that you shalt continue Christ's faithful soldier and servant throughout the ages of ages. R. Amen.

The Lord's Prayer is recited

A white silk handkerchief is brought and the priest, having blessed it, places it upon the shoulders of the child, saying

These words in brackets are usually to be omitted when the person has already received baptism in some other church or by lay ministration

Receive from holy church this white vesture as a pattern of the spotless purity and brightness of him whose service you have entered [today] and as a token of your fellowship with Christ and his holy angels, that your life may be filled with His peace.

Delivering a lighted candle to the child, the priest says

Take this burning light, enkindled from the fire of God's holy altar, for a sign of the ever-burning fight of your spirit. God grant that hereafter his love shall so shine through your heart that you may continually enlighten the lives of your fellow human beings.

170

The priest places his hand on the head of the child, saying

N., go in peace and may the Lord be with you. R. Amen.

THE FINAL CHARGE

The priest then addresses the neophyte, saying

You who have come here to be baptized, seeing that now you are regenerate of water and the Holy Spirit and grafted into the mystical body of Christ's church, remember that there lies upon you the duty of following God's holy will and commandment, as it was spoken by our Lord himself when he said: 'You shalt love the Lord your God with all your heart and with all your soul and with all your mind and with all your strength. This is the first and great commandment; and the second is like unto it: you shalt love your neighbor as yourself. On these two commandments hang all the law and the prophets.'

Also you shall further study the doctrine of the Holy Catholic Church, into which you have been admitted, and come in due course before the bishop to be confirmed by him.

FORM TO BE USED FOR ADULTS

THE INVOCATION

Priest. In the name of the Father ☦ and of the Son and of the Holy Spirit. R. Amen.

The people are seated
The candidate comes forward and kneels

THE EXORCISM

P.   In the name which is above every name, in the power of the ☦ Father and of the ☦ Son and of the Holy ☦ Ghost, be so purified that you may be rightly prepared to receive this first sacrament of Christ's holy church; (the priest places his hand on the head of the candidate) for he who is the Lord of love and compassion has deigned to call you to his holy grace and blessing and to the font of baptism.

The priest stretches out his right hand towards the candidate and says

Do, O Lord, with your ever-abiding power, watch over this your chosen servant whom we dedicate to your service that, using well the beginnings of your glory and heedfully observing your holy laws, he/she may be found worthy to attain to the fullness of the new birth; through Christ our Lord. R. Amen.

THE FIRST ANOINTING

The priest takes upon his right thumb a little of the oil of catechumens. At the first two crosses the priest touches respectively the can&date's breast or throat and the nape of his neck, making a small cross at each with the oil; he then, without touching the body, makes two crosses, respectively before and behind the candidate, reaching to the entire length of the body.

The Apostle's Creed is recited

All: **We believe in God, the Father almighty, creator of heaven and earth.**

We believe in Jesus Christ, his only Son, our Lord. He was conceived by the power of the Holy Spirit and born of the Virgin Mary. He suffered under Pontius Pilate, was crucified, died, and was buried. He descended to the dead. On the third day he rose again. He ascended into heaven, and is seated at the right hand of the Father. He will come again to judge the living and the dead.

We believe in the Holy Spirit, the holy catholic Church, the communion of saints, the forgiveness of sins, the resurrection of the body, and the life everlasting.

AMEN.

P.   In the name of Christ our Lord, I ✝ anoint thee with oil for your safeguarding; may his holy angel ✝ go before thee and ✝ follow after thee; may he be with you in your downsitting and your uprising and keep you in all your ways.

THE BAPTISM

While the candidate leans over the font the priest pours some of the consecrated baptismal water thrice over his head and forehead, pronouncing these words

N., I baptize thee in the name of the ✝ Father and of the ✝ Son and of the Holy ✝ Ghost. Amen.

If the baptism be sub condtione, the following is the formula

N., if you are not already baptized, then do I baptize thee in the name of the ✝ Father and of the ✝ Son and of the Holy ✝ Ghost. Amen.

THE ANOINTING WITH CHRISM

The priest takes upon his thumb some of the sacred chrism and, anointing the candidate on the top of the head in the form of a cross, says

With Christ's holy chrism do I ✝ anoint thee, that his strength may prevent you in your going out and your coming in and may guide you into life everlasting.

THE RECEPTION

With his thumb, still moist with chrism, the priest makes a cross upon the neophyte's brow; at the last clause he lays his hand on the neophyte's head

P.   I receive thee into the fellowship of Christ's holy church and do ✝ sign thee with the sign of the cross in token that hereafter you shall not be

ashamed to confess the faith of Christ our Lord, to acknowledge him when he shall come and manfully to fight under his banner against sin and selfishness and that you may continue as Christ's faithful soldier and servant throughout the ages of ages. R. Amen.

The Lord's Prayer is read or sung

The giving of the white vesture and light may then follow (or not) at the option of the priest and candidate

He places his hand on the head of the neophyte, saying

N., go in peace and may the Lord be with you. R. Amen.

A MARRIAGE SERVICE

Note: Various other components, such as readings, music, etc., may be added to this basic service. See, for example, a variety of consents, vows, ring exchanges, readings, and so forth, contained in The Wedding Service Guide.

INTRODUCTORY WORDS

INVOCATION

Priest: **In the name of the Father (or Creator) and the ✝ Son (or Word Made Flesh), and the Holy Spirit. Amen.**

ADDRESS TO THE PEOPLE

Priest: **Dearly beloved, we are gathered here together in the sight of God, and in the face of this congregation, to join together these two people in holy matrimony, which is an honorable estate, not to be entered into lightly or wantonly, but reverently, discreetly, advisedly and soberly, in the sight of God.**

Into which estate these two persons come now to be joined. Therefore if anyone can show any just cause why they may not be joined, let them now speak or forever hold their peace.

PRESENTATION OF THE BRIDE
[OPTIONAL]

Priest: **Who presents this (these) person(s) to be married**

Presenter(s): **I do.**

[CONSENT]

Priest: Of your own free will, N., is it your it your intnet to have N. to be your lawfully wedded wife [or spouse]?

R: **It is.**

Priest: Of your own free will, N., is it your it your intnet to have N to be your lawfully wedded husband [or spouse]?

R: **It is.**

[BLESSING BY THE CONGREGATION]

Brief explanation about the nature of a blessing. Members of the congregation are advised that not only are we here to ask God's blessing but to extend ours as well. As part of their own blessing the congregation is asked if they promise to do all that they can to uphold and support this new marriage

[LITURGY OF THE WORD]

If a reading is to be included in the marriage liturgy it is inserted here in the service

[VOWS]

This having been said, the woman presents the man with her right hand and the man cradles it in his own

Priest: Very well, then. N., please repeat after me.

Priest: I, N., take you, N., to be my wife [or spouse, or other preferred term], to have and to hold, from this day forward, for better, for worse, for richer, for poorer, in sickness and in health, to love, to cherish and to honor; and thereunto, in the presence of God, and with all that I am and all that I have. R. And so be it.

Priest: N., please repeat after me.

Priest: I, N., take you, N., to be my husband [or spouse, or other preferred term], to have and to hold, from this day forward, for better, for worse, for richer, for poorer, in sickness and in health, to love, to cherish and to honor; and thereunto, in the presence of God, and with all that I am and all that I have. R. And so be it.

[RING BLESSING]

The bridegroom and bride place the rings on a salver held before them by a server. The priest sprinkles the rings with holy water in the form of a cross and then blesses them saying

Priest: Bless † O Lord and † hallow these rings, that they who wear them may ever keep true faith to the other, and so, abiding in your peace and in conformity with your holy will, may ever live together in unchanging love; through Christ our Lord. R. Amen.

[RING EXCHANGE]

The ring bearer is motioned to come closer

Priest: *(to first party)* **N., as you give N. your ring, please repeat after me.**

Turning to giver the priest asks the first party to take the other's ring from the salver

Priest: **With this ring I thee wed; my truest love I thee pledge; with my body I give you reverence, and with all my strength I thee shield. R. Amen.**

First party is then asked to place the ring on their spouse's finger

Priest: *(to second party)* **N. as you give N. your ring, please repeat after me.**

Turning to second party the priest asks the second party to take ring from the salver

Priest: **With this ring I thee wed; my truest love I thee pledge; with my body I give you reverence, and with all my heart I thee unfold. R. Amen.**

Second party is then asked to place the ring on first party's finger

The priest joins their hands together. Here an anointing may take place

[UNITY CANDLE - *Optional*]

If the unity candle is to be lit it should be done here. While music is playing the bride and groom bring their lit candle to the large unity candle and then rejoin the officiant in the center of the sanctuary area.

[ANOINTING - *This is a non-traditional innovation*]

Brief explanation of anointing with oil as an ancient practice going back thousands of years, and an act designed to consecrate or set people or things aside for special purposes. Here we will consecrate the head, heart, and hands of each marriage partner.

Head - making the sign of the cross on each forehead

Priest: **With this holy oil we bless and consecrate your minds and your consciousness, that you might always remember the commitments you made today, that you grow in wisdom, and that you achieve a deep understanding of each other.**

Heart - making the sign of the cross before each of the couple's hearts

Priest: **With this holy oil we bless and consecrate your hearts, that deep love and compassion for each other may grow and** abide there, and that they are never dark or empty.

Hands - with palms up, and fingers touching, the priest draws a circle such that their hands are encompassed with the oil

Priest: **With this holy oil we bless and consecrate your hands, uniting the two of you. May it be that these hands are always used to hold and support each other; and to bring each other love and never hurt.**

[This concludes the anointing with oil.]

[DECLARATION & PRESENTATION]

Priest: **Those whom God has joined, let no one put asunder.**

Priest: **Forasmuch as N. (first party) and N. (second party) have consented together in holy wedlock and have witnessed the same before God and this company, and thereto have given and pledged their troth each to the other, and have declared the same by giving and receiving of a ring and joining hands: By the authority vested in me by the Church ([optional] and the State/Province/County of …) I declare that they are husband and wife [or other preferred terms].**

In the name of the Father ✝ and of the ✝ Son and of the Holy Spirit ✝.

Or

> May God the Father hold you in the palm
> of his hand ✝, the love of Christ be in your
> heart ✝, and may the Holy Spirit light
> your path ✝.

Priest: **You may now embrace and kiss one
another**

Priest: **Ladies and gentlemen, it my pleasure to
present to you N. (first party) and N.
(second party), husband and wife [or
other preferred terms].**

THE NUPTIAL MASS

THE CANTICLE

Antiphon
Now abideth faith, hope, love.
But the greatest of these is love.

1. **Blessed are all they that love the Lord: and walk in his ways.**

2. **For thou shalt eat the labor of thine hands: O well art thou and happy shalt thou be.**

3. **They that put their trust in the Lord shall be even as the mount Zion: which may not be removed, but standeth fast for ever.**

4. **The hills stand about Jerusalem: even so standeth the Lord round about his people, from this time forth for evermore.**

Antiphon

Now abideth faith, hope, love.
But the greatest of these is love.

THE COLLECT

P. **O God, who has consecrated the state of marriage to be such a great mystery that in it is signified the spiritual marriage and unity between Christ and his Church, grant to these your servants that, casting** aside all fear and selfishness and abiding in your holy love, they may successfully pass through all travails that may befall them and continually grow in wisdom and the knowledge of eternal things; through Christ our Lord. R. Amen.

THE EPISTLE

The epistle is taken from the thirteenth chapter of the First Epistle of St. Paul the Apostle to the Corinthians, beginning at the first verse.

Though I speak with the tongues of men and of angels and have not love, I am become as sounding brass, or a tinkling cymbal. And though I have the gift of prophecy and understand all mysteries and all knowledge; and though I have all faith, so that I could remove mountains, and have not love, I am nothing. And though I bestow all my goods to feed the poor and though I give my body to be burned and have not love, it profiteth me nothing. Love suffereth long and is kind; love envieth not; love vaunteth not itself, is not puffed up, doth not behave itself unseemly, seeketh not her own, is not easily provoked, thinketh no evil; rejoiceth not in iniquity, but rejoiceth in the truth; beareth all things, believeth all things, hopeth all things, endureth all things. Love never faileth: but whether there be prophecies, they shall fail; whether there be tongues, they shall cease; whetherthere be knowledge, it shall vanish away. For we know in part and we prophesy in part. But when that which is perfect is come, then that which is in part shall be done away. When I was a child, I spake as a child, I understood as a child, I thought as a child: but when I became a man, I put away childish things. For now we see through a glass, darkly; but then face to face: now I know in part; but then shall I know even as also I am known. And now abideth faith, hope, love, these three; but the greatest of these is love.

V. This is the word of the Lord
R. Thanks be to God

THE GRADUAL

1. The just shall shine and shall run to and fro: like sparks among the reeds.

2. They shall judge nations and rule over people: and their Lord shall reign for ever.

3. They that trust in him shall understand the truth: and they that are faithful in love shall rest in him; for grace and peace is to his elect.

4. He that loveth wisdom loveth life: and they that seek her early shall be filled with joy.

5. He that holdeth her fast shall inherit glory: and wheresoever she entereth the Lord will bless†

6. They that serve her shall minister to the Holy One: and them that love her the Lord doth love.

7. She is more precious than rubies: and all the things thou canst desire are not to be compared unto her.

8. Her ways are ways of pleasantness: and all her paths are peace.

THE GOSPEL

The holy gospel is taken from the fifteenth chapter of the Gospel according to St. John, beginning at the first verse.

I am the true vine and my Father is the husbandman. Every branch in me that beareth not fruit he takes away: and every branch that bears fruit, he prunes it, that it may bring forth more fruit. Now you are clean through the word which I have spoken unto you. Abide in me and I in you. As the branch cannot bear fruit of itself, except that it abides in the vine; no more can you, except that you abide in me. I am the vine, you are the branches; he that abides in me and I in him, the same brings forth much fruit: for without me you can do nothing. If a person abides not in me, that person is cast forth as a branch and is withered; and people gather them and cast them into the fire and they are burned. If you abide in me and my words abide in you, you shall ask what you will and it shall be done for you. Herein is my Father glorified, that you bear much fruit; so shall you be my disciples. As the Father has loved me, so have I loved you; continue in my love. If you keep my commandments, you shall abide in my love; even as I have kept my Father's commandments and abide in his love. These things have I spoken to you that my joy might remain in you and that your joy might be full.

V: This is the Gospel of the Lord
R: Praise be to you, Lord Jesus Christ

BEFORE THE COMMEMORATION OF THE SAINTS

OR INTERCESSORY PRAYERS

The priest stands at the epistle corner of the altar, turning towards the newly-married pair who kneel

The following versicles and responses and prayers are then sung or said

P.   O Lord, bless you servant and your handmaid.
C.   Who put their trust in you.

P.   Pour forth upon them of the fullness of thy love.
C.   And lighten them with thy heavenly grace.

P.   Send them wisdom from thy sanctuary.
C.   And do thou dwell in their understanding.

P. Be unto them, O Lord, a tower of strength.
C. And evermore defend them.

P. The Lord be with you.
C. And with thy spirit.

P. Let us pray.

P. O eternal God, creator and preserver of all people, giver of all spiritual grace, the author of everlasting life, send your blessing upon these your servants, this man and this woman, whom we ✝ bless in your name; that they may surely perform and keep the vows and covenant made between them and may so maintain in their lives in the knowledge and love of You, that they may dwell together in holy love and peace; through Christ our Lord. R. Amen.

If desired, the above collect may be followed by another specially selected prayer.

COMMUNION

The eye of the Lord is upon those that love him: even upon those that rest in his loving-kindness.

The human spirit is the candle of the Lord: and the righteous shall shine forth as the sun in the kingdom of their Father.

For every good gift and every perfect gift is from above and comes down from the

Father of Lights, in whom there is eternal light and strength.

POSTCOMMUNION

P. **O Lord Christ, thou who arte the well of infinite compassion, look with the tender eyes of your love upon this man and woman; strengthen them that the light of your glory may ever burn brightly in their hearts, O great King of love, to whom be praise and adoration from human beings and from the angel host. Amen.**

OFFICE OF THE HEALING SERVICE

Go to sanctuary by short way. Genuflect by lowest step stand at middle and say

IN THE NAME OF THE FATHER (Cross Self) ✝ and **OF THE SON**, and **OF THE HOLY SPIRIT**.

Response: **Amen.**

(Receive aspergill and cross self while saying)

May the Lord purify me that I may worthily perform His service.

(Asperse altar: first to center, then to left, then to right while saying)

In the strength of the Lord do I repel all adverse influence from this His holy altar and sanctuary;

(Face people, aspersing them first to center, then to left, then to right while saving)

and from this House, wherein we worship Him;

If you have a server, return aspergil to him/her; if not, retain it until the Cotifiteor; it can readily be placed in holder when you kneel; Face altar

And I pray our heavenly Father that He will send His healing Angel to minister unto these His servants here present, that they may be restored to health of mind and body; through Christ our Lord.

Response: **Amen**.

Kneel at lowest altar step to lead as people join in Confiteor

Oh Lord, thou hast created us to be immortal, and made him to be an image of Thine own eternity; yet often we forget the glory of our heritage, and wander from the path which leads to righteousness. But Thou, O Lord, hast made us for Thyself, and our hearts are ever restless till they rind their rest in Thee. Look with the eyes of Thy love upon our manifold imperfections, and pardon all our shortcomings, that we may be filled with the brightness of the everlasting light, and become the unspotted mirror of thy power and the image of Thy goodness; through Christ our Lord. Amen.

If not a priest, remain kneeling to pray the following prayer alone. If a priest, stand, go to altar, bow, extend hand toward people changing US to YOU; and making Cross over people instead of over self

God the Father, God the † Son (cross self), God the Holy Spirit, bless, preserve and sanctify us; O Lord in Thy loving kindness look upon us and be gracious unto us; absolve (cross self) us from all our sins, and grant us the grace and comfort of Thy Holy Spirit.
Response: **Amen**.

(Go to altar and bow. Turn by the right to people and announce hymn. Stand at epistle side during the hymn. The Following hymn is traditional in this

service; but it may be omitted or another substituted for it.)

Immortal Love, forever full, for ever flowing free,

Forever shared, forever whole, a never-ebbing sea.

Our outward lips confess the Name all other names above;

Love only knoweth whence it came, and comprehendeth love.

We need not climb the heavenly steps to bring the Lord Christ down,

Alike within the lowest deeps is He, of heaven the Crown.

But warm, sweet, tender, even yet a present help is He;

And faith has still its Olivet, and love its Galilee.

The healing of His seamless dress is by our beds of pain;

We touch Him in life's throng and press, and we are whole again.

Through Him the first fond prayers are said, our lips of childhood frame;

The last low whispers o'er our dead are uttered in His Name.

Alone, O love ineffable, thy holy Name is given;

A thousand saints Thy glories tell who in that Name have striven.

192

Lord Christ, of Love and Joy the Sun, undying praise to Thee,

With Father and with Spirit One, through all eternity. Amen.

Go to epistle side of altar, face people and read

Hear the words of the Apostle James: Is any sick among you? Let him call for the elders of the Church: and let them pray over him, anointing him with oil in the Name of the Lord. And the prayer of faith shall save the sick, and the Lord shall raise him up; and if he has committed sins, they shall be forgiven him. Pray for one another that ye may be healed. The effectual fervent prayer of a righteous person availeth much.

Go to altar center; announce the following Prayer Hymn, or substitute; turn by your back to the altar, and kneel during the singing

O Lord, Who hast given unto humankind bodily health and vigor wherewith to serve Thee, we pray Thee to free Thy servants from their sickness so far as may be expedient for them; and by the might of Thy (cross self) † blessing to restore unto them full health, both outwardly in their bodies and inwardly in their souls; through Christ our Lord.
Response. Amen.

Go to place where anointing will be given and say

Let those who desire to be anointed come forward.

The following three prayers, to be prayed over each one receiving healing, are to be memorized; when spoken, use a moderate tone of voice. Offer yourself as a channel, and do not attempt to apply any personal power of healing. Remind yourself of this as you wash and dry your hands in preparation for serving the first applicant. Raise right hand, palm toward the person, making the Sign of the Cross where shown over the person's head

In the Name which is above every name, in the power of the ✝ Father, and of the ✝ Son, and of the Holy ✝ Spirit, I exorcise all adverse influences, that you may be rightly purified to receive this Sacrament of Holy Anointing.

Moisten right thumb slightly with Oil for the Sick, making Cross upon person's forehead where shown

In the Name of our Lord Christ, and invoking the help of the holy Archangel Raphael, I ✝ anoint you with oil, that you may gain refreshment, both of soul and body.

Silently proceed to anoint the center at the top of the head, intending that Christ shall be the crowned head of this person; anoint the center at the throat, intending that peace shall fill the words of this one; additionally anoint the center at the nape of the neck, intending the Initiate Intelligence in the body shall redirect and realign all forces and functions with the Perfect Original Pattern of expression

All anointings are made in the form of a small cross. When clothing makes the physical touch impossible, make the sign as near as possible.

Now place both hands lightly upon the head of the person, dwelling totally in the Christ and His omnipotent Will-to-Heal every member of His Body, and say:)

Christ, the Son of God, pour down His healing power upon you, and enfold you in the Light of His Love.

(Assist the person to rise, if necessary. Wash and dry hands. Repeat all that precedes on this page with each individual.)

The forms following are for use of healers who are not priests. Priests are referred to the liturgy for the form appropriate to their use. Return to the altar, kneel and pray

As with this visible oil our bodies are outwardly anointed, Almighty God, our heavenly Father, grant of Thy infinite goodness that our souls may be anointed Inwardly with the Holy Spirit, Who is the Spirit of strength, relief, and gladness. And may He so replenish us with the spirit of His wisdom and strengthen us with His mighty power, that we may persevere in the Way of Holiness and ever serve Him joyfully in the course that He hath appointed for us; through Christ our Lord.

Response: **Amen**

The Grace *(cross self)* † **of our Lord Jesus Christ and the love of God and the fellowship of the Holy Spirit be with us all evermore.**

Response: **Amen.**

Rise; exit to sacristy

A LITURGY OF RENEWAL

Introductory Comments

What follows is called a liturgy of renewal, for it is designed to help facilitate and mark the beginning of a renewed life for people making the transition back into "the world" after having spent 21-days in an intensive inpatient substance abuse recovery program.

John Bradshaw, a former minister and a popular figure in the substance abuse recovery field, describes one of the reasons for why people start using alcohol and drugs in the first place as there being "a hole in the soul." In his book, *The Restless Heart*, Fr. Ron Rolheiser, suggests that loneliness and restlessness may be a natural state for human beings, who being separated from God, ache and yearn until reunited with the Divine. Substance abuse may be but one of many misguided ways of trying to cope with our estrangement from God, a route fraught with its own dangers and problems.

Spirituality is very much a part of the recovery process, especially programs that use a "12-Step" approach based upon the model developed by Alcoholics Anonymous. This approach explicitly asks the sufferer to start relying upon a Higher Power, take steps to undo some of the harm caused others in the past, and to commit to a new way of life.

The author's own experience with the inpatient substance abuse recovery process is that in addition to providing new tools for dealing with life and new hope it also provides an opportunity to start or renew the journey on the spiritual path. But, as the day approaches when it's time to leave inpatient programs, patients sometimes feel afraid about the prospects ahead of them. The liturgy that follows is intended to build upon the recovery work already begun and to provide a spiritually-oriented venue in which to start the transition back into "the real world," a world full of both temptations and opportunities for spiritual growth and renewal.

THE PREPARATION

Ideally the "candidate" for this ritual should begin preparing about seven days before the actual ceremony. In consultation with the person's primary counselor, chaplain, 12-step sponsor, or other mentor, the candidate takes a look at what happened in the past as a result of their substance abuse, what they've been experiencing while in the program, and what they hope for in their life in the future. For those who express themselves well in writing, this could be condensed into the form of a story or mini-biography, emphasizing those aspects the person feels are most important. For those who express themselves best via other means (verbally, through music, and so forth), they could be asked to prepare a talk, bit of music, poetry, and so forth, that will tell their story during the ritual.

SELECTION OF THE RESPECTED ONES

The person should also identify and recruit three individuals to play important roles during the ritual (the person might need to get help from a mentor with this). One respected person (who must also be invested in the candidates renewal) from the person's old life, one respected person who has been a positive influence on their recovery while in the program, and one respected individual who symbolizes what is hoped for in the future.

THE LITURGY

This liturgy can be a "free-standing" ritual, done by itself, or incorporated into a community worship service. Unless otherwise reserved, the various readings can be read by any number of the people present

An area where the ritual will take place is clear except for a small table, with a small cloth and a votive candle

INTRODUCTORY WORDS

The minister, chaplain, presider, or facilitator, makes a few introductory comments about the purpose of the ritual and it's importance to the candidate

THE INVOCATION

The three respected individuals and candidate approach the table. The candidate lights the votive candle to open the ceremony

> *First elder* (from past): **O God, we ask that you bless what we do here today.**
>
> *2nd elder* (positive influence from the present): **O Christ, we ask that you pour out your love for us and that you walk with us as we journey from darkness to light.**

3rd elder (person representing what is hoped for): **O Holy Spirit, we ask that you inspire us with your wisdom, and that you light our path.**

The candidate and elders take their seats

THE READINGS

First reading/presentation: *The candidate reads a selection from his/her story/biography, or else makes a verbal presentation about his/her life, reads a meaningful poem, plays a special tune, or makes another type of presentation*

First psalm reading: Ps 6: 1-2; 6.

O Lord, do not rebuke me in your anger, or discipline me in your wrath. Be gracious to me, O Lord, for I am languishing ... I am weary with my moaning; every night I flood my bed with tears.

2nd Reading: Ex 13: 3; 21

Moses said to the people, "Remember this day on which you came out of Egypt, out of the house of slavery ... The Lord went in front of them in a pillar of cloud by day, to lead them along the way, and in a pillar of fire by night, to give them light, that they might travel by day and by night.

2nd Psalm Reading: Ps 7: 1

O Lord, my God, in you I take refuge; save me from all my pursuers, and deliver me ....

3rd Reading: Rom 12:2

Do not be conformed to this world, but be transformed by the renewing of your minds, so that you may discern what is the will of God – what is good and acceptable and perfect.

GOSPEL & ACCLAMATION

Gospeller: **May the Lord be in my heart and on my lips that through my heart the love of God may shine forth and through my lips his spiritual powers be manifest.**

Gospel: Lk 15: 4-10

Alleluia! The reading is taken from the Gospel according to Luke: Which one of you, having a hundred sheep and losing one of them, does not leave the ninety-nine in the wilderness and go after the one that is lost until he finds it? When he has found it, he lays it on his shoulder and rejoices. And when he comes home, he calls together his friends and neighbors, saying to them, 'rejoice with me, for I have found my sheep that was lost.' Just so, I tell you, there will be more joy in heaven over one sinner who repents than over ninety-nine righteous persons who need no repentance.

This is the Gospel of the Lord.
R. Praise to you, Lord, Jesus Christ

REDEDICATION & RENEWAL CEREMONY

Testimonials of the elders

The three elders and minister proceed to a place near to the votive candle.

Each of the three elders comments upon the steps the candidate is taking to renew his/her commitment to a positive way of life, one talking about things from the past that are changing, one talking about the good things the candidate has been doing in the recovery center, and one talking about steps the candidate is taking toward a better future.

Consecration. *Brief explanation of anointing with oil as an ancient practice going back thousands of years, and an act designed to consecrate or set people or things aside for special purposes. Here we consecrate the head, heart, and hands to help prepare the candidate for renewal in his/her life.*

The candidate is then asked to join the elders and minister near the votive candle and to kneel. The elders hold their hands over the head of the candidate while the minister leads a short prayer and then proceeds to sign the candidates head, heart (not touching the clothing) and hands with the consecrated oil. The elders keep their hands extended over the head of the candidate while the anointing is occurring.

Head - signing forehead

Minister. **With this oil we bless and consecrate your mind and your consciousness, that you might grow in wisdom, and that you achieve a deep understanding and respect for yourself and others, and the way to true happiness.**

Heart - signing in front of the person's heart

Minister: **With this oil we bless and consecrate your heart, that your heart may be opened to giving and receiving love and compassion. May you also find the courage and patience you will need as your transformation unfolds.**

Hands - with palms up, the minister draws a circle on the hands with the oil

Minister: **With this oil we bless and consecrate your hands. May it be that these hands are strengthened that they might accomplish all the good things that will be necessary in your life.**

CLOSING

The candidate is asked to rise. The members of the congregation are invited to congratulate the candidate and to exchange hugs or another sign of Peace

Concluding prayer

The Lord's Prayer is said or sung

PENANCE

A TRADITIONAL SACRAMENT OF PENANCE

Instruction and Prayer
for Confession

Whoever you are, O Christian soul, that approaches the holy Sacrament of Penance, remember that you are going to undertake a work on the good performance of which, more than any other duty, your eternal welfare depends.

Therefore, retire apart from every external source of distraction, place yourself in the presence of God, and humbly adore Him. Represent to yourself that this may be the last confession you will ever have the opportunity of making. Let this reflection induce you to discharge every part of your duty, both as to the examination of your conscience, your sorrow for your sins, your firm purpose of amending your life, and the sincerity of your confession, in the most perfect manner possible.

Begin by imploring the light and grace of Almighty God, Who alone can discover to you the malice of your sins, and can give you true repentance:

COME, HOLY GHOST, divine Spirit of light and truth, assist me to discover all my sins, to be truly sorry for them, to confess them sincerely, and to amend my life. Amen.

HOLY MARY, Pray for me. St. Joseph, pray for me.
MY GUARDIAN ANGEL, help me that I

may make a good confession.

Examination of Conscience

The Ten Commandments

1. I am the Lord Thy God. Thou shalt not have any other gods before Me.
2. Thou shalt not take the Name of the Lord thy God in vain.
3. Remember thou keep holy the Sabbath day.
4. Honor thy father and thy mother.
5. Thou shalt not kill.
6. Thou shalt not commit adultery.
7. Thou shalt not steal.
8. Thou shalt not bear false witness against thy neighbor.
9. Thou shalt not covet thy neighbor's wife.
10. Thou shalt not covet thy neighbor's goods.

Six Traditional Precepts of the Church

1. To hear Mass on Sundays and Holy days of Obligation.
2. To fast and abstain on the days appointed.
3. To confess at least once a year.
4. To receive the Holy Eucharist during the Easter season.
5. To contribute to the support of our Pastors.
6. Not to marry persons who are not Christians, or who are related to us within the third degree of kindred, nor privately without witnesses, nor to solemnize marriage at forbidden times.

Sins Against The Holy Spirit

- Presumption of God's mercy – Despair
- Impugning the known truth
- Envy at another's spiritual good
- Obstinacy in sin/final impenitence.

Sins Crying to Heaven for Revenge

- Willful murder
- The sin of Sodom
- Oppression of the poor
- Defrauding laborers of their wages.

Nine Ways of Being Accessory to Another's Sin

- By counsel
- By command
- By consent
- By provocation
- By praise or flattery
- By concealment
- By partaking
- By silence
- By defense of the ill done

The Seven Deadly Sins

- Pride
- Lust
- Gluttony
- Sloth
- Covetousness
- Anger
- Envy

Prayer After Examination of Conscience

O MY God, I cry to Thee with the prodigal son: "Father, I have sinned against heaven and before Thee; I am no longer worthy to be called Thy son.' Thou Whose property is always to have mercy and to spare the penitent, O meet me in pity, embrace me in love and forgive me all my sins. I confess my sins unto Thee, O Christ, Healer of our souls, Lord of Life. Heal me of my spiritual sickness, Thou Who art long suffering and of tender mercy; heal me, O Lord Christ. Thou, O God, seest me in all the foulness of my sins! Blessed Jesus, speak for me, plead for me, come between my soul and my offended God, that I perish not. Amen.

Form for Confession

Before beginning confession, make a thorough examination of conscience. Have you loved God? Have you harmed him, His creation, yourself or another by what you have said or done?

Enter the confessional or kneel in front of the priest and say

"Bless me Father, for I have sinned. It is (state the time) since the last confession."

Then, confess your sins. The Priest may interrupt you several times to ask questions. When you have finished, say,

"For these and all the sins of my past life, especially, (here mention, in general, sins against charity, obedience, purity, anger, etc.) I am heartily sorry."

The Priest will assign you a penance to do; some good work, prayers, or reparation for wrongs. Remember that the words of absolution are of no value to you if you do not perform the penance, nor if you are not truly sorry for your sins and intend to make every effort to avoid sinning again.

Having assigned you a penance, he will then ask you to say an "Act of Contrition" that he may hear your words of repentance and sorrow for your sins.

Act of Contrition

O MY GOD, I am heartily sorry for having offended Thee, and I detest all my sins, because I dread the loss of heaven and the pains of hell, but most of all because they offend Thee, my God, Who art all good; and deserving of all my love. I firmly resolve,with the help of thy grace, to confess my sins, to do penance, and to amend my life. Amen.

With you head bowed, the Priest will place his hand over your head and pronounce the absolution.

I absolve you from your sins, in the name of the Father, and of the † Son, and of the Holy Spirit. Amen." *He will dismiss you with the words,* **"Go in peace and sin no more."**

Thanksgiving After Confession
and Performing Penance

ETERNAL FATHER! I thank Thee for Thy goodness and mercy. Thou hast had compassion on me, although in my folly I had wandered far away from Thee and offended Thee most grievously. With fatherly love Thou has received me anew after so many relapses into sin and forgiven me my offenses through the holy sacrament of Penance. Blessed be Thy infinite mercy! Never again will I offend Thee. All that I am, and all that I have, shall be consecrated to Thy service and Thy glory. Amen.

Prayer to St. Joseph

O FAITHFUL GUARDIAN and Father of virgins, Blessed Joseph, to whom was confided the care of Jesus, and of Mary the Queen of Virgins, I most humbly supplicate thee, by the love thou didst bear Jesus and Mary, to obtain for me that, being preserved from every stain during my whole life, I may be ever able to serve them with unspotted purity of mind and body.

Why Confess Your Sins?

Penance is the Sacrament by which sins committed after baptism are forgiven through the absolution of the priest. Our Lord gave Peter the power to forgive sins, saying to him, "And whatever thou shalt bind on earth shall be bound in heaven, and whatever thou shalt loose on earth shall be loosed in heaven." (Mt. 16:19) Christ later made the same promise to the other Apostles saying, "Amen, I say to you, whatever you bind on earth shall be bound also in heaven; and whatever you loose on earth shall be loosed also in heaven." (Mt. 18:18). It was instituted by Jesus Christ on the first Easter Sunday night when he appeared to his Apostles and said, "Peace be to you. As the father has sent me, I also send you. " When He had said this, He breathed upon them and said to them, "Receive the Holy Spirit whose sins you shall forgive, they are forgiven them; and whose sins you shall retain, they are retained. " (John 20:21-23.)

The power to forgive sins was not given to the Apostles alone, but also to their successors,the bishops and priests of the Church, until the end of time.

The words of Christ oblige us to confess our sins, because the priest cannot know whether he should forgive or retain our sins unless we tell them to him. In order to be able to give a just decision the priest must know the facts of each case. Thus the penitent must tell his or her sins. The penitent is his or her own accuser and his or her own witness.

Very few of us are horrible, evil people. But none of us have been the best that we could have been. We are all guilty of sins of one sort or another. If we say that we are not sinful, then we are like the publican who Christ criticized for praying that he was proud not to be a sinner. His sins were not forgiven; but the poor man at the back of the temple, who said, "Lord forgive me a sinner. " was praised by Christ.

A LIBERAL RITE OF RECONCILIATION
(Based upon the Rite of the Liberal Catholic Church)

Absolution is a sacrament by which persons may be restored to a state of spiritual health after the commission of sin. (See John 20: 22-23.) The word is derived from the Latin *ab,* 'from,' and *solvere,* 'to loosen.' Absolution must not be thought of as enabling a person to escape the consequences of their misdeeds. It is a spiritual process, a loosening from the bondage of sin, a process of at-onement with the higher self, a restoration of that inner harmony of being which is disturbed by wrongdoing, so that the person can make a fresh effort towards righteousness, fortified by the uninterrupted flow of the divine power within him. That this absolution may be fully effective, it is requisite that the candidate be anxious to rise above his or her imperfections of nature and to live a higher life. A person cannot escape the consequences of misdeeds, though one can neutralize them by sowing fresh causes of a righteous kind. 'Be not deceived; God is not mocked: for whatsoever you soweth, that shall you also reap' (Galatians 6: 7).

At ordination a priest is given authority to withhold absolution and this passage sometimes causes much heart searching among people unfamiliar with the subject. It is a duty to be used with the greatest moderation and discretion. But it is the priest's duty, in the first place, to be satisfied that the candidate is sincere before granting absolution; secondly, he or she may be justified in reserving absolution to a person until the individual has made an act of restitution.

In the Catholic Apostolic Church of Antioch auricular confession is entirely optional and is not required before the the reception of the holy communion. It should be noted that most Eucharistic liturgies contain a general confession, or confiteor, and absolution. Reconciliation is intended primarily for those who may feel their conscience to be troubled with some weighty matter. In keeping with the traditions of Christ's church, what is shared during this sacrament is held as sacred. It is strictly forbidden for the priest to disclose it to anyone, for any reason, without the explicit permission of the suppliant.

It is also strictly forbidden to the priest and the suppliant for absolution respectively to ask and disclose the identity of others implicated in any wrongdoing confessed. The suppliant comes to confess his/her own faults, not those of others. The priest should be as sympathetic, natural, and humane as possible with those who come to him to receive absolution.

Children under seven are not subjects for confession, since it is the tradition of the church that they are not capable of serious and responsible sin. Above that age and until they are responsible agents they may, in the Catholic Apostolic Church of Antioch, make auricular confession (save in emergency) only with the consent of a parent or guardian.

The person desiring absolution may sit facing the priest as in normal conversation, kneel at a prie-dieu in the church or chapel beside the priest, or speak with the priest in a confessional, depending upon local practice.

212

THE INVOCATION

Suppliant (crossing himself). **In the name of the Father and of the † Son and of the Holy Spirit. Amen. Father, give me your blessing, for I have sinned.**

Priest. **The Lord be in thy † heart and on thy † lips, that you might rightly confess your offenses.**

THE CONFESSION

Suppliant. **I confess before God almighty, Father, † Son and Holy Spirit and to you, Father (or Mother), that I have sinned in thought, in desire, in word and deed. Especially I have ...**

For these and all my other offenses which I cannot now remember, I am heartily sorry, firmly purpose amendment, and most humbly ask remission of almighty God, and of you, Father, absolution and the benefit of spiritual counsel and advice.

The priest hears the confession without interruption, unless that be necessary. He then gives such counsel as he may think well. In the Catholic Apostolic Church of Antioch the priest may or may not impose a penance. The priest may also suggest that the supliant should attend the Holy Eucharist, with the desire that the power which then comes to him shall be used against some particular fault or set of faults. This being done, he proceeds to the absolution.

THE ABSOLUTION

P. Our Lord Christ, who has left power on earth to his church to absolve all those that with heartfelt repentance and true faith turn to him, of his tender compassion forgive you your offenses; and by his authority committed to me I † absolve you from all your sins. In the name of the Father and of the † Son and of the Holy Spirit. R. Amen.

P. May the King of love and fountain of all goodness restore to you the fellowship of the Holy Spirit and give you the grace to continue in the same, that you may inherit the kingdom of heaven and be made like his own pure and glorious image. R. Amen.

NEW RITE OF PENANCE
(Roman Rite since Vatican II)

Texts for the Penitent

The penitent is encouraged to prepare for the celebration of the sacrament by prayer, reading of scripture, and silent reflection.

RECEPTION OF THE PENITENT

The penitent enters the confessional or other place set aside for the celebration of the sacrament of penance. After the welcoming of the priest, the penitent makes the sign of the cross saying:

In the name of the Father, and of the † Son, and of the Holy Spirit. Amen.

The penitent is invited to have trust in God and replies: **Amen.**

READING OF THE WORD OF GOD

The penitent then listens to a text of Scripture which tells about God's mercy and calls human beings to conversion.

CONFESSION OF SINS AND ACCEPTANCE OF SATISFACTION

The penitent speaks to the priest in a normal, conversational fashion. The penitent tells when he or she last celebrated the sacrament and then confesses his or her sins. The penitent then listens to any advice the priest may give and *accepts the satisfaction from the priest. The* penitent *should ask* any *appropriate questions.*

PRAYER OF THE PENITENT AND ABSOLUTION

Before the absolution is given, the penitent expresses sorrow for sins in these or similar words:

My God, I am sorry for my sins with all my heart. In choosing to do wrong and failing to do good, I have sinned against you whom I should love above all things. I firmly intend, with your help, to do penance, to sin no more, and to avoid whatever leads me to sin. Our Savior Jesus Christ suffered and died for us. In his name, my God, have mercy.

Several other prayer options are available for the penitent.

ABSOLUTION

If the penitent is not kneeling, he or she bows his or her head as the priest extends his hands (or at least extends his right hand).

God, the Father of mercies, through the death and resurrection of his Son has reconciled the world to himself and sent the Holy Spirit among us for the forgiveness of sins; through the ministry of the Church may God give you pardon and peace, and I absolve you from your sins in the name of the Father, and of the ✝ Son, and of the Holy Spirit. Amen.

216

PROCLAMATION OF PRAISE OF GOD AND DISMISSAL

Penitent and priest give praise to God.

Priest:　　　　　Give thanks to the Lord, for he is good.
Penitent: His mercy endures for ever. *Then the penitent is dismissed by the priest.*

RITE OF EXTREME UNCTION
(Last Rites)

The purposes of the Sacrament of Holy Unction are: (a) to aid in the restoration of bodily health, (b) to prepare a person for death, (c) to which may be added remission of sin, since it also involves a form of absolution.

Extreme Unction is a form of unction which with the giving of holy communion, is used in the case of a person who appears to be about to die.

The name is sometimes said to originate from the idea that it is the last of the unctions given to the ordinary Christian, those of Baptism and Confirmation preceding it.

If convenient, a table should be provided, covered with a linen cloth and bearing upon it a cross and two lighted candles. The Priest wears a violet stole. Portions in square brackets [ ] may be omitted.

THE INVOCATION

P. In the name of the Father and of the ✝ Son and of the Holy Spirit. R. Amen.

CONFITEOR

The priest should exhort the dying person to make a momentary act of contrition and then to turn with love and devotion to his Master.

If the person is very weak, the Confiteor may be said on his behalf by the priest.

The Confession

Priest: Let us ask forgiveness for our wrong doings and admit our human imperfections.

I admit to God, to the saints, and to you, that I failed to love God and my neighbor as I ought to have, committing wrongs in thought, word, and deed, by what I have done and by what I have not done. I acknowledge these failings and that I have missed the mark many times. I now seek God's forgiveness and ask blessed Mary, the angels, the saints, and you, to pray for me to the Lord our God.

Priest: May almighty God have mercy on us, forgive us for our wrong doings, and bring us all, in peace, to eternal spiritual life.

God the Creator, ✝ Son, and Holy Spirit, bless, preserve and sanctify you; the Lord in his loving kindness look down upon you and be gracious unto you; the Lord ✝ free you from the burden of your wrong doings and grant you the grace and comfort of the Holy Spirit.
R: Amen.

If the person is very weak or about to die, the priest pronounces the absolution using, if necessary, the following shortened form

P.   I ☦ absolve thee from all your transgressions, in the name of the Father and of the ☦ Son and of the Holy Spirit. R. Amen.

THE UNCTION

[Taking upon his thumb some of the holy oil for the sick, the Priest anoints in the form of a cross the organs of sense, using the words herein under specified:

Upon the closed eyelids

P.   By this holy ☦ unction and of his most tender love, the Lord pardon thee whatever faults you have committed through seeing. R. Amen.

Upon the ears:

P.   By this holy ☦ unction and of his most tender love, the Lord pardon thee whatever faults you have committed through hearing. R. Amen.

Upon the nostrils

P.   By this holy ☦ unction and of his most tender love, the Lord pardon thee whatever faults you have committed through smelling. R. Amen.

Upon the closed lips

P.   By this holy ☦ unction and of his most tender love, the Lord pardon thee whatever faults you have committed through tasting. R. Amen.

Upon the inside of the palms of the hands (but outside in the case of priests): The feet and reins (i.e. the small of the back) may also at this time be anointed, but this is optional

P.   By this holy ✝ unction and of his most tender love, the Lord pardon thee whatever faults you have committed through touch. R. Amen.]
In cases of extremity, or at the option of the Priest , the forehead only need be anointed, with these words:

P.   By this holy ✝ unction and of his most tender love, the Lord pardon thee whatever faults you have committed through thy thoughts and desires and the senses of thy body. R. Amen.

The priest may now proceed to anoint the sacral plexus (at the base of the spine), the spleen, the solar plexus, the heart, the pharyngeal plexus (at the front of the throat) and the center at the top of the head, in that order.

Of these it is sufficient to anoint the last four or five, more especially if the person's infirmity be great.

If impracticable to reach any center the sign of the cross is made with the thumb (moist with oil) in the air as close as possible to the center with the intent to affect the center. The nape of the neck may be anointed in place of the sacral plexus.

VIATICUM

The viaticum is then given, unless there be danger of the body's rejecting, or being unable to swallow, the sacred Host. The Host may be placed in a spoon and given with a little wine or water.

P.   Brother (or Sister), receive the viaticum of the most holy Body of our Lord Jesus Christ and may the peace of the Lord go with you. R. Amen.

THE BENEDICTION

P.   Unto God's gracious love and protection we commit you; the Lord ✝ bless you and keep you; the Lord make his face to shine upon you and be gracious to you; the Lord lift up the light of his countenance upon you and give you his peace, now and for evermore. R. Amen.

If death takes place, the priest may at once proceed to the absolution, as set forth in the order of the burial of the dead

In the absence of a priest, a deacon may administer a blessing (not extreme unction). He uses the.following form for the absolution

D.   May the Lord ✝ bless us and absolve us from all our transgressions; in the name of the Father and of the ✝ Son and of the Holy Spirit. R. Amen.

The grace of our Lord Jesus Christ and the love of God and the fellowship of the Holy Spirit, be with us all evermore. R. Amen.

THE BURIAL OF THE DEAD

The funeral rites of the Church may be grouped into two divisions: the first including those offices, foremost in importance, whose purpose it is to surround the liberated soul with peace and spiritual power. Of these the offering of the holy sacrifice for the repose of the soul in the form of the Requiem Eucharist is the most important and efficacious. The other and less important part of the rite consists in the hallowing of the ground or grave and the consigning to it of the ashes or the cast-off body. To this must be added the work of giving comfort and assurance to the relatives and friends.

This work of giving help and peace to the departed person is inevitably hindered if we surround him with feelings of depression and unhappiness. Every effort should therefore be made to put aside our own very natural sense of sorrow and loss and to think rather of the happiness and peace of the departed soul. In proportion as we can accomplish this, do we also gain comfort and strength for ourselves.

The priest should be asked to commemorate the deceased person, as soon after the death as possible, at one of his regular celebrations. It is strongly recommended that wherever possible the physical body of the deceased person shall be cremated, that is, disintegrated rapidly by fire rather than by process of slow decay. If there is to be a special Requiem Eucharist the body should if possible be taken to the church where that Eucharist is offered.

After the death, it is well that the body be sprinkled by the relatives with holy water.

The coffin should similarly be sprinkled before the funeral procession leaves the house. The absolution hereafter printed should be performed as soon after the death as is convenient, unless the deceased person received absolution shortly before death. It may be repeated at the burial service. In the case of a child of tender years the absolution is omitted.

THE FUNERAL SERVICE

As the burial customs vary in different countries and places, the clergy must use their discretion in rearranging the several portions of the ceremony. Hymns may be introduced at suitable places, also addresses and readings from various sources

According to the arrangements made, the portion of this ceremony preceding the burial itself will take place in the cemetery out of doors, in the cemetery or crematorium chapel, in a funeral parlor, in a private house, or in the church. The committal usually takes place at the crematorium or the cemetery

The priest may either accompany the funeral procession or meet it at the church, the cemetery or the crematorium

All stand

As the body is carried through the cemetery or the church, some of the following passages are read by the priest or chanted by the choir

I am the resurrection and the life, saith the Lord: he that believeth in me, though he were dead yet shall he live; and whosoever liveth and believeth in me shall never die.

Lay not up for yourselves treasures upon earth: where moth and rust do corrupt and where thieves break through and steal.

But lay up for yourselves treasures in heaven: where neither moth nor rust doth corrupt

and where thieves do not break through and steal.

For where your treasure is: there will your heart be also.

I know that my redeemer liveth: whom I shall see for myself and mine eyes shall behold.

Be not deceived; God is not mocked: for whatsoever you soweth, that shall you also reap.

For he that soweth to his flesh, shall of the flesh reap corruption: but he that soweth to the spirit, shall of the spirit reap life everlasting.

And let us not be weary in well-doing: for in due season we shall reap, if we faint not.

As we have therefore opportunity: let us do good unto all men.

The souls of the righteous are in the hand of God: and
there shall no torment touch them.

In the sight of the unwise they seemed to die and their departure is taken for misery and their going from us to be utter destruction: but they are in peace.

For God created us to be immortal: and made him to be an image of his own eternity.

Glory be to the Father and to the Son: and to the Holy Spirit.

As it was in the beginning, is now and ever shall be: world without end. Amen

THE INVOCATION

When the priest has arrived at the chancel or grave and the above sentences are finished, he says

Priest. **In the name of the ✝ Father and of the ✝ Son and of the Holy Spirit ✝. Amen.**

THE CHARGE

The people are seated

The priest turns to the people and says

P.   Brothers and sisters, we meet together here today on the occasion of the passing into a higher life of our dear *brother or sister* N. It is but natural that we who have known and loved *him/her* should regret *his/her* departure from among us; yet it is our duty to think not of ourselves, but of *him/her*. Therefore let us endeavor to lay aside thoughts of our personal loss and dwell upon *his/her* great and most glorious gain.

To this end I call upon you to join with me in the recitation (or singing) of part of the twenty-third psalm *(or the Te Deum).*

PSALM 23

The Lord gave and the Lord hath taken
away. Blessed be the name of the Lord.

1.   The Lord is my shepherd: therefore can I
lack nothing.

2.   He shall feed me in a green pasture: and
lead me forth beside the waters of comfort.

3.   He shall convert my soul: and bring me
forth in the paths of righteousness, for his
name's sake.

4.   Yea, though I walk through the valley of
the shadow of death, I will fear no evil: for
thou art with me; thy rod and thy staff
comfort me.

Glory be to the Father and to the † Son and
to the Holy Spirit.
As it was in the beginning, is now and ever
shall be, world without end. Amen.

Antiphon

The Lord gave and the Lord hath taken
away.

Blessed be the name of the Lord.

THE ABSOLUTION

During the following passages the priest encompasses the body and sprinkles it with holy water thrice on either side, after which he again encompasses it and censes it thrice on If the body be not present, these ceremonies are omitted, but the words, nevertheless, are said. The absolution is omitted in the case of young children.

P. Rest in the eternal grant unto *him/her, O* Lord.

C. And let light perpetual shine upon *him/her.*

P. Come forth to meet *him/her,* ye angels of the Lord.

C. Receive *him/her* into your fellowship, O ye saints of God.

P. May the choirs of angels receive *him/her.*

C. And guide *him/her* into eternal peace.

P. Rest in the eternal grant unto *him/her, O* Lord.

C. And let light perpetual shine upon *him/her.*

P. O God, in whose unspeakable love the souls of the departed find rest and peace, in thy name we † absolve from every bond of sin thy servant who has cast off this garment of flesh. May thy holy angels bear *him/her* in their tender care, that *he* may enter the brightness of the everlasting light and find *his* peace in thee; through Christ our Lord. †. Amen.

P. The Lord be with you.

C. And with your spirit.

THE COLLECTS

The following collects are recited, unless a special Requiem Eucharist is to be celebrated. In that event the Eucharist begins and the collects will be said in the usual place therein. In the case of children, the words 'this thy child' are used instead of 'this thy servant'.

P. Let us pray. *The people kneel*

P. Almighty God, who hast dominion over both the living and the dead and dost hold all thy creation in the everlasting arms of thy love, we pray thee for the peace and repose of thy servant, that *he*, being dead unto this world, yet ever living unto thee, may find in thy continued and unceasing service the perfect consummation of happiness and peace; through Christ our Lord. R. Amen.

P. Likewise, O Lord, we pray thee for those who love thy servant, those whom thou hast called to sacrifice the solace of *his* earthly presence; do thou, O Lord, comfort them with the balm of thy loving-kindness that, strengthened by thee and resting upon the surety of thy wisdom, they may put aside their thoughts of sorrow and grief and pour out upon *him/her* only such thoughts of love as may help *him/her* in the higher life of service to which thou hast now called *him/her;* through Christ our Lord. R. Amen.

The epistle, gospel and communio from the Requiem Eucharist may follow here if desired

COMMITMENT OF THE BODY

From this point onwards the ceremony is conducted either at the grave, in the crematorium chapel or at the place where the ashes are to be deposited. If the funeral service is held in a church and is to be followed by a Requiem Eucharist the committal may be said at the conclusion of the Requiem instead of at the cemetery or crematorium.

In the case of cremation the committal begins as follows

P.   Forasmuch as it hath pleased almighty God of his great love to take unto himself our dear *brother* hence departed, we therefore commit this *his* cast-off body to be consumed by fire, ashes to ashes, dust to dust, that in that more glorious spiritual body which now he weareth, he may be free from earthly chains to serve God as *he* ought.

In the case of burial in a grave the procession bearing the coffin or casket goes to the grave. Before the coffin is lowered the grave or ground is sprinkled with holy water and censed.

The following prayer is said by the priest

P.   O God, who in thy providence hast appointed a wondrous ministry of angels, we pray thee to up hallow this grave *(or* ground) and send down thy holy angel from heaven to † bless and sanctify it; through Christ our Lord. . Amen.

P. Forasmuch as it hath pleased almighty God of his great love to take unto himself our dear *brother hence* departed, we therefore commit this his cast-off body to the ground, earth to earth *(here some earth is cast upon the coffin by the priest or someone standing by)*, ashes to ashes, dust to dust, that in that more glorious spiritual body which now *he* weareth, *he* may be free from earthly chains to serve God as *he* ought.

In the case of the disposal of the ashes, the urn or casket containing the ashes is sometimes buried in a grave or sometimes deposited in a niche and sometimes the ashes are scattered on the ground. When the ashes are buried in a grave, the ground may be sprinkled with holy water and censed. The priest may bless the grave as in the case of the burial of the body

P. Forasmuch as it hath pleased almighty God or his great love to take unto himself our dear *brother* hence departed, we therefore commit *his* ashes to their resting place *(or* to the ground), ashes to ashes, dust to dust, that in that more glorious spiritual body which now he *weareth, he* may be free from earthly chains to serve God as he ought.

The priest continues

For I say unto you: Blessed are the dead which die in the Lord; for the souls of the righteous are in the hand of God and there shall no torment touch them. In the sight of the unwise they seem to die and their departure is taken for misery and their going from us to be utter destruction: but they are in peace. For God created us to be immortal and made us to be an image of his own eternity. The Lord sitteth above the water floods; the Lord remaineth a king for ever. The universe is his temple; wisdom, strength and beauty are about his throne as pillars of his works; for his wisdom is infinite, his strength is omnipotent and his beauty shines through the whole universe in order and symmetry. The heavens he has stretched forth as a canopy; the earth he has planted as his footstool; he crowns his temple with stars as with a diadem and from his hands flow all power and glory. The sun and the moon are messengers of his will and all his law is concord. If we ascend up into heaven, he is there; if we go down into hell, he is there also. If we take the wings of the morning and dwell in the uttermost parts of the sea, even there also his hand shall lead us and his right hand shall hold us. In his almighty care we rest in perfect peace and equally in his care rests this our loved one, whom he has deigned to draw nearer to the vision of his eternal beauty.

Ever praising him therefore, in firm but humble confidence we call upon him and say the following *(or the Lord's Prayer)*:

O Father of light, in whom is no darkness at all, we pray that you will fill our hearts with calm and peace and to open within us the eyes of the soul, that we may see by faith the radiance and the glory that you are pouring upon us, your servants. For you have ever given us far more than we can ask or think, and it is only through our feebleness and faithlessness that we ever need crave anything from your omnipotence. But thou know well the weakness of the human heart and in your limitless love thou will make allowances for our human love when we pray that you grant eternal rest to this our dear *brother/sister* and that light perpetual may shine upon *him/her.* We thank you that in your loving providence thou have drawn *him/her* from the unreal to the real, from the darkness of earth into your glorious light, through the gates of death into a splendor beyond our comprehension. Our loving thought shall follow and surround *him/her; O God,* take this our gift of thought, imperfect though it be, and touch it with the eternal fire of your love, so that it may become for *him/her* a guardian angel to help *him/her on his/her* upward way. Thus, through your loving-kindness, may we in deep humility and reverence become fellow-workers with your boundless power and may our weakness be supported by your infinite strength; that we, with this our dearly beloved *brother/sister,* may in due time attain to the wisdom of the Spirit, who with the Father and the Son lives and reigns, God throughout all ages of ages. R. Amen.

The following prayer may be added

P. Almighty God, in whose light lives the souls of those that depart hence in the Lord and with whom the faithful, after they are delivered from the burden of the flesh, are in joy and felicity; we give you hearty thanks, that it has pleased you to deliver this our *brother/sister* out of the miseries of this mortal world and we do pray to you that we may be found worthy, together with all those that are departed in the true faith of thy holy name, to stand before you hereafter in the ranks of your glorious church triumphant; through Christ our

Lord. R. Amen.

P. ✟ **May the souls of all the departed through the love of God rest in peace. R. Amen.**

P. ✟ **The grace of our Lord Jesus Christ and the love of God and the fellowship of the Holy Spirit be with us all evermore. R. Amen.**

If a priest is not available any member of the clergy, whether deacon, subdeacon, or one in minor orders, or any lay member of the church, may conduct its funeral rites with the following modifications

At the absolution *holy water, if available, will be sprinkled as usual, but incense will not be used, and the form of absolution shall be modified so that the first sentence shall read 'O God, in whose unspeakable love the souls of the departed find rest and peace, we pray to you to absolve from every bond of sin. your servant who has cast off this garment of flesh (omitting the sign of the cross)*

If burial takes place at a gravesite, the grave may be aspersed (but not censed) and the usual prayer said, omitting the two signs of the cross

THE REQUIEM MASS

*In the Requiem Eucharist violet is the color used,
save in the case of children of tender years, when the
color is white. In such case also the word 'child' is
substituted for 'servant'. The order of service is as
usual, except for the points hereunder noted. The
words in italics will be altered according as the
requiem is general or particular.*

PSALM 90

To be used instead of the canticle.

Antiphon

> **God is our hope and strength.**
> **A very present help in trouble.**

1. **Lord, thou hast been our refuge: from one
   generation to another.**

2. **Before the mountains were brought forth,
   or ever the earth and the world were made:
   thou art God from everlasting and world
   without end.**

3. **Thou turnest us to destruction: again thou
   sayest, Come again, ye children.**

4. **For a thousand years in thy sight are but as
   yesterday: seeing that is past as a watch in
   the night.**

5. **The days of our age are three score years
   and ten; and though men be so strong that**

they come to fourscore years, yet is their strength then but labor and sorrow: so soon passeth it away and we are gone.

6. So teach us to number our days: that we may apply our hearts unto wisdom.

7. Show thy servants thy work: and their children of thy glory.

8. And the glorious majesty of the Lord our God be upon us: prosper thou the work of our hands upon us, O prosper thou our handiwork.

Glory be to the Father and to the † Son: and to the Holy Spirit.

As it was in the beginning, is now and ever shall be: world without end. Amen.

Antiphon

God is our hope and strength.
A very present help in trouble.

INTROIT

Rest in the eternal grant unto *them, O* Lord: and let light perpetual shine upon *them.*

The righteous shall be in everlasting remembrance: he shall not be afraid of evil tidings.

Blessed is the one whom thou choosest and receivest unto thee: that person shall dwell in thy court and shall be satisfied with the pleasures of thy house, even of thy holy temple.

Rest in the eternal grant unto *them, O* Lord: and let light perpetual shine upon *them.*

THE COLLECTS

The collect for the day is first said.

The second and third collects are as follows:

P.   Almighty God, who has dominion over both the living and the dead and does hold all your creation in the everlasting arms of your love, we offer this holy sacrifice that it may avail for the peace and repose of thy servants(s) [N.] and that *he/she,* being dead to this world, yet be ever living to you in the next, may find in your continued and unceasing service, the perfect consummation of happiness and peace; through Christ our Lord. R. Amen.

The collect of All Souls' day may be substituted for the above when the Requiem is general.

P.   Likewise, O Lord, we pray to you for those who love your servant, those whom you has called to sacrifice the solace of *his/her* earthly presence; do, O Lord, comfort them with the balm of your loving-kindness, that, strengthened by you and resting upon the surety of your wisdom, they may put aside their thoughts of grief and sorrow and pour out upon *him/her* only such thoughts of love as may help *him/her* in the higher life of service to which you have now called *him/her;* through Christ our Lord. R. Amen.

THE EPISTLE

The epistle is taken from the fifteenth chapter of the First Epistle of St. Paul the Apostle to the Corinthians, beginning at the fifty-first verse.

Behold, I show you a mystery: there is a natural body and there is a spiritual body; for this corruptible must put on incorruption and this mortal must put on immortality. So when this corruptible shall have put on incorruption and this mortal shall have put on immortality, then shall be brought to pass the saying that is written: Death is swallowed up in victory. O death, where is thy sting? O grave, where is thy victory? But thanks be to God, who giveth us the victory through our Lord Jesus Christ. Therefore, my beloved brethren, be ye steadfast, unmovable, always abounding in the work of the Lord, forasmuch as ye know that your labor is not in vain in the Lord.

Here ends the epistle

THE GRADUAL

1. **Remember now thy creator in the days of thy youth: while the evil days come not, nor the years draw nigh, when thou shalt say, I have no pleasure in them.**

2. **While the sun, or the light, or the moon, or the stars, be not darkened: nor the clouds**

return after the rain.

3.   In the day when the keepers of the house shall tremble and the strong men shall bow themselves: and the grinders cease because they are few and those that look out of the windows be darkened.

4.   And the doors shall be shut in the streets, when the sound of the grinding is low: and he shall rise up at the voice of the bird and all the daughters of music shall be brought low.

5.   Also when they shall be afraid of that which is high and fears shall be in the way and the almond tree shall flourish and the grasshopper shall be a burden and desire shall fail: because we goeth to his long home and the mourners go about the streets.

6.   Or ever the silver cord be loosed, or the golden bowl be broken: or the pitcher be broken at the fountain, or the wheel broken at the cistern.

7.   Then shall the dust return to the earth as it was: and the spirit shall return unto God who gave it.

or

THE GRADUAL (2)

Psalm 139

1. **O Lord thou has searched me out: and thou knowest me.**

2. **Thou knowest my downsitting and mine up-rising: thou discernest me thoughts even from afar.**

3. **I will give thanks unto thee for the wonder of my birth: marvelous are thy works and that my soul knoweth right well.**

4. **My body was no mystery to thee: when it was made in secret and wrought in the world below.**

5. **Thine eyes beheld my unformed substance and in thy book were all the days of my life written: the days that were formed for me when as yet there were none of them.**

6. **How precious are thy counsels unto me O Lord: how great is the sum of them!**

7. **If I count them they are more in number than the sand: were I to come to the end I am still with thee.**

THE GOSPEL

The holy gospel is taken from the eleventh chapter of the Gospel according to St. John, beginning at the twenty first verse.

Then said Martha unto Jesus: Lord, if thou hadst been here, my brother had not died. But I know that even now, whatsoever thou wilt ask of God, God will give it thee. Jesus saith unto her: Thy brother shall rise again. Martha saith unto him: I know that he shall rise again in the resurrection at the last day. Jesus said unto her: I am the resurrection and the life; he that believeth in me, though he were dead, yet shall he live. And whosoever liveth and believeth in me shall never die. Believest thou this? She saith unto him: Yea, Lord; I believe that thou art the Christ, the Son of God who should come into the world.

In the case of children, the following gospel is used:

The holy gospel is taken from the tenth chapter of the Gospel according to St. Mark, beginning at the thirteenth verse.

And they brought young children to him, that he should touch them; and his disciples rebuked those that brought them. But when Jesus saw it, he was much displeased and said unto them: Suffer the little children to come unto me and forbid them not; for of such is the kingdom of God. Amen, I say unto you: Whosoever shall not receive the kingdom of God as a little child, he shall not enter therein. And 'he took them up in his arms, put his hands upon them and blessed them.

COMMUNION

Amen. Blessing and glory and wisdom and thanksgiving and honor and power and might be unto our God for ever and ever. Amen.

[The Lord our God lives for ever and ever: and we his children live in him.

They who do not know the Lord are filled with fear: they have no sure stay and their life lies in darkness.

But they who love him walk in safety: neither do they fear the shadow of death.

For he is the Lord of life and death alike: and all the worlds are in his hand.]

The portion in brackets may be omitted.

POSTCOMMUNION

P. We praise you, O Lord, that your compassionate wisdom which guides your *child* through the portal of birth has [now] called *him/her* through death's gateway to a fuller life with you. Enlighten *him/her, O* heavenly Father, with the knowledge of your laws that, casting out all fear, *he/she* may grow in grace as *he/she* labors in your holy service; through Christ our Lord. R. Amen.

(In very exceptional cases the usual form of the Postcommunio may be used.)

> P.   The Lord be with you.
> C.   And also with you.
>
> P.   May *he/she* rest in peace.
> C.   And may light perpetual shine upon *him/her.*

THE BENEDICTION

P.   **Unto God's gracious love and protection we commit you; the Lord † bless you and keep you; the Lord makes his face to shine upon you and be gracious to you; the Lord lift up the light of his countenance upon you and give you his peace, now and for evermore. R. Amen.**

VESTING PRAYERS

Each piece of liturgical clothing, which are called vestments, has symbolic significance. It is traditional to offer specific prayers when each item of liturgical clothing is donned. Included below are two versions of vesting prayers, one quite traditional (in a tradition that precedes the Second Vatican Council) and one which is more contemporary. Servers are encouraged to get into the practice of offering vesting prayers in preparation for their service at the liturgy. Later, even if not recited out loud, it helps the offering of the vesting prayers to become second nature to recall the prayers to mind and offer them non-verbally.

CONTEMPORARY VESTING PRAYERS

The following prayers are relatively contemporary in nature.

Washing of hand before putting on articles of liturgical attire - Cleanse my hand, O Lord, that in your strength I might render unto you a pure offering and a perfect work.

Alb (white baptismal robe) - Endow me, O Lord, with the garment of praise and innocence and the vesture of light, that I might worthily receive and dispense Your holy gifts.

Tying the cinture (rope belt or girdle) - I bind unto myself the Name, the Holy Name, the Mighty and Immortal Name, with this cord of love and purity, that Your power might dwell in me.

Amice - Place, O Lord, on my head the helmet of salvation, that your servant may be free from adversity.

Chasuble (priests) **Dalmatic** (deacons) - May this vestment of grace, which I accept, and the service I prepare for be a labor of righteousness and a holy work. That it will be to the glory of God and to His angel host, to the joy of all saints and great ones, and toward the liberation of humankind. I will go unto the altar of our God, and He shall declare His victory unto us, through Jesus Christ, our Lord.

Stole (worn over neck by priests/draped diagonally by deacons) - (Kiss the cross at the center of the stole). You who said, 'My yoke is easy and my burden is light,' grant that I might yoked with you in this service and bring your blessings to the whole world.

TRADITIONAL VESTING PRAYERS

The following traditional vesting prayers were graciously given to us by Bishop Lucas Graywolf, bishop of the Diocese of Texas.

Washing the Hands - Cleanse my hands, O Lord, in thy strength, that I may so render unto Thee a pure offering and a perfect work.

Alb (white baptismal robe) - Purify me, O Lord, from all stain and cleanse my heart, that washed in the Blood of the Lamb, I may enjoy eternal delights.

Tying the girdle/cincture (rope belt) - Gird me, O Lord, with the cincture of purity, and quench in my heart the fire of concupiscence, that the virtue of continence and chastity may remain in me.

Amice - Place, O Lord, unto my head the helmet of salvation, that I may overcome the assaults of the devil.

Stole - (Kiss the cross at the center of the stole. Priests cross in the middle). Restore to me, O Lord, the state of immortality which was lost to me by my first parents, and although unworthy to approach Thy sacred mysteries, grant me nevertheless eternal joy. As a sign of his full priestly powers the bishop does not cross the stole in front.)

Chasuble - O Lord, Who hast said, "My yoke is sweet and my burden is light," grant that I may carry it so as to obtain Thy grace.

Maniple - (Hangs on the left forearm). Let me deserve, O Lord, to bear the maniple of tears and sorrow, so that one day I may come with joy into the rewards of my labors.

Preparatory Prayers (before the saying of the Holy Mass) - Let no Priest or Bishop come to the Altar of the Lord without asking for the full grace and authority of God, stating his intentions to make present the Body and Blood of our Lord, Jesus Christ.

HOLY ORDERS

Holy Orders is the sacrament by which, in their various degrees, ministers of the church receive the power and authority to perform their sacred duties. Our Lord works through human agency and so that those who are chosen for this sacred ministry as bishops, priests or deacons, will become readier channels for his grace, he has ordained that they be linked closely with him by this holy rite, and shall thereby be empowered to administer his sacraments and act as almoners of his blessing. But it's vital that we remember that they receive all sacraments from the hand of Christ himself and that the officiant is but an instrument in that hand.

While some churches, the Roman Catholic Church for example, have done away with the historic minor orders, there are two ancient and historic groups of orders within Christ's church, the minor and the major, and in our church there is a preliminary stage leading up to each group. The minor orders are four; the major three, as outlined below:

MINOR ORDERS

Preliminary step: Cleric (initiation symbol is the **surplice or alb**)

1. Doorkeeper (initiation symbols are the **key and bell**)
2. Reader (initiation symbol is the **book**)
3. Healer/Exorcist (initiation symbols are the **sword and a book**)
4. Acolyte (initiation symbols are **cruet; candlestick with lighted candle**)

MAJOR ORDERS

Preliminary step: Subdeacon (ordination symbols - **empty chalice and paten, cruets and lavabo bowl with towel; amice; maniple; tunic; book of epistles**)

1. Deacon (ordination symbols - **white stole, dalmatic, book of gospels**)
2. Priest (ordination symbols - **white stole, chasuble, chalice with wine & water, paten with a host**)
3. Bishop (consecration symbols - **pastoral staff, pectoral cross, ring, mitre, gloves**)

THE CONFERRING OF MINOR ORDERS

Traditionally, the degrees from cleric to acolyte inclusive may be conferred apart from the celebration of the Holy Eucharist, but only in the morning, except in the case of cleric, which may be, given at any hour. If, however, they are given during the Eucharist, the ordination to the degree of cleric shall take place after the introit and to the other four degrees after the kyrie. It is the practice within the Catholic Apostolic Church of Antioch to confer all orders during the Eucharist. The minor orders of Cleric through Acolyte may be conferred by an authorized archpriest (monsignor), but only a bishop may confer the orders of Subdeacon through Bishop. Portions of the charges enclosed between brackets may be omitted. The charges may be read by priests at the discretion of the bishop.

THE ADMISSION OF A SERVER

The priest stands at the entry-way of the sanctuary, the candidate standing before him.

Priest. **In the name of the Father and of the † Son and of the Holy Spirit. R. Amen.**

P. **You should understand that in being admitted as a server in the church a great privilege is being given to you. The altar of a church is the throne of God and a center of most powerful spiritual influences. You are admitted to the sanctuary, the specially sacred part of the church immediately around the altar, and it is part of your duty and privilege to be a channel of this spiritual influence and to help to pour it out upon the people.**

Therefore you take upon yourself certain responsibilities, of which you should be ever mindful. You must be scrupulously clean in your person. You must follow attentively the services, that your thoughts may be fixed upon high and holy things and that you are ever in readiness to carry out punctually and accurately whatever work is entrusted to you. Remember that your best, and only your best, must be offered to God. Therefore, be punctual and regular in your attendance at church and never allow yourself to perform any action carelessly and negligently, without proper thought. Your actions should be the outcome of thoughts of devotion and reverence, so that whatever you do is done as beautifully and as perfectly as possible. Try to enter into the spirit of service, remembering that

even the Son of Man came not to be ministered to, but to minister. So shall you find joy and peace in the service of God's holy church and the hand of Christ be laid upon you in tender love and blessing.

P.   Will you strive earnestly to practice these duties?

Candidate. I will.

P.   The Lord keep you in all these things, well-beloved *son/daughter,* and strengthen you in all goodness. R. Amen.

The candidate kneels before the priest.

The priest says the following prayer with hands extended towards the candidate

P.   O Lord Christ, who is ever ready to receive and strengthen the earnest aspirations of your children, look down in your love upon this your servant, who desires to minister as a server in your holy church. Sanctify † *him/her,* O Lord, with your heavenly grace that, growing continually in virtue, *he/she* may rightly practice the duties of *his/her* office and so be found acceptable in your sight, O thou great King of love and wisdom, to whom be glory for ever and ever. R. Amen.

The priest lays his hand upon the candidate's head, raising his hand to make the sign of the cross, and says

P.   The blessing of God almighty, the Father, the

† So and the Holy Spirit come down upon you, that you may rightly fulfill that which today you have undertaken.
R. Amen.

If it is thought well to admit in a solemn manner persons appointed to other duties in the church, or to bless any who engage in good works, the priest should use the above form with modifications, omitting the charge and promise or substituting another.

THE INITIATION OF CLERICS

The people are seated.

At the appointed time those about to be made clerics are summoned by a priest, as follows:

Priest. **Let those who are to be initiated to the office of cleric come forward.**

*The candidates rise from their seats and advance a, few paces towards the bishop or archpriest, **bearing lighted candles** in their hands. They bow to him, the candles are then taken from them and they are seated. The bishop charges them as follows:*

Bishop or archpriest. **In ancient times those who wanted to dedicate their lives to the service of Christ's holy church were admitted, as a preliminary step, to this order of cleric. Set apart from the life of the world, they were admonished to put away worldly distractions and secular desires, the abandonment of which, as typified by outer adornment of the person, was indicated by** the shaving of hair from the head and the relinquishment of secular garb. This is called tonsuring.

You, who now come before us, are likewise reminded to dedicate yourselves to the Christ's service, and that you are making a commitment to prepare yourself(ves) for this. In these times it is no longer necessary to be ritually tonsured or to wear a special garb outside the church; nevertheless, it is true that those who wish to serve the Christ faithfully must set themselves apart from the world, in that considerations of Christ's work must take preeminence over the fulfillment of merely personal desires.

In this grade of cleric you set before yourselves a great and glorious ideal - to become fellow workers with God, to cooperate in his plan for perfecting creation. For this you must learn self-control and acquire additional powers. Instead of allowing your body to direct and enslave you, you must endeavor to live for the soul. Wherefore, as a first step you must learn in the grade of cleric to control, and to appropriately express yourselves through your physical body, [as in the next stage, that of doorkeeper, it will be your duty to control, and to develop, the emotions, so that whatever power lies in them may be used for God's service. In the grade of reader you will need to learn to handle the powers of the mind and devote those also to God's service. Having thus diligently labored at the training of the body, the emotions, and the mind, you may endeavor to enter upon a higher phase of your work in the order of healer/exorcist, where you will work to develop more definitely the power of the will, that you may conquer evil in yourselves and such evil suggestions as may be imposed upon you from outside. Also, you will then be more able to help others to cast out evil from their natures. Above the grade of exorcist lies that of acolyte, wherein your task is to quicken the intuition and open yourself(ves) to higher spiritual influences.

Beyond these grades, which among us are intended for the many, there lies for the few a higher level of service, in which the person sets himself or herself wholly apart for the service of the Christ. Having passed the probationary grade of subdeacon, the candidate enters the greater orders of deacon and priest. But even should you elect not to enter upon this higher path, yet happy indeed will you be, for even in the minor orders you will have unfolded many powers within yourselves, and with those powers rightly developed and trained you will be better prepared to offer acceptable service to Christ, in whose service alone is perfect freedom to be found.

In this order of cleric, then, you must learn self-control with regard to the body. It must be trained to habits of accuracy and neatness; it must be kept in perfect health and cleanliness and you must see that its energies are devoted to God's service, not in disorderliness and selfishness, but in harmony and rhythm. In your gestures, manners, and your speech, strive to exemplify the ideal of beauty, never forgetting that our physical bodies are the temple of the Holy Spirit. Moreover, as you learn to respect your own body, so must you scrupulously respect the bodies of others.

The charge being ended, the candidates kneel before the bishop or archpriest, who rises and says

B.   Let us pray.

B.   O Lord Christ, who is ever ready to receive and to strengthen the earnest aspirations of his children, look down in your love upon these your servants, who desire to become worthy to serve you as clerics in your holy church. Sanctify ✝ them, O Lord, with thy heavenly grace, that growing continually in virtue they may rightly practice the duties of their office and so be found acceptable in your sight, O great King of love, to whom be glory for ever and ever. R. Amen.

The candidates kneel before the bishop or archpriest in succession
He places his right hand on the head of each, as he says

B.   In the name of Christ our Lord, I admit thee to the order of cleric.

*The bishop or archpriest places a **surplice** on each of the candidates, saying to him:*

I clothe you with the vesture of holiness and do admonish you to diligently develop the powers that are in you, that your service may be to good effect.

Having ordained the several candidates, he blesses the new clerics with the following words, unless they are immediately to receive another order:

B. The blessing of God almighty, the † Father, the † Son and the Holy † Spirit come down upon you, that you may rightly fulfill that which you have undertaken today . R. Amen.

THE INITIATION OF DOORKEEPERS

The people are seated. At the appointed time those about to be made doorkeepers are summoned by a priest, as follows:

Priest. **Let those who are to be initiated to the office of doorkeeper come forward.**

The ordinands rise from their seats and advance a few paces towards the bishop or archpriest, bearing lighted candles in their hands. They bow to him, the candles are then taken from them and they are seated.

The bishop or archpriest charges them as follows

Bishop or archpriest. **It was the duty of the doorkeeper in ancient times to ring the church bells, to open the church at the appointed times to the faithful, to keep it ever closed to unbelievers, to open the book for the preacher, and to guard with diligence the church furniture, lest any should be lost. Today, these specific functions no longer appertain to the order of doorkeeper; rather, we relate to them symbolically, and invest them with a moral significance. [It will thus be your duty as doorkeepers to keep the keys of your heart, to open the heart at all times for the expression of that which is noble and good, but to sternly keep it closed to evil and unworthy suggestions. As it is your duty to safeguard your own heart, you should** also seek to encourage the hearts of others to aspire things which are holy and beautiful. May you then carry out a ministry which spiritually builds upon the groundwork of our predecessors.]

In this order, it will be your task to learn control of the emotions and passions, as before you learned to master the crude instincts of the physical body. There are those who thought of emotion as necessarily evil, and have taught others to uproot it from the nature. Not is not for you to think this way. God has given us the power to feel emotion and it, too, is a power which can become mighty in his service. At whatever stage a person's emotions may be, they represent the working of the divine power within and should not be suppressed, but raised and consecrated to God's service. If through carelessness or selfishness the emotions have been allowed to become self-centered, it is our duty not to kill them, but to purify and raise them; to substitute devotion to God and humanity for devotion to our own pleasure; to put aside, as far as possible, concern for self and replacing it with love for others. Hence it is your task as doorkeepers to train your emotions, laying them as gift on Christ's holy altar, that they too may be used in his service.

The charge being ended, the candidates kneel before the bishop or archpriest, who rises and says

B.   Let us pray.
B.   O Lord Christ, who art ever ready to receive and to strengthen the earnest aspirations of thy children, look down in thy love upon these thy servants who desire to become worthy to serve

thee as doorkeepers in thy holy church. Sanctify ✝ them, O Lord, with thy heavenly grace that, growing continually in virtue, they may rightly practice the duties of their office and so be found acceptable in thy sight, O thou great King of love, to whom be glory for ever and ever. R. Amen.

The candidates kneel before the bishop or archpriest in succession. He places his right hand on the head of each as he says

B.   In the name of Christ our Lord, I admit thee to the order of doorkeeper.

*The bishop or archpriest hands a **key and a bell** to each candidate in turn, saying*

Like as he who bears the key throws open the church for the use of all mankind, so shalt thou throw open the doors of thy heart for the service of thy brethren. And as he who rings the bell summons men to divine worship so by the force of good example shalt thou also summon men to the service of God.

Each candidate rings the bell thrice

Having ordained the several candidates, the bishop or archpriest blesses the new doorkeepers in the following words, unless they art, immediately to receive another order

B.   The blessing of God almighty, the ✝ Father, the ✝ Son and the Holy ✝ Spirit come down upon you, that you may rightly fulfill that which to-day you have undertaken. R. Amen.

THE INITIATION OF READERS OR LECTORS

The people are seated

At the appointed time those about to be made readers are summoned by a priest, as follows

Priest. **Let those who are to be initiated to the office of reader come forward.**

*The candidates rise from their seats and advance a few, paces towards the bishop or archpriest, **bearing lighted candles** in their hands. They bow to him, the candles are then taken from them and they are seated. The bishop charges them as follows*

Bishop or archpriest. **We know from the traditions of the church that in ancient times it was the duty of the reader to read for him who was about to preach, to intone the lessons, to bless bread and all first fruits. The passage of time has stripped the office of reader of these duties and its functions, but it is still of the essence of this office that the reader dedicate the gifts of his mind to the glory of God. [You have learned in the preceding orders that you should control the physical body and train the emotions for service, and you will have seen from experience that, in so far as your affection has been bestowed upon others, you have greatly helped to develop affection in them. It will now become your responsibility to train your own mind in order to positively influence the minds of others. As you have had to conquer and control wrong tendencies of emotion, it is now also necessary that you learn to discipline your** thinking, for just as you know that the physical body is not yourself, or your emotions, however glorious or wonderful they may be, it is also true that your mind is not you. In your thoughts there is a power, splendid and great, given to you for the service of God; it also has to be your servant and not your master. It too needs careful training, and that training is the special purpose of this step, which you are about to undertake. You will find yourselves prone to wandering thoughts; this you must conquer. You must develop within yourself(ves) the power of concentration, that you might study effectively, and be able to communicate the results of this study to others.]

As you had to learn to purify emotion, you must also learn to purify your mind. As you learned to perceive the necessity for physical cleanliness, or to cast off the baser emotions, you must also endeavor to cast out unworthy thoughts, remembering that all thought is unworthy that is impure, selfish, mean or base; for example, finding fault instead of looking for the gifts in others. All such thought is impure beside the light of the the Christ, who is our pattern and perfect example. Wherefore, as a reader it will be your duty to train and develop the powers of your mind, to study, and make yourself fit so that you may be better able to help others develop their minds.

The charge being ended, the candidates kneel before the bishop or archpriest, who rises and says

B.   Let us pray.
B.   O Lord Christ, who is ever ready to receive and to strengthen the earnest aspirations of your

children, look down in your love upon these your servants, who desire to become worthy to serve you as readers in your holy church. Sanctify ✝ them, O Lord, with your heavenly grace that, growing continually in virtue, they may rightly practice the duties of their office and so be found acceptable in your sight, O you great king of love, to whom be glory for ever and ever. R. Amen.

The candidates kneel before the bishop or archpriest in succession. He places his right hand on the head of each, as he says

B. In the name of Christ our Lord, I admit thee to the order of reader.

*The bishop or archpriest hands a **book** to each candidate, saying*

Study diligently the sacred sciences, that you may become better be able to devote your mind with all its powers to the service of God.

Having ordained the several candidates, he blesses the new readers in the following words, unless they are immediately to receive another order

B. The blessing of God almighty, the ✝ Father, the ✝ Son and the Holy ✝ Spirit come down upon you, that you may rightly fulfill that which you have undertaken today. R. Amen.

THE INITIATION OF HEALER/EXORCISTS

The people are seated.

At the appointed time those about to be made healer/exorcists are summoned by a priest, as follows

Priest. **Let those who are to be initiated to the office of healer/exorcist come forward.**

The candidates rise from their seats and advance a few, paces towards the bishop or archpriest, bearing lighted candles in their hands. They bow to him, the candles are then taken from them and they are seated. The bishop or archpriest charges them as follows

Bishop or archpriest. **It was the duty of the exorcist in the ancient church to cast out devils, to warn the people that noncommunicants should make room for those who were going to communion, and to pour out the water needed in the divine service. The book of exorcisms was handed to him with the words: 'Take and commit this to memory and receive the power to lay hands on demoniacs, whether they be baptized or catechumens.' [The candidate was admonished that as he cast out devils from the bodies of others he should rid his own mind and body of all uncleanliness and wickedness, lest he be overcome by those whom he drove out of others by his ministry. For then only would he be able safely to exercise mastery over the demons in others, when he should first have overcome their manifold wickedness within himself.]**

Such exorcism as is now performed in the church is undertaken only by those who have been ordained to the priesthood, and even for then only with a special authorization from the church. Also, with the passage of time, the other duties associated with the office of exorcist have fallen into abeyance. [Moreover, our conception of these matters is different in some respects from that entertained in former times. Men of old thought of temptation as being due to the attacks of demons without. But in truth this is not generally so. There lies behind each one of us a past which, since we are growing in grace, must have been less desirable than the present. Each of us are subject to habits, instincts, and other influences, which rise against us when we try to live the higher life. What we try to conquer is not always a devil from outside, nor is it always inherent wickedness in ourselves. It is often the consequence and a relic of earlier behavior, which was permitted in the days of our ignorance.]

In this grade of healer/exorcist it will be your duty, by strenuous effort, to develop the power of the will, and by its exercise to endeavor to cast out whatever selfishness may reside there. Learning to control your own evil habits, you will be better equipped to help others cast out whatever evil is in them, not only by example but by precept and even by direct action on your part. In earlier times, it was often true and still is in rare cases that, through weakness or by persistence in evil, men allowed their bodies to become truly obsessed or partially controlled by evil spirits. To some, special power and authority are given to hold unclean spirits in check and to cast out this evil influence from the bodies of others. There are some, too, who possess the gift of healing and are able by the virtue flowing from them to alleviate suffering and to soothe afflictions of the body; this gift may likewise be strengthened in the order of healer/exorcist; indeed, in ancient times the exorcist was regarded as a healer in the church.

Wherefore, dearly beloved, strive diligently in this new office to which you are called to exercise mastery over yourselves, that you may more effectively help others to gain a similar mastery over their weaknesses.

The charge being ended, the ordinands kneel before the bishop or archpriest, who rises and says

B.   Let us pray.
B.   O Lord Christ, who is ever ready to receive and to strengthen the earnest aspirations of your children, look own in your love upon these your servants, who desire to become worthy to serve you as healer/exorcists in your holy church. Sanctify ✝ them, O Lord, with your heavenly grace, that growing continually in virtue they may rightly practice the duties of their office and so be found acceptable in your sight, O thou great king of love, to whom be glory for ever and ever. R. Amen.

The ordinands kneel before the bishop or archpriest in succession. He places his right hand on the head of each, as he says

B.   In the name of Christ our Lord, I admit you to the order of healer/exorcist.

*The bishop or archpriest hands a **sword and a book** to each ordinand, saying*

Take this sword as a symbol of the will and this book as a symbol of knowledge, that you might be strong in the warfare of the spirit.

Having ordained the several candidates, he blesses the new exorcists in the following words, unless they are immediately to receive another order

B.   The blessing of God almighty, the ✝ Father, the ✝ Son and the Holy ✝ Spirit come down upon you, that you might fulfill that which you have undertaken today. R. Amen.

THE INITIATION OF ACOLYTES

The people are seated

At the appointed time those about to be made acolytes are summoned by a priest, as follows

Priest. **Let those who are to be initiated to the office of acolyte come forward.**

The ordinands rise from their seats and advance a few paces towards the bishop or archpriest, bearing lighted candles in their hands. They bow to him, the candles are then taken from them and they are seated. The bishop or archpriest charges them as follows

Bishop or archpriest. **It was the duty of the acolyte in earlier times to carry the candlestick, to light the tapers and lamps of the church, and to present** wine and water for the Eucharistic offering. These duties are no longer confined to the acolyte, therefore, as in the case of the previous orders, we treat these duties symbolically, and invest them with spiritual significance. Where the acolyte served before the altar of the church, you now serve before the altar of the human heart, on which each of us must truly offer ourselves as a sacrifice to God. [You will have noticed that in the former degrees the training consisted partly of the cultivation of your own powers, and also to learn to use them to help others. Assuredly, this training, through which you have already passed, was vain if it not lead you, for Christ's sake, to use them for the wider interests humanity. Remember the words of the Christ, when he said, 'Whosoever will be great among you let him be your minister; and whosoever will be chief among you let him be your servant, even as the Son of Man came not to be ministered to but to minister.' Wherefore, as you are about to offer yourself(ves) to him, thereby to become enrolled in the fellowship of those who serve, endeavor with singleness of heart to perform the office you now undertake, for then only will you truly present wine and water to be used in sacrifice to God, when by the continual practice of unselfishness you will have offered yourself(ves) as an acceptable sacrifice to God.]

In the ancient symbolism of this order, the candidate, in addition to receiving a cruet as the visible token of this sacrifice, is also given a candlestick with a candle and told that he is bound to light the lights of the church in the name of the Lord. This lighting of lights will be your duty in the literal sense, and this you should do. But, it is

266

also you duty, with the spiritual light of Christ's holy presence, to enkindle the sense of his presence within the hearts of others, who form the body of the universal church. [In many forms of religious faith light has been taken as a symbol of deity - the light which lighteth everyone who comes into the world. That light is universal, but it also dwells in the heart of humankind. It is our duty to find the light in everyone, however dimly it may burn, however veiled and darkened it may appear. Having learned to recognize the light in ourselves and others, we are better equipped to help others let their inner divinity to shine forth, in its pristine glory and splendor, until it becomes one with the universal light. To this end, indeed, let us be constantly admonished by the words of scripture: 'Let your light so shine before men that they may see your good works and glorify your Father who is in heaven.' 'They that be wise shall shine as the brightness of the firmament, but they that turn many to righteousness as the stars for ever and ever.' 'Let your loins be girded about and your lights burning.' Again, the apostle Paul says: 'In the midst of a crooked and perverse generation, among whom shine ye as lights in the world.' 'Let us therefore cast off the works of darkness and let us put on the armor of light.' 'For ye were sometimes darkness, but now are ye light in the Lord; walk as children of light.']

This order of acolyte is intended to help you to quicken your spiritual faculties, especially the intuition through which the light of divine love and wisdom may enlighten your understanding. As you fulfill your ministry by helping others, so shall you be helped by the great ones, whose ears are never deaf, whose hearts are never closed against the world they love.

The charge being ended, the candidates kneel before the bishop or archpriest, who rises and says

B.   Let us pray.
B.   O Lord Christ, who is ever ready to receive and to strengthen the earnest aspirations of your children, look down in your love upon these your servants, who desire to become worthy to serve you as acolytes in your holy church. Sanctify ✝ them, O Lord, with your heavenly grace that, growing continually in virtue, they may rightly practice the duties of their office and so be found acceptable in your sight, O thou great king of love, to whom be glory for ever and ever. Amen.

The candidates kneel before the bishop or archpriest in succession. He places his right hand on the head of each, saying

B.   In the name of Christ our Lord, I admit thee to the order of acolyte.

The bishop or archpriest hands a candlestick with lighted candles to each candidate, saying

As you bear this visible light, may you forever shed the brightness of the divine light around you.

The bishop or archpriest hands a cruet to each candidate, saying

See to it that you pour out your life, in union with the great sacrifice, by which the world is sustained.

The bishop or archpriest endues each candidate with the badge of the order, saying:

I endue thee with the badge of the order of acolyte; see that you use it as a channel of Christ's love.

B. Let us pray. O Christ, the Lord of love, we worship at your feet, and once more we dedicate ourselves to your service; let the light of your ineffable glory shine forth through these sacred symbols, that they might be as radiant suns to those who wear them, and fountains of light and blessings to all your faithful people, you who lives and reigns for ever. Amen.]

Having ordained the several candidates, he blesses the new acolytes in the following words, unless they are immediately to receive another order:

B.   The blessing of God almighty, the ✝ Father, the ✝ Son and the Holy ✝ Spirit come down upon you, that you may with steadfastness and zeal persevere in that which today you have undertaken. Amen.

THE ORDINATION OF SUBDEACONS

The bishop celebrates the Holy Eucharist, using the following special collect

THE COLLECT

ALMIGHTY, everlasting God, by whose Spirit the whole body of the church is made holy and governed, pour forth your sanctifying grace into the hearts of these your servants, who are about to be numbered among the subdeacons of your church, that with pure heart and open mind they may faithfully receive your blessing from on high; through Christ our Lord. R. Amen.

The collect of the day and such other collects as are usual follow here

The collects being ended the people are seated and the bishop takes his seat upon a footstool before the altar. Those about to be ordained are summoned by a priest as follows

Priest. **Let those who are to be ordained to the order of subdeacon come forward.**

*The candidates come forward **bearing lighted candles**. They bow to the bishop, the candles are then taken from them and they are seated. The bishop charges them as follows*

Bishop. **Dearly beloved, the order of subdeacon is a preparatory grade for the orders of deacon and priest. It gives to those who receive it greater strength and steadfastness of purpose that, with** singleness of heart, they might strengthen their dedication to the service of Christ in his holy church. So great, indeed, are the responsibilities put upon those, who in the greater orders become Christ's representatives, that a season of trial in the preparatory grade of the subdeacon is often required, wherein those who aspire to so sublime an estate may test themselves, if need be, especially if they are young in years or ecclesiastical experience, that they not enter lightly or unadvisedly into so solemn an undertaking.

You, having already offered yourselves to the service of God, and to help forward his kingdom upon earth, are now moved in your hearts to devote yourselves still further to his service and to that of your brethren. For this reason we hereby invoke the divine blessing; and, with the help and ready concurrence of the faithful here assembled, shall now proceed in the exercise of our office to bring you as a holy oblation into the presence of Christ, not doubting that at the latter end you, having the witness of faithful service, will shine, pure and lustrous, as jewels in the crown of our Master.

The bishop rises and addresses the congregation as follows

B.   Let us then pray that almighty God, in his great loving-kindness and watchful care over his church, may bestow a plentiful portion of grace upon these acolytes, who are now about to be raised to the order of subdeacon.

LITANY

All kneel and sing the following litany, during which the ordinands lie prostrate:

If it should happen that the candidates are all to receive the diaconate immediately after this, the litany given in the service for the ordination of a deacon is substituted here.

God the Father, seen of none,
God the co-eternal Son,
God the Spirit, with them one;
Hear us, Holy Trinity.

God eternal, mighty king,
Unto thee our love we bring;
Through the world thy praises ring;
We are thine, O Trinity.

Holy Spirit, heavenly dove,
Dew descending from above,
Breath of life and fire of love;
Hear us, Holy Spirit.

Source of strength, of knowledge clear,
Wisdom, godliness sincere,
Understanding, counsel, cheer;
Hear us, Holy Spirit.

Source of courage, love and peace,
Patience, pureness, faith's increase,
Hope and joy that cannot cease;
Hear us, Holy Spirit.

Spirit guiding us aright,

Spirit making darkness light,
Spirit of resistless might;
Hear us, Holy Spirit.

Thine is an unchanging love
Higher than the heights above;
Lord, life-giver, holy dove;
Hear us, Holy Spirit.

Come to aid the souls who yearn
More of truth divine to learn,
And with deeper love to burn;
Hear us, Holy Spirit.

Keep us in the narrow way,
Warn us when we go astray,
Fill us with thy glorious ray;
Hear us, Holy Spirit.

May we from temptation turn,
Secrets of thy kingdom learn,
Feel thy fire within us burn;
Hear us, Holy Spirit.

Help us nobly to endure,
Keep us faithful, keep us pure,
Ever wiser, stronger, truer;
Hear us, Holy Spirit.

Light and strength on us bestow,
Guide us, lead us here below,
Where thou wiliest we shall go;
Hear us, Holy Spirit.

To the outcast and forlorn,
To the weary and the worn,

Let thy hope and peace be borne;
Bless them, Holy Spirit.

Fount of love, by all adored,
Let the wisdom of the Lord
On his waiting church be poured;
Hear us, Holy Spirit.

Still unsheathe be thy sword,
Till the world, from sin restored,
Is the kingdom of the Lord;
Hear us, Holy Spirit.

Holy, loving as thou art,
All thy sevenfold gift impart,
Nevermore from us depart;
Hear us, Holy Spirit.

*The three verses which follow are sung by the bishop
alone*

We beseech thee, hear our prayer;
Bless † thy servant(s), prostrate there;
Hold *them* in thy loving care;
Hear us, Holy Trinity.

Hear thy servants as they pray;
Help thy chosen one(s) to-day,
Bless † and † hallow *them* for aye;
Hear us, Holy Trinity.

Pour thy loving kindness great
On each *(this)* chosen candidate,
Bless †† *them,* † hallow, † consecrate;
Hear us, Holy Trinity.

274

God the Father, seen of none,
God the co-eternal Son,
God the Spirit, with them one;
We are thine, O Trinity.

The people are seated.

The bishop and ordinands are again seated and the bishop charges them in this way:

B. **Dearly beloved, you who are about to be admitted to the office of subdeacon, should know what manner of ministry was in former times committed to your order. It appertained to the subdeacon to provide water for the service of the altar, to minister to the deacon, to wash the altar cloths and corporals, to present to the deacon the chalice and paten to be used at the sacrifice, to guard the church doors or the gates of the sanctuary, and in later times to read the epistles before the people. Endeavor, then, by fulfilling readily with meetness and diligence such of these visible ministries as are still part of your office, to show true reverence for the invisible things they may be said to typify. For the altar of holy church is the throne of Christ himself, and it is indeed fitting that they who minister before it should walk circumspectly and realize that upon them is laid the high honor of its guardianship.**

Also take heed that you become watchful sentinels of heavenly warfare, so that growing ever in virtue, you may shine, lustrous and chaste, in the company of the saints. Strive earnestly to pattern

yourselves after the example of our divine Master, that you might meetly minister at the divine sacrifice, in the invisible sanctuary of your hearts as well as in the visible sanctuary of the holy church.

From ancient times, also, it has been required of those who enter this order that they strive to acquire certain virtues of character, such as are typified by the vestments delivered to them. By the amice, control of speech; by the maniple, the love of service; by the tunic, the spirit of joy and gladness and confidence in the good law, which may be interpreted as a recognition of the plan revealed by almighty God for the perfecting of his creation.

The ordinands rise.

B.   Will you then strive to order your lives in accordance with these precepts?

Ordinands. I will.

B.   The Lord keep you in all these things and strengthen you in all goodness. R. Amen.

The bishop rises and, with hands extended towards the ordinands who kneel before him, and says the following prayer:

B.   O Lord Christ, the fountain of all goodness, who bestows upon all who serve you in your holy church, the gifts pertaining to their several offices. Graciously regard these your servants, whom we now present for the order of the subdiaconate, and so ✝ open their hearts and minds to your heavenly grace that they may be steadfast in your holy service. Increase in them, O Lord, the sevenfold gift of the Spirit that, growing in the knowledge of things eternal, they may offer their lives as a holy and continual sacrifice to you, O great king of love, to whom be praise and adoration from human beings and the angel host alike. Amen.

The ordinands kneel before the bishop in succession. He places his right hand on the head of each and says

B.   In the name of Christ our Lord, I admit you to the order of subdeacon.

The bishop is seated. He hands an empty chalice and paten, cruets and lavabo bowl with towel to each ordinand, who touches them with the right hand, while the bishop says

B.   Take heed of that the ministry which is committed to you. I admonish you to comport yourself in your ministry in such a way as to bring credit in the sight of God.

The bishop touches the amice which is upon the neck of each ordinand, saying

Take the amice, by which restraint of the tongue is signified. In the name of the ✝ Father and of the ✝ Son and of the Holy ✝ Spirit. Amen.

The bishop places the maniple on the left arm of each saying

Take the maniple, by which is meant the fruit of good works. In the name of the ✠ Father and of the ✠ Son and of the Holy ✠ Spirit. Amen.

The bishop vests one after another in the tunic, saying

May the Lord clothe thee with the garment of gladness and the vesture of joy. In the name of the ✠ Father and of the Son and of the Holy ✠ Spirit. R. Amen.

The bishop hands to each the book of epistles, saying as he touches it with the right hand

Take the book of epistles and receive authority to read them in God's holy church, both for the living and the dead. In the name of the ✠ Father and of the ✠ Son and of the Holy ✠ Spirit. R. Amen.

He rises and blesses them in this wise

B. The blessing of God almighty, the ✠ Father, the ✠ Son and the Holy ✠ Spirit come down upon you, that with steadfastness and zeal you may persevere in that which you have undertaken today. R. Amen.

One of the newly ordained subdeacons, vested in tunic, reads the epistle of the day

The Holy Eucharist is then continued

IN THE PRAYER OF CONSECRATION

In the prayer of consecration the following clause is inserted after the words: 'for all our bishops, clergy and faithful:

Especially for *these* whom in Christ's holy name we have admitted to the order of the subdiaconate.

THE ORDINATION OF A DEACON

Bishop Almighty God, to you all hearts are open, all desires known, and from you no secrets are hid. Cleanse the thoughts of our hearts by the inspiration of your Holy Spirit, that we may perfectly love you, and worthily praise your holy Name; through Christ our Lord. *Amen.*

The Presentation

The bishop and people sit. A Priest and a Lay Person, and additional presenters if desired, standing before the bishop, present the ordinand, saying

Presenters N.N, Bishop in the Church of God, on behalf of the clergy and people, we present to you N. to be ordained a deacon in Christ's one, holy, catholic, and apostolic Church.

Bishop Have you selected him to be your deacon? And, do you believe *his* manner of life is compatible with the exercise of this ministry?

Presenters We have chosen him, and we believe *him* to have the divine gifts necessary for this office.

Bishop (*to the ordinand*) Will you be faithful to the stirrings of the Holy Spirit, to God, and the people you will serve? And will you, in accordance with our canons, be a faithful colleague to your bishop and the other ministers of Christ's Church?

Ordinand   I will. I solemnly declare that I believe in Holy Scripture as Divinely inspired, that I will be open to the promptings of Holy Spirit as it speaks to me today, and that I will be a faithful servant to the people of God.

The Ordinand then signs the above Declaration in the sight of all present. All stand

Bishop   Dear friends in Christ, I know you are aware of the importance of this ministry, and the weight of your responsibility in presenting *N.* for ordination to this office. Therefore if any of you know any reason why we should not proceed, speak now, and make it known.

If there is no objection the Bishop continues

Bishop   Is it your will that *N.* be ordained a deacon?

People   It is.

Bishop   Will you support and uphold *him* in this ministry?

People   We will.

The Bishop then calls the people to prayer with these or similar words

Bishop	In peace let us pray to the Lord.

All kneel, and the person appointed leads the Litany for Ordinations, or some other approved litany.

Bishop	The Lord be with you
People	And also with you.

Let us pray. O God of unchangeable power and eternal light: Look favorably on your whole Church, that wonderful and sacred mystery; by the effectual working of your providence, carry out in tranquillity the plan of salvation; let the whole world see and know that things which were being cast down are being raised up, and things which had grown old are being made new, and that all things are being brought to their perfection by him through whom all things were made, your Son Jesus Christ our Lord; who lives and reigns with you, in the unity of the Holy Spirit, one God, for ever and ever. *Amen.*

The Examination

All are seated except the ordinand, who stands before the Bishop. The Bishop addresses the ordinand as follows

Bishop	My *brother*, every Christian is called to follow Jesus Christ, serving God the

Father, through the power of the Holy Spirit. God now calls you to a special ministry of servanthood directly with your bishop. In the name of Jesus Christ, you are to serve all people, particularly the poor, the weak, the sick, and the lonely. As a deacon in the Church, you are to engage in intense praxis, study Scripture, and listen for the voice of God, seeking spiritual nourishment and guidance from. You are to make Christ and his redemptive love known, by your example, and if necessary by word. You are to speak to the Church on the needs, concerns, and hopes of the world. You are to assist your bishop and his priests. At all times, your life and teaching are to show Christ's people that in serving the helpless they are serving Christ himself.

Bishop	My *brother*, do you believe that you are truly called by God and his Church to the life and work of a deacon?
Ordinand	I do.
Bishop	Do you now in the presence of the Church commit yourself to this trust and responsibility?
Ordinand	I do.
Bishop	Will you support and respect the leadership of your bishop in all matters canonical?
Ordinand	I will.

Bishop	Will you be faithful in prayer, in praxis, and in the study of Holy Scripture?
Ordinand	I will.
Bishop	Will you look for Christ in all others, being ready to help and serve those in need?
Ordinand	I will.
Bishop	Will you do you best to pattern your life [and that of your family, or household, or community] in accordance with the teachings of Christ, so that you may be a wholesome example to all people?
Ordinand	I will.
Bishop	Will you in all things seek not your glory but the glory of the Lord Christ?
Ordinand	I will.
Bishop	May the Lord by his grace uphold you in the service he lays upon you.
Ordinand	Amen.

The Consecration

All now stand except the ordinand, who kneels facing the Bishop.

Hymn Veni Creator Spiritus, or the hymn, Veni Sancte Spiritus

A period of silent prayer follows, the people still standing.

Bishop   O God, most merciful Father, we praise you for sending your Son Jesus Christ, who took on himself the form of a servant, and humbled himself, becoming obedient even to death on the cross. We praise you that you have highly exalted him, and made him Lord of all; and that, through him, we know that whoever would be great must be servant of all. We praise you for the many ministries in your Church, and for calling this your servant to the order of deacons.

Here the Bishop lays hands upon the head of the ordinand, and prays

Bishop   Therefore, Father, through Jesus Christ your Son, give your Holy Spirit to *Chalres*; fill *him* with grace and power, and make *him* a deacon in your Church.

Bishop   Make *him*, O Lord, modest and humble, strong and constant, to observe the discipline of Christ. Let *his* life and teaching so reflect your commandments, that through *him* many may come to know you and love you. As your Son came not to be served but to serve, may this deacon share in Christ's service, and come to the unending glory of him who, with

285

you and the Holy Spirit, lives and
reigns, one God, for ever and ever.

The People in a loud voice response   Amen.

*The new deacon is now vested according to the order
of deacons.*

*The Bishop then gives a Bible to the newly ordained,
saying*

Receive this Bible as the sign of your authority to
proclaim God's Word and to assist in the ministration
of his holy Sacraments.

THE ORDINATION OF A PRIEST

Bishop   Almighty God, to you all hearts are open, all desires known, and from you no secrets are hid. Cleanse the thoughts of our hearts by the inspiration of your Holy Spirit, that we may perfectly love you, and worthily praise your holy Name; through Christ our Lord. *Amen.*

The Presentation

The bishop and people sit. A Priest and a Lay Person, and additional presenters if desired, standing before the bishop, present the ordinand, saying

Presenters   *N.N*, Bishop in the Church of God, on behalf of the clergy and people, we present to you *N.* to be ordained a Priest in Christ's one, holy, catholic, and apostolic Church.

Bishop   Do you believe he has the Divine Gifts necessary and manner of life compatible with the exercise of Christ's priesthood?

Presenters We do.

Bishop   *(to the ordinand)* Will you be faithful to the stirrings of the Holy Spirit, to God, and the people you will serve? And will you, in accordance with our canons, be a faithful colleague to your bishop and the other ministers of

Christ's Church?

Ordinand   I will. I solemnly declare that I believe in Holy Scripture as Divinely inspired, that I will be open to the promptings of Holy Spirit as it speaks to me today, and that I will be a faithful servant to the people of God.

The Ordinand then signs the above Declaration in the sight of all present. All stand

Bishop   Dear friends in Christ, I know you are aware of the importance of this ministry, and the weight of your responsibility in presenting *N.* for ordination to this office. Therefore if any of you know any reason why we should not proceed, speak now, and make it known.

If there is no objection the Bishop continues

Bishop   Is it your will that *N.* be ordained a Priest?

People   It is.

Bishop   Will you support and uphold *him* in this ministry?

People   We will.

The Bishop then calls the people to prayer with these or similar words

Bishop   In peace let us pray to the Lord.

All kneel, and the person appointed leads the Litany for Ordinations, or some other approved litany.

Bishop	The Lord be with you
People	And also with you.

Let us pray. O God of unchangeable power and eternal light: Look favorably on your whole Church, that wonderful and sacred mystery; by the effectual working of your providence, carry out in tranquillity the plan of salvation; let the whole world see and know that things which were being cast down are being raised up, and things which had grown old are being made new, and that all things are being brought to their perfection by him through whom all things were made, your Son Jesus Christ our Lord; who lives and reigns with you, in the unity of the Holy Spirit, one God, for ever and ever. *Amen.*

The Examination

All are seated except the ordinand, who stands before the Bishop. The Bishop addresses the ordinand as follows

Bishop   My *brother*, the Church is the family of God, the Mystical Body of Christ, and the temple of the Holy Spirit. All baptized people are called to make

Christ known as Savior and Lord, and to share in the renewing of his world. Now you are called to work as pastor, priest, and teacher, together with your bishop and fellow presbyters, and to take your share in the councils of the Church. As a priest, it will be your task to proclaim by word and deed the Gospel of Jesus Christ, and to fashion your life in accordance with its precepts. You are to love and serve the people among whom you work, caring alike for young and old, strong and weak, rich and poor. You are to preach, to declare God's forgiveness to penitent sinners, to pronounce God's blessing, to share in the administration of Holy Baptism and in the celebration of the mysteries of Christ's Body and Blood, and to perform the other ministrations entrusted to you. In all that you do, you are to nourish Christ's people from the riches of his grace, and strengthen them to glorify God in this life and in the life to come.

Bishop   My *brother*, do you believe that you are truly called by God and his Church to the life and work of a Priest?

Ordinand   I do.

Bishop   Do you now in the presence of the Church commit yourself to this trust and responsibility?

Ordinand   I do.

Bishop	Will you support and respect the pastoral leadership of your bishop in all matters canonical?
Ordinand	I will.
Bishop	Will you be faithful in prayer, in praxis, and in the study of Holy Scripture?
Ordinand	I will.
Bishop	Will you endeavor to minister the Word of God and the sacraments of the Church, that the reconciling love of Christ may be known and received?
Ordinand	I will.
Bishop	Will you undertake to be a faithful pastor to all whom you are called to serve, laboring together with them and with your fellow ministers to build up the family of God?
Ordinand	I will.
Bishop	Will you do your best to pattern your life [and that of your family, or household, or community] in accordance with the teachings of Christ, so that you may be a wholesome example to all?
Ordinand	I will.
Bishop	Will you persevere in prayer, both in public and in private, asking God's grace, both for yourself and for others, offering all your labors to God, through the mediation of Jesus Christ, and in the sanctification of the Holy

| | Spirit? |
| *Ordinand* | I will. |

| *Bishop* | May the Lord who has given you the will to do these things give you the grace and power to perform them. |
| *Ordinand* | Amen. |

The Consecration

All now stand except the ordinand, who now lays prostrate before the Bishop and any other presbyters who stand to the right and left of the ordaining bishop.

Hymn Veni Creator Spiritus, or the hymn, Veni Sancte Spiritus

After the Veni Creator Spiritus or Veni Sancte Spiritus is concluded the ordinand kneels.

| *Bishop* | God and Father of all, we praise you for your infinite love in calling us to be a holy people in the kingdom of your Son Jesus our Lord, who is the image of your eternal and invisible glory, the firstborn among many brethren, and the head of the Church. We thank you that by his death he has overcome death, and, having ascended into heaven, has poured his gifts abundantly upon your people, making some apostles, some prophets, some evangelists, some pastors and teachers, to equip the saints for the work of ministry and the building up of his |

Mystical Body.

Receive the Holy Spirit for the work of God.

Here the Bishop lays hands upon the head of the ordinand, then any other Priests who are present also lay hands upon the head of the ordinand. The bishop prays.

Bishop Therefore, Father, through Jesus Christ your Son, give your Holy Spirit to *N.*; fill *him* with grace and power, and make *him* a Priest in your Church.

The new priest is now vested in chasuble and stole

Then, the bishop and priest are seated, facing each other. A towel, chrism oil, and a strip of cloth is brought to the bishop. The towel is placed on the laps of the bishop and new priest

The bishop anoints the hands of the priest with Chrism Oil

Bishop Be pleased, O Lord, to consecrate and hallow these hands by this anointing and our † blessing; that whatsoever they † bless may be blessed and whatsoever they consecrate may be consecrated and hallowed, in the name of our Lord Jesus Christ. R. Amen.

The bishop closes the hands together, palm to palm, and they are bound together with a white linen strip. The bishop places a chalice between the hands of the new priest , saying

> Take the authority to offer sacrifice to God and to celebrate the Holy Eucharist, both for the living and for the dead; in the name of the Father, Son, and Holy Spirit. R. Amen.

Bishop

> May *he* exalt you, O Lord, in the midst of your people; offer spiritual sacrifices acceptable to you; boldly proclaim the Gospel; and rightly administer the sacraments of the Church. Make *him* a faithful pastor, a patient teacher, and a wise councelor. Grant that in all things *he* may serve without reproach, so that your people may be strengthened and your Name glorified. All this we ask through Jesus Christ our Lord, who with you and the Holy Spirit lives and reigns, one God, for ever and ever.

The People in a loud voice respond

Amen.

A tray with lemon and bread is brought to the bishop and new priest to clean their hands with. Afterward, the towel and chairs are taken away. The bishop greets and congratulates the new priest.

The new priest joins the bishop and any other priests who may be present. The Holy Eucharist is continued to its close.

RITE OF CONSECRATION
OF A BISHOP

The Rite of Consecration of a Bishop begins after the Indroit Liturgy of the Eucharistic Celebration, except Collect

(Opening Prayer)

After the conclusion of he purification rites in the Indroit Liturgy the consecrating bishop says

Consecrator: May God Creator, Word, and Spirit, + bless, strengthen, preserve, and sanctify you. May the Lord in loving kindness look upon you that you may receive the grace and comfort of the Holy Spirit.

Assembly: Amen.

THE PRESENTATION

Assistant Bishops and Bishop-Elect rise. Senior Assistant Bishop addresses the Consecrator in these words

The Bishop-Elect comes forward

S.A.B.: *N,* Bishop in the Church of God, the clergy and people of God, trusting in the guidance of the Holy Spirit, have chosen *N. N.* to be a bishop and chief pastor. We therefore ask you to lay your hands upon *him/her* and in the power of the Holy Spirit to consecrate *him/her* a bishop in the one, holy, Catholic, and apostolic Church.

Consecrator: Thanks be to God. Have you the Charge of Election?

S.A.B.: We have.

Consecrator: Let it be read.

An individual selected by the bishop-elect reads the testimonial (Charge of Election)

Consecrator, assisting bishops, and bishop-elect sit while the testimonial (Charge of Election) is read

EXAMINATION AND PLEDGE

When the reading of the testimonial (Charge of Election) is ended the bishop-elect kneels while putting his/her hands together between those of the Consecrator while the consecrating bishop asks the bishop-elect the following:

Consecrator: In the name of God, who is Creator, Word made Flesh, and Holy Spirit, do you, *N. N.,* chosen bishop of the Church Universal, solemnly declare that you believe in Holy Scripture as Divinely inspired and in the promptings of the Holy Spirit that speaks to people in today's world? Do you solemnly declare that you will be faithful to the stirrings of the Holy Spirit, to God, and the people you serve? Do you solemnly declare that in accordance with our canons and traditions, you will be a faithful colleague to your Presiding Bishop, your fellow bishops, the clergy, and members of Christ's Church?

Bishop-Elect: I, *(Name)* ..., chosen bishop of the Church Universal, do promise all due reverence and loyalty to the Holy Tradition of the Church, and loving respect to you as Presiding Bishop of the Ascension Alliance, and to your successors, the guardians of our Apostolic Succession. I also promise vigilance in all matters canonical, from this hour, until I have been formally released by the Grace of God.

The Consecrator presses the hands lightly and says

Consecrator: The peace of the Lord be with you.

Bishop-Elect: Amen.

Consecrator: The established Order teaches and commands that whoever is elected to the Episcopal Order and serves the Church Catholic shall be diligently examined beforehand concerning the qualifications and virtues suitable to this charge. Our stewardship was committed to us by Jesus Christ, and we must remember how great and vast our responsibility is. In the Lord's name and authority we now ask you: if you are raised to this sacred charge will you exercise its powers for the benefit of our Lord Jesus Christ, the Church Universal, and Ascension Alliance and for no other purpose whatsoever, laying aside all thought of personal predilections and advancement?

Bishop-Elect: With my whole heart I will endeavor to do so.

Consecrator: According to the measure of your understanding and the powers of your mind, do you believe in the Holy Trinity, Father/Mother, Son, and Holy Spirit, from whom, by whom, and in whom all things are created, in heaven and on earth, visible and non-visible, bodily and spiritual?

Bishop-Elect: I do.

Consecrator: Will you cherish as a most sacred trust the power committed to you, and solemnly pledge yourself to exercise all care and discretion in the choice of those upon whom in Christ's name you bestow the gift of Holy Orders?

Bishop-Elect: I will.

Consecrator: Do you believe that the soul and

	spirit of the human being is immortal and eternal, having neither beginning or end, and that it advances itself by growing toward perfection in this embodiment?
Bishop-Elect:	I do.
Consecrator:	Will you set your affection on things above and not on things of earth, as far as human frailty will permit, serving God faithfully?
Bishop-Elect:	I will.
Consecrator:	Will you be gentle and compassionate to the sorrowful and afflicted?
Bishop-Elect:	I will.
Consecrator:	Will you ever be watchful and defend the Church and its clergy against all slander?
Bishop-Elect:	I will.
Consecrator:	As we now proceed to bestow upon you the powers of Bishop and Guardian of the Apostolic Succession, will you remember that the noblest title of a Bishop is "Servant of the Servants of God," and that you are called to lead your people to a knowledge of Divine Wisdom?

Bishop-Elect: I will.

The bishop-elect is presented with a written declaration to sign

Consecrator: May the Lord keep you in all good things and strengthen you in all goodness.

Response: (all Bishops) This we Bishops of the Church Univrsal, accept, state, and pledge: We will not forget your pledge nor fail to honor and regard that which is given.

The Consecrator now reads the Collect, or opening prayer

Consecrator: **Let us pray: Holy God, be merciful to your people. Fill us with your gifts and   make us always eager to serve you in faith, hope, and love. We ask this through Jesus Christ, who lives and reigns with you and the Holy Spirit, one God for ever and ever. Amen.**

The assembly is seated

LITURGY OF THE WORD

1st Reading

At the end of the reading: **This is the word of the Lord.**

Assembly: **Thanks Be To God.**

300

Responsorial Psalm

2nd Reading

At the end of the reading: **This is the word of the Lord.**

Assembly: **Thanks Be To God.**

ALLELUIA: *(form optional)*

GOSPEL READING *(to be chosen)*

Deacon (or Priest): A reading from the holy gospel according to N.
All   Glory to You, Lord.

Deacon (or Priest): This is the Gospel of the Lord
(Upon conclusion of the Gospel)

All   Praise to you, Lord Jesus Christ.

HOMILY

Following the homily, the assembly remains seated.

The Consecrator puts on the miter and stands

THE CHARGE

Consecrator: It pertains to a Bishop to consecrate, ordain, celebrate the Eucharist, anoint, bless, baptize, confirm, interpret, and judge. Let us pray that Almighty God, Father/Mother may bestow upon this/these Bishop(s)-Elect grace for the performance of their sacred ministry.

All stand while the Bishop(s)-Elect lies prostrate. All sing the response.

THE LITANY

Cantor	Assembly
Lord, have mercy	
	Lord, have mercy
Christ have mercy	
	Christ have mercy
Lord, have mercy	
	Lord, have mercy
Holy Mary our Mother	
	pray for us
Saint Michael	
	pray for us
Holy angels of God	
	pray for us
Saint John the Baptist	
	pray for us
Saint Joseph	
	pray for us
Saints Peter and Saint Paul	

pray for us

Saint Andrew

pray for us

Saint John

pray for us

Saint Mary Magdalene   pray for us

Saint Jane   pray for us

Saint Stephen   pray for us

Saint Ignatius of Antioch

pray for us

Saint Lawrence   pray for us

Saint Perpetua and St. Felicity

pray for us

Saint Sergius and St. Bacchus

pray for us

Saint Agnes   pray for us

Saint Diana   pray for us

Saint Patricia   pray for us

Saint Gregory

pray for us

Saint Martin   pray for us

Saint Benedict	pray for us
Saint Francis	pray for us
Saint Dominic	pray for us
Saint Catherine	pray for us
Saint Teresa All holy men and women	pray for us pray for us
Lord be merciful	Lord, save your people
From all evil	Lord, save your people
From all sin	Lord, save your people
By your incarnation	Lord, save your people
By your death and resurrection	Lord, save your people
By your Holy Spirit	Lord, save your people
Guide and protect your Church	Lord, hear our prayer

Keep all the clergy in faithfulservice to your people
> Lord, hear our
> prayer

Bring all people together in trust and peace
> Lord, hear our
> prayer

Strengthen us in your service
> Lord, hear our
> prayer

Bless these chosen women
> Lord, hear our
> prayer

Bless these chosen women and make them holy
> Lord, hear our
> prayer

Bless these chosen women make them holy, and consecrate them for their sacred duties

> Lord, hear our
> prayer

Jesus, Son of the living God

> Lord, hear our
> prayer

Christ, hear us   Christ, hear us

Lord Jesus, hear our prayer

> Lord Jesus, hear our
> prayer

VENI CREATOR SPIRITUS

Come thou Creator Spirit Blest,
And in our souls take up thy rest;
Come with thy grace and heavenly aid,
To fill the hearts which thou hast made,

Great Paraclete, to thee we cry,
O highest gift of God most high;
O living font, O fire, O love,
And sweet anointing from above.

Far let us drive our tempting foe
And thine abiding peace bestow;
So shall we not, with thee for guide,
Turn from the path of life aside.

O may thy grace on us bestow
The Father and the Son to know
And thee, through endless time confessed,
Of both eternal Spirit blest.

All glory while the ages run
Be to the Father and the Son,
Who gave us life; the same to thee,
O Holy Ghost, eternally.

The Bishop(s)-Elect kneels before the Consecrator. The Bible Bearers place an open Bible over the neck and shoulders of the Bishop(s)-Elect.

The Consecrator, with hands extended, offers the following prayer.

Consecrator: O Lord Christ, who has appointed many orders in Your Church and Who pours down Your gifts abundantly upon Your people, grant to these Your servants, the fullness of the Holy Spirit that in the Episcopal dignity, to which we are about to raise them, they may shine with all manner of heavenly virtues.

The Consecrator places both hands over the head of the Bishop(s)-Elect saying the words of Consecration

"RECEIVE THE HOLY SPIRIT FOR THE OFFICE AND WORK OF A BISHOP IN THE CHURCH OF GOD."

Consecrator lays hands on the bishop-elect in silence

Each of the Assistant Bishops, one by one, places their hands on the head of the bishop-elect, silently in prayer. The Bible is now removed from the back of the new Bishop.

After a pause, the Consecrator and Assistant Bishops extend their hands over the new Bishop(s), and together they pray the following.

Consecrator and Assistant Bishops:

> O God, Father/Mother, Son and
> Spirit, you have bestowed upon
> these chosen Your power and has
> consecrated them/him/her as Your
> Apostle(s) + open their/his/her
> hearts and minds to Your Grace,
> that they may handle wisely that
> which they have received, and that
> they may exercise this sacred trust
> to Your Honor. Fulfill in them the
> perfection of Your service, and
> sanctify them with power from
> above.

*(The new Bishops kneel before the Consecrator. The
Bishop's head is bound with a cloth band and a
binding is placed between the neck of the bishop-elect
and hands, and is then anointed with Holy Chrism.)*

Consecrator: May your head be anointed and
consecrated with heavenly blessing
in the Episcopal Order, so that the
power which you receive from on
high may flow forth from you in
ever greater abundance and glory.
In the Name of God, + Creator , +
Son, and + Holy Spirit. Amen.

*After the new Bishop has been anointed, the
Consecrator and Assistant Bishops with hands
extended offer the following prayer*

Consecrator and Assistant Bishops:

> O God, Holy Spirit, Sophia, who is wisdom, strength and beauty, show forth Your glory in these your servants. Let Your wisdom dwell in their minds and enlighten their understanding, that they may be true in judgment, a wise counselor for the people, and discerning in spiritual knowledge. May they be strong and of good courage, sustaining their people in the face of darkness and despondency, a tower of strength to those that falter on the way. Let the beauty of holiness shine forth in their conversation and actions. Fill them, O Holy One, with reverence and make them devout and steadfast in Your service. May gentleness encompass their lives, that they may win the hearts of people and open them to the light of the Holy Spirit. Above all, may they be so filled with your love that they may touch the hearts of people with the fire from heaven and bring all into your gracious light.

Assembly: Amen.

Bread and lemons are brought to the Consecrator for cleansing his hands.

PRESENTATION OF THE INSTRUMENTS OF OFFICE

The new bishop faces the people. The instruments of the Bishop's office, which have been previously blessed and consecrated, are now presented to him/her.

THE BIBLE

Consecrator: Receive this book of Sacred Wisdom. Be a teacher of the divine wisdom to the people entrusted to you.

THE RING

Consecrator: Receive this ring in token of the link which binds you to our Lord, and for a symbol of your office as Legate to the people. In Our Lord's Most Holy Name, be a healer of the souls of your brothers and sisters and a channel of Christ's love.

THE PECTORAL CROSS

Consecrator: Receive this cross, remembering that by your sacrifice of the lower nature to the higher, you will be able to bear it worthily. Go forth in the power of the Cross, and may the Light of the Holy Spirit shine through you, that you may win others to the beauty of the cross.

THE MITER

Consecrator: Receive this miter for the service of our Lord, who is both God and human, not two, but One in Christ. May you forever unite within yourself the attributes of wisdom and love.

THE CROZIER

Consecrator: Receive this staff and care for your people as a shepherd of Christ's flock. By virtue of the Holy Spirit, be all things to all people; giving strength to the strong, showing gentleness and compassion to the weak, offering wisdom to the wise, and guiding your people with love.

AD MULTOS ANNOS

(The new Bishop(s) gives an ascription of well-being and many years to the Patriarch of the Church of Antioch and advances by 3 stages toward the Patriarch, genuflecting each time and saying: "Ad Multos Annos" (Unto Many Years).

OBLIGATION

New Bishop: I. ... *(Name)* ..., Bishop of Ascension Alliance, do hereby promise to respect, maintain, and support the rights, obligations, and liberties of this Holy Catholic and Apostolic Church, to be loyal to its

Presiding Bishop, and to his/jrt successors, to uphold the Bylaws of the Church, and the Holy Sacraments of the Church; and to show myself as a faithful example in all things. So help me God. Amen.

SEATING OF THE NEW BISHOP

The new Bishop(s) is/are seated. The Consecrator and Assistant Bishops offer this prayer

Consecrator and Assistant Bishops:

O Lord, Shepherd of the Church, be forever enthroned within the hearts and minds, spirits and souls, of the men and women who are servants of your people. May their ministry, by word and deed, be an example to their people and help further Your kingdom here on earth.

People: Amen.

SALUTATION OF PEACE OF THE BISHOPS

All Bishops: The peace of the Lord be with you.

New Bishop: And also with you.

HAIL MARY *(recited)*

Presider: **Let us offer our prayer to the Holy Mother, as we say: Hail Mary, full of grace, the Lord is with you. Blessed are you among women and blessed is the fruit of your womb, Jesus. Holy Mary, Mother of God, pray for us now and at the hour of our death. Amen.**

All are seated

The mass resumes with the Liturgy of the Eucharist, as normally celebrated. The consecrator and the newly consecrated bishop stand together, or the newly consecrated bishop may resume as principal celebrant for the remainder of the Eucharist.

WHO CAN PERFORM WHAT SACRAMENTAL FUNCTIONS

Type of Service	L	EM	D	P	B
Prime	x	x	x	x	x
Compline	x	x	x	x	x
Burial	x*	x*	x	x	x
Reading at Mass	x	x	x	x	x
Healing	x	x	x	x	x
Teaching	x	x	x	x	x
Baptism	x*	x*	x	x	x
Extreme Unction				x	x
Matrimony			x	x	x
Reserved Sacrament		x*	x*	x	x
Celebrate Mass			x*	x	x
Hear Confession				x	x
Benediction Service				x	x
Blessing of Places & Objects				x	x
Confirmation				x*	x
Elevate to Minor Orders				x*	x
Ordain to Major Orders					x
Consecrate Bishops					x

L = Lay
EM = Eucharistic Minister
D = Deacon
P = Priest
B = Bishop

* "With authorization and modification

314

BLESSINGS

The following blessings are reserved to bishops (with the exceptions noted):

1. The consecration of the holy oils.

2. The consecration of a church, cemetery or altar stone. (A priest *may bless* these for temporary use, but cannot consecrate them.)

3. The blessing of a chalice and paten, Ciborium, Monstrance and large church bell. (In case of necessity, a priest may perform these blessings.)

   It is desirable, but not essential, that a bishop bless church vestments of silk and metal.

Priests may perform all other blessings.

THE BLESSING OF HOLY WATER

THE EXORCISM AND BLESSING OF THE SALT

The priest prepares the salt as follows:

Priest. I exorcise you, O creature of salt, by the living God, by the holy ✝ God, by the omnipotent ✝ God, that you may be purified from all evil influence, in the name of him who is Lord of angels and of men, and who fills the whole earth with his majesty and glory. R. Amen.

P. We pray, O God, in your boundless loving kindness to stretch forth the right hand of your power upon this creature of salt which we ✝ bless and ✝ hallow in your holy name. Grant that this salt may make for health of mind and body to all who partake thereof and that there may be banished from the place where it is used every power of adversity and every illusion or artifice of evil; through Christ our Lord. R. Amen.

THE EXORCISM AND BLESSING OF THE WATER

The priest prepares the water as follows:

P. I exorcise you, O creature of water, by the living ✝ God, by the holy ✝ God, by the omnipotent ✝ God, that you may be purified from all evil influence, in the name of him who is Lord of angels and of men, and who fills the whole earth with his majesty and glory. R. Amen.

P. O God, who for the helping and safeguarding

316

of human beings, does hallow the water set apart for the service of your holy church, send forth your light and your power upon this element of water which we ✝ bless and ✝ hallow in your holy name. Grant that whosoever uses this water in faithfulness of spirit may be strengthened in all goodness and that everything sprinkled with it may be made holy and pure and guarded from all assaults of evil; through Christ our Lord. R. Amen.

The priest casts the salt thrice into the water in the form of a cross as he says the following:

P.   Let salt and water mingle together in the name of the ✝ Father and of the ✝ Son and of the Holy ✝ Ghost. R. Amen.

P.   The Lord be with you.
C.   And with your spirit.

P.   O God, the giver of invincible strength and king of irresistible power, whose splendor shines throughout the whole of creation, we pray to you that you will look upon this your creature of salt and water, to pour down upon it the radiance of your ✝ blessing and to ✝ hallow it with the dew of your loving kindness, that wherever it shall be sprinkled and your holy name shall be invoked in prayer, every noble aspiration may be strengthened, every good resolve made firm and the fellowship of the Holy Spirit vouchsafed to us who place our trust in you; O God, who with the Son lives and reigns in the unity of the same Holy Spirit, God throughout all ages of ages. R. Amen.

THE BLESSING OF HOLY WATER FOR BAPTISM

The priest takes holy water and says over it the following blessing:

Priest. **O Lord Christ, who in the mystery of your boundless love did take upon yourself the limitations of human form and in your gracious compassion did gather little children into your arms; stretch forth, we pray, the right hand of your power over this holy water and fill it with your heavenly † grace and † blessing, that *those* to be baptized with it will receive the fullness of your love and ever remain your faithful children. R. Amen.**

THE BLESSING OF A CHURCH BELL

The bell to be blessed should be thoroughly cleansed beforehand, both within and without and should be suspended so that its lip may be three or four feet above the ground. Before the service is begun, four small crosses should be marked with chalk upon the upper pare of the sides of the bell, denoting the north, east, south and west points respectively. Also seven small crosses should be marked with chalk at equal distances upon the outside of the lip of the bell, to indicate to the bishop where the oil is to be applied. An acolyte or other assistant should precede the bishop as he walks round the bell and should wipe off with a damp cloth each of the chalk crosses just before the bishop touches the spot with the holy oil.

The thymiama (which according to ancient custom is a mixture of ground myrrh, resin and incense) should be prepared beforehand and a brazier with glowing embers or charcoal. If the ingredients of thymiama are not procurable, a plentiful supply of incense shall suffice.

Holy water having been made in the usual way, the bishop begins the service with:

THE INVOCATION

Bishop. **In the name of the Father and of the ✝ Son and of the Holy Spirit. R. Amen.**

The bishop takes the aspergill and sprinkles the bell both outside and inside, saying:

B. **In the name of God, I exorcise all influences of evil that they may be banished and driven forth from this bell which we are about to dedicate to his service. In the power of the Father and of the ✝ Son and of the Holy ✝ Ghost.** **Amen.**

The bishop takes upon his thumb some of the oil for the sick and therewith makes the sign of the cross four times upon the outside of the upper half of the bell, first upon the north side, then (passing by the east) upon the south, then on the west side and finally upon the east, saying:

In the name of the Most High and invoking the aid of the holy Archangel Raphael I anoint this bell for the healing of Christ's faithful followers, that wherever its sound may penetrate it may bear help and strength both to soul and body, through Christ the Lord of heaven and earth. R. Amen.

The bishop intones the following prayer, moving round the bell and making the sign of the cross upon it with the oil for the sick at the seven points indicated

O Christ, who are yourself the great exemplar of all divine virtues, we pray to you that pour down your blessing upon this bell, that its voice may arouse in the hearts of your loving children the discernment clearly to perceive and the will humbly to copy your ✟ strength, your ✟ wisdom, your ✟ loving kindness, your ✟ beauty, your ✟ justice, your ✟ devotion and your ✟ guiding power, that so your servants, being of your grace made perfect in you, may finally attain the glory which you have ordained for them, you who lives and reigns with the Father and the Holy Spirit, one God throughout the ages of ages. R. Amen.

The bishop then takes upon his thumb the sacred chrism and therewith anoints the inside of the lip of the bell at the four cardinal points, saying

To the glory of ✟ God Most High and of his servants Mary, Queen of Heaven, Blessed ✟ Michael the Archangel and the holy ✟ St.'........ I solemnly dedicate this bell. May its sound peal forth ever to the praise of God and the blessing of man;

Making five large crosses in the air over the whole bell, he continues

may it be ✟ hallowed and ✟ consecrated to God's service for ever, in the name of the   Father and of the ✟ Son and of the Holy ✟ Ghost. Amen.

The thymiania is then cast upon the slowing charcoal in the brazier and the latter is placed upon a stool under the bell. The bishop intones

As the sweet savor fills this bell and rises up before you, so pour down, O Holy Spirit, the dew of your all-powerful blessing upon it and upon us your servants, you who lives and reigns with the Father and Son, one God throughout the ages of ages. R. Amen.

A hymn may be sung while the bishop cleanses his hands. When it is ended he pronounces this blessing

B.   Unto God's gracious love and protection I commit you: the Lord bless † you and keep you; the Lord make his face to shine upon you and be gracious unto you; the Lord lift up the light of his countenance upon you and give you his peace and blessing, now and for evermore. Amen.

THE BLESSING OF OBJECTS IN GENERAL

THE EXORCISM

Priest. **In the name of God, I exorcise all influences of evil that they may be banished and driven forth from this .... which we are about to dedicate to his service. In the power of the ✝ Father and of the ✝ Son and of the Holy ✝ Ghost. R. Amen.**

The object may now be sprinkled with holy water and censed

THE BLESSING

P.   Let us pray.

P.   O God, who in the mystery of your boundless love did breath forth your own divine life into the universe and are yourself the continual source of its existence, stretch forth, we pray, the right hand of your power over this . . . . which has in divers ways been purified, and fill this creature with heavenly ✝ grace and ✝ blessing; grant that whosoever shall *use* this ... may be enlightened in heart and mind and serve you in all good works; through Christ our Lord, who lives and reigns with you in the unity of the Holy Spirit, God throughout all ages of ages.

THE BLESSING OF A HOUSE

The priest, having vested with stole, formally enters the house and says

Priest: Peace be to this house and to all who dwell herein.

The priest draws a line with holy water at the entrance and says

P. We pray, O Lord, that you will bless this doorway by your mighty power, that those who enter here may leave behind them all unworthy thoughts and feelings, and that your children, who dwell in this place, may ever serve you in peace and a holy life; through Christ our Lord. R. Amen.

He then goes to all other entrances to the house and draws a line of holy water before each, repeating the same prayer

He next blesses incense and, attended by one bearing the censer and another the aspergill, he/she sprinkles the various rooms with holy water. After which he says

P. O God, who in your providence hast appointed a wondrous ministry of angels, we pray that you will send down your holy angel to ✝ bless and to ✝ hallow this house, that those who dwell herein may live in the power and love of Christ, our Lord and Master, and may continually serve you in all good works; through the same Christ our Lord. R. Amen.

A SIMPLE EXORCISM

Prayer to St. Michael the Archangel

In the Name of the Father, and of the Son, and of the Holy Spirit. Amen.

Most glorious Prince of the Heavenly Armies, Saint Michael the Archangel, defend us in "our battle against principalities and powers, against the rulers of this world of darkness, against the spirits of wickedness in the high places" (Eph 6:12). Come to the assistance of men whom God has created to His likeness and whom He has redeemed at a great price from the tyranny of the devil. Holy Church venerates thee as her guardian and protector; to thee, the Lord has entrusted the souls of the redeemed to be led into heaven. Pray therefore the God of Peace to crush Satan beneath our feet, that he may no longer retain men captive and do injury to the Church. Offer our prayers to the Most High, that without delay they may draw His mercy down upon us; take hold of "the dragon, the old serpent, which is the devil and Satan," bind him and cast him into the bottomless pit ... "that he may no longer seduce the nations" (Rev 20:2-3).

Exorcism

In the Name of Jesus Christ, our God and Lord, strengthened by the intercession of the Immaculate Virgin Mary, Mother of God, of Blessed Michael the Archangel, of the Blessed Apostles Peter and Paul and all the Saints. (and powerful in the holy authority of our ministry)*, we confidently undertake to repulse the attacks and deceits of the devil. * Lay people

324

omit the parenthesis above.

Psalm 67

God arises; His enemies are scattered and those who hate Him flee before Him. As smoke is driven away, so are they driven; as wax melts before the fire, so the wicked perish at the presence of God.

V.   Behold the Cross of the Lord, flee bands of enemies.
R.   The Lion of the tribe of Juda, the offspring of David, hath conquered.

V.   May Thy mercy, Lord, descend upon us.
R.   As great as our hope in Thee.

The crosses below indicate a blessing to be given if a priest recites the Exorcism; if a lay person recites it, they indicate the Sign of the Cross to be made silently by that person.

We drive you from us, whoever you may be, unclean spirits, all satanic powers, all infernal invaders, all wicked legions, assemblies and sects. In the Name and by the power of Our Lord Jesus Christ, † may you be snatched away and driven from the Church of God and from the souls made to the image and likeness of God and redeemed by the Precious Blood of the Divine Lamb. †

Most cunning serpent, you shall no more dare to deceive the human race, persecute the Church, torment God's elect and sift them as wheat. † The Most High God commands you, † He with whom, in your great insolence, you still claim to be equal. "God

325

who wants all men to be saved and to come to the knowledge of the truth" (1 Tim 2:4). God the Father commands you. † God the Son commands you. † God the Holy Spirit commands you. † Christ, God's Word made flesh, commands you; † He who to save our race outdone through your envy, "humbled Himself, becoming obedient even unto death" (Phil 2:8); He who has built His Church on the firm rock and declared that the gates of hell shall not prevail against Her, because He will dwell with Her "all days even to the end of the world" (Mat 28:20). The sacred Sign of the Cross commands you, † as does also the power of the mysteries of the Christian Faith. † The glorious Mother of God, the Virgin Mary, commands you; † she who by her humility and from the first moment of her Immaculate Conception crushed your proud head. The faith of the holy Apostles Peter and Paul, and of the other Apostles commands you. † The blood of the Martyrs and the pious intercession of all the Saints command you. †

Thus, cursed dragon, and you, diabolical legions, we adjure you by the living God, † by the true God, † by the holy God, † by the God "who so loved the world that He gave up His only Son, that every soul believing in Him might not perish but have life everlasting" (John 3: 16); stop deceiving human creatures and pouring out to them the poison of eternal damnation; stop harming the Church and hindering her liberty. Begone, Satan, inventor and master of all deceit, enemy of man's salvation. Give place to Christ in Whom you have found none of your works; give place to the One, Holy, Catholic and Apostolic Church acquired by Christ at the price of His Blood. Stoop beneath the all-powerful Hand of God; tremble and flee when we invoke the Holy and terrible Name of Jesus, this Name which causes hell to tremble, this Name to which the Virtues, Powers and Dominations of heaven are humbly submissive, this Name which the Cherubim and Seraphim praise unceasingly repeating: Holy, Holy, Holy is the Lord, the God of Hosts.

V. O Lord, hear my prayer.
R. And let my cry come unto Thee.

V. May the Lord be with thee.
R. And with thy spirit.

Let us pray.

God of heaven, God of earth, God of Angels, God of Archangels, God of Patriarchs, God of Prophets, God of Apostles, God of Martyrs, God of Confessors, God of Virgins, God who has power to give life after death and rest after work: because there is no other God than Thee and there can be no other, for Thou art the Creator of all things, visible and invisible, of Whose reign there shall be no end, we humbly prostrate ourselves before Thy glorious Majesty and we beseech Thee to deliver us by Thy power from all the tyranny of the infernal spirits, from their snares, their lies and their furious wickedness. Deign, O Lord, to grant us Thy powerful protection and to keep us safe and sound. We beseech Thee through Jesus Christ Our Lord. Amen.

V. From the snares of the devil,
R. Deliver us, O Lord.

V.   That Thy Church may serve Thee in peace and liberty:

R.   We beseech Thee to hear us.

V.   That Thou may crush down all enemies of Thy Church:

R.   We beseech Thee to hear us.

Holy water is sprinkled in the place where we may be

A SUGGESTED SERVICE FOR CLEANSING A HAUNTED HOUSE

We gratefully acknowledge Rev. Mtr. Millicent Mountjoy for sharing this rite of cleansing with us. It has been edited and adapted.

The following is based upon a shortened form of a requiem with the intention, which is expressed in the opening prayer, for the release and response of any souls which are still earthbound or tied to the place concerned. This can be further adapted and modified according to the needs and preferences of the celebrant. A full Eucharistic liturgy is not required, though sometimes desirable.

The Prayer of Intention (this is important)

O divine and loving Father, God, we pray Thee to send Thy ministering angels into this household, to take away any fallen angels who might be disturbing your children on Earth. We ask it through Jesus Christ, our Lord. Amen.

The Mass or Requiem Holy Communion

I.   Collect for Purity
II. Three-fold Kyries
III. Collect (St Michael and A.A. adapted)

Almighty and everlasting God, who has ordained and constituted the service of Angels and human beings in a wonderful order, mercifully grant that as your holy angels always do your service in heaven, so by your appointment they will succor and defend us, your children on earth, and especially those Guardian Angels whom you have appointed to look after each person here present today, who work in the Name, in the Power and in the Service of Jesus Christ, your Son, our Lord. Amen.

IV.   Epistle and Gospel if desired. These should be short, e.g.:

> Epistle: Phil. 3: 20-1;
> or I Cor 15: 12-14, 20.
> Gospel: Jn 14: 1-3 or 1-6; Lk 23:
> 32-4, 39-43: Mt 16:19

V.   Prayer. We now have prayer, which is usually mainly extempore. Since we believe we are dealing not with 'devils' or 'demons' but with unhappy discarnate human beings, who have got lost or stuck amid the unhappy the surroundings of their former earthly life, whether because of ignorance, lack of spiritual development, an earthly minded and materialistic outlook, a complete disbelief in the possibility of an afterlife, or possibly owing to the memory of sorrow or tragedy, or even of some unfulfilled task, which they are not able to efface, we do not as a rule 'exorcise them (with bell, book and candle!) by commanding them to depart into 'outer darkness,' as medieval exorcism did, but rather we pray *for* them, and help them to progress forward and upward into the Light.

So you address the unseen spirit as though you could see him (her or them), "Whoever you may be, you have died, and have shed the physical body and are now clothed in a spiritual body; having died, you should not now be remaining around the scenes of your former life, causing distress and disturbance to those present; we shall pray for you, and with the help of our prayers and of the ministering angels or messengers who now are with us, you will be taken away from this place (or person) and helped to find your proper resting place, and to a better understanding of your condition. If you are perplexed and bewildered and in the darkness, call out for a loved one who has already passed over (e.g. a mother or father or husband/wife, especially if you have so e of who the "haunter" may be), and pray, pray to Jesus Christ that He will send one of these to be with you, and guide you into the realms of Light.'

Concluding perhaps with this lovely old prayer

O unquiet spirit, who at your departure from the contagions of the flesh chose to remain earthbound and to haunt this place, go your way rejoicing that the prayers of the faithful shall follow you, that thou might enjoy everlasting rest, and might find your rightful place at the throne of Grace, through Jesus Christ, our Lord, Amen.

Rest eternal grant unto them O Lord, and let light perpetual shine upon them as you promised in times of old to Abraham and to his seed. Amen.'

VI. Short confession and absolution or if those present are not familiar with these, a combined confession and absolution such as the Collect for Ash Wednesday, or this adapted collect: Grant, we beseech you, merciful Lord, to give us, your children, pardon and peace, and that being cleansed from our sins, we might serve you with quiet minds, through Jesus Christ, our Lord, Amen.

VII. Sursum Corda, with 'Benedictus', followed by the prayer of consecration and 'Agnus Dei', perhaps finishing at 'do this in remembrance of me' in which case the manual acts will be done during the prayer.

The real problem in this sort of service is to get the folk there to take part, since they are almost certainly unfamiliar with church. It might be a good thing to get them to say 'Grant, we beseech Thee' etc. (VI) clause by clause after you.

VIII. Administration to whoever present is able or willing to receive. (It might better to have the Lord's Prayer *after* the administration, especially in the cases where the householders are non-communicants - it gives them a feeling of being in the picture.)

IX.   Post Communion Prayers

And now let us all join together in saying the family prayer, 'Our Father   . . .' (with Gloria).

We thank Thee O loving Father that you do send your holy angels to take away from this place those unquiet spirits, who having lost their way, have been for so long imprisoned in the darkness of their own earthly imaginings, those lost sheep of your flock, whom your Son, the Good Shepherd, came into this world to help, and who shed His precious blood to save. Amen.

Visit O Lord we beseech you, this place, and drive from it all the snares of the enemy. Let your holy angels dwell herein to preserve us in peace, and may the blessing of God, Father, Son and Holy Spirit be with us now and always. Amen.

A bowl of holy water, incense & censor, and chrism oil should be available. Divesting yourself of surplice or vestments, (for convenience sake) you should get someone to hold the bowl for you, together with a small towel, and then go round the house, censing each room, hallway, and space, and sprinking each with holy water. Make the sign of the cross on every door, window (not necessarily every pane of glass), wall, and mirror (particularly those areas which seem most affected), saying as you do so, "In nomine Patris et Filii, et Spiritus Sancti, Amen " - or in English. This should protect the house against unwanted visitors. It is also advisable to make the same sign over the forehead, nape, and solar plexus of each one of those present. Also do it to yourself, and this should also be done by the celebrant before he begins the service.

BLESSING OF AN ORATORY

To be used where the service of Consecration is not appropriate.

The blessing precedes the Holy Eucharist.

The altar-stone or antiminsion must previously have been blessed by a bishop.

All stand.

THE INVOCATION

Priest. **In the name of the Father and of the ✝ Son and of the Holy Spirit. R. Amen.**

P.   O God, omnipotent and omnipresent, who does deign especially to hallow and to dwell within those places set apart for your worship, we pray you will purify this temple by the influence of your Holy Spirit, that no evil thought may enter herein; through Christ our Lord, who lives and reigns with you in the unity of the same Holy Spirit, one God throughout all ages of ages. R. Amen.

The priest takes the aspergill and, standing before the altar, sprinkles it thrice with holy water; he goes once round the altar, sprinkling it meanwhile; then he faces the people and asperses them.

P.   Guide us, almighty Father, in all our doings and from your heavenly throne send down your holy angel to be with your people, who have met together to serve and to worship you; through Christ our Lord. R. Amen.

The people are seated.

The priest moves clockwise round the oratory sprinkling the walls with holy water. He then censes the whole area. Meanwhile a hymn may be sung.

THE BLESSING

P. Let us pray.

The people kneel or are seated.

P. God the Father, God ✝ the Son, God the Holy Spirit, accept, hallow and bless this place to the end to which we have dedicated it, even to be a sanctuary of the Most High and a church of the living God. May the Lord, with his favor, graciously regard our work and so send down his spiritual benediction and grace, that it may be to him the house of God and to his people, worshiping herein, the gate of heaven.

Therefore we now ✝ dedicate this place to the glory of God, to the perfecting of humanity, and in honor of his glorious martyr, or servant, angel, archangel, or holy deed ... In the name of the Father and of the ✝ Son and of the Holy Spirit. R. Amen.

The altar is dressed, the chalice and paten arranged upon it as usual and the candles lighted

The Holy Eucharist is then continued, beginning with the Canticle

When it is desirable to use a church before the bishop can conveniently attend to consecrate it, the priest should use the above service, omitting the dedication at the end

THE CONSECRATION OF A CHURCH

Based on the form used in the
Liberal Catholic Church

The clergy and acolytes enter the chancel singing a
hymn and group themselves around the altar, which
is uncovered and unadorned.

THE INVOCATION

Bishop. **In the name of the Father and of the ✝ Son**
and of the Holy Spirit. R. Amen.

A short address appropriate to the occasion may be
given by the bishop or by one of the clergy appointed
for the purpose; or the homily which follows may be
read.

It is the immemorial custom of holy church to
consecrate the building in which her services are
permanently held; and it is for this purpose that we
gather together today. Our first step in this ceremony
is to purify the mental and spiritual atmosphere of the
building by the use of holy water and incense, so that
worldly thought and influence may be banished from
it. Our thoughts during the first procession are
devoted to that end. Having performed the ritual of
purification, we call upon almighty God to consecrate
and hallow the various parts of the building, for the
purpose of dedicating each for which they are
destined. To that end we anoint with special centers
of influence with holy oil. In this second procession,
our minds should be strongly fixed upon the idea that
this church shall be not only a place free from selfish

or worldly thought but also an active center of good, not merely free from evil, but actively good. When this great act of consecration has been duly performed, we at once begin our first service - the highest and holiest service that we know - the Holy Eucharist, which Christ himself ordained. In the course of this celebration, the third procession will take place and the sacred Host will be borne round the church as a crowning benediction. During that time our hearts should be filled with deepest adoration to our Lord, and with heartfelt thanks for his wondrous love. Remember, then, these three keynotes of the different portions of the service -- purification, then consecration and, lastly, adoration and thankfulness.

THE PURIFICATION

B.   Let us pray.

All   kneel.

B.   O God, omnipotent and omnipresent, who does deign especially to hallow and to dwell within those places set apart for you worship, we pray that you will so purify this temple by the influence of your Holy Spirit that no evil thought may enter; through Christ our Lord, who lives and reigns with you in the unity of the same Holy Spirit, one God throughout all ages of ages. R. Amen.

All rise and the people are seated

The Purification of the Altar

The bishop takes the aspergill and, standing before the altar, sprinkles it three times with holy water; he goes once round the altar, sprinkling it meanwhile; then he faces the people and asperses them.

B. Let us pray.

The people kneel

B. **Guide us, Almighty Father, in all our doings and from your heavenly throne send down your holy angel to be with your people, who have met together to serve and to worship you; through Christ our Lord; R. Amen.**

The people are seated

The Procession of Purification

The procession forms, leaves the chancel by the center and encircles the church, the bishop sprinkling the walls. Meanwhile a hymn is sung by all

The procession returns to the chancel

THE CONSECRATION

B. **Let us pray.**

All   kneel.

B. **God ✝ the Father, God ✝ the Son, God ✝ the Holy Spirit, accept, hallow and bless this place for the purpose we have separated it, even to be a sanctuary of the Most High and a church of the living God. We ask, O Lord, that with your favor you graciously regard our work and so send down your spiritual benediction and grace, that it may**

be the house of God and to your people worshiping herein the gate of heaven itself. R. Amen.

The Consecration of the Altar

The people are seated. The bishop goes to the altar and with his thumb makes the sign of the cross with chrism upon the five crosses carved upon the altar-stone (or upon the altar itself if it be made of stone). He then anoints the cross of the tabernacle (or the altar cross) with chrism, and says

B. O God, whose wisdom mightily and sweetly orders all things, look down, we pray, upon the handiwork of your servants and fill this house with heavenly wisdom, that those who serve you here may be so filled with the spirit of wisdom and love that they will constantly labor to raise your people from the darkness of ignorance to the light of your holy truth.

Wherefore do we ✝ consecrate and ✝ hallow this altar to the glory of God, to the perfecting of humanity and in honor of ✝ his holy work ... or glorious saint or martyr, the holy St. ... In the name of the ✝ Father and of the ✝ Son and of the Holy ✝ Spirit. Amen.

The altar is dressed, the chalice and paten arranged upon it as usual and the candles lighted

The altar is censed by the bishop, assisted by his ministers

The Procession of Consecration

The people stand

The procession is formed and leaves the chancel by the center. The following verses are sung as the procession moves to the cross in the south-east corner

> Blessed city, heavenly Salem,
> Vision dear of peace and love,
> Who of living stones art builded
> In the height of heaven above
> And, with angel hosts encircled,
> As a bride doth earthward move;
>
> From celestial realms descending,
> Bridal glory round thee shed,
> Meet for him whose love espoused thee,
> To thy Lord shalt thou be led;
> All thy streets and all thy bulwarks
> Of pure gold are fashioned.

The bishop anoints this cross with chrism and says

B.   O thou whose beauty shines through the whole universe, grant that as in this your shrine we seek to mirror the beauties of your celestial glory, so may we continually irradiate our lives with the light of your indwelling presence.

Wherefore do we ✝ consecrate and ✝ hallow this temple to the glory of God, to the perfecting of humanity and in honor of his glorious work ... (or martyr, the holy St. . . . In the name of the ✝ Father and of the ✝ Son and of the Holy ✝ Spirit. R. Amen.

*The third verse of the hymn is sung as the procession
moves to the cross in the south-west corner*

> Many a blow and biting sculpture
> Polished well those stones elect,
> In their places now compacted
> By the heavenly architect,
> Who therewith bath willed for ever
> That his palace should be decked.

The bishop anoints this cross with chrism and says

**B.   O thou great Master-Builder, who has laid
the foundations of the universe in order and
symmetry, grant that your people may so mould
and polish the rude material of their natures that
they may be found just and accurate in your sight.**

**Wherefore do we to consecrate and ✝ hallow this
temple to the glory of God, to the perfecting of
humanity and in honor of his glorious work ...
(saint, or martyr, the holy St. ...)**

**In the name of the ✝ Father and of the ✝ Son and
of the Holy ✝ Spirit. Amen.**

*The fourth verse of the hymn is sung as the procession
moves to the cross in the West*

> Christ is made the sure foundation,
> Christ the head and corner-stone,
> Chosen of the Lord and precious,
> Binding all the church in one,
> Holy Zion's help for ever
> And her confidence alone.

The bishop anoints this cross with chrism and says

B.   O God, the King of angels, ruler of all the hosts of heaven, we praise thee for the help which these thy radiant servants so joyously do render unto us; may we find strength to unfold within ourselves such courage, such wisdom and such purity that we may be found worthy to be fellow workers with them in thy most glorious service.

Wherefore do we ☦ consecrate and ☦ hallow this temple to the glory of God, to the perfecting of humanity and in honor of his glorious work … (saint, or martyr, the holy St. …)

In the name of the Father and of the ☦ Son and of the Holy ☦ Spirit. Amen.

The fifth verse of the hymn is sung as the procession moves to the cross in the north-west corner

> All that dedicated city,
> Dearly loved of God on high,
> In exultant jubilation
> Pours perpetual melody,
> God the One in Three adoring,
> In glad hymns eternally.

The bishop anoints this cross with chrism and says

B.   O Christ, the Lord of love, we lay our hearts upon your shrine; in this your house of praise may the fervent adoration of your servants rise ever before you like incense, until the light of their love becomes one with your own infinite light.

Wherefore do we ✝ consecrate and ✝ hallow this temple to the glory of God, to the perfecting of humanity and in honor of his glorious work (saint, or martyr, the holy St. . . .) In the name of the ✝ Father and of the ✝ Son and of the Holy ✝ Spirit. Amen.

The sixth verse of the hymn is sung as the procession moves to the cross in the north-east corner

To this temple, where we call you, Come, O Lord of hosts, today; With your loving kindness Hear your servants as they pray: And your full benediction Shed within its walls always.

The bishop anoints this cross with chrism and says

B.   O God, who meets every everyone upon that path who draws nigh to you, grant us the grace to see you in the hearts of all people that we may never fail in courtesy and understanding; and as you, O Lord, fulfills yourself in many ways so may we rightly discern your purpose amid the tumult of our earthly life.

Wherefore do ✝ consecrate and ✝ hallow this temple to the glory of God, to the perfecting of humanity and in honor of his glorious work ... (saint, or martyr, the holy St. ...) In the name of the ✝ Father and of the ✝ Son and of the Holy ✝ Spirit. Amen.

The seventh verse of the hymn is sung as the procession moves to the cross in the center

Here vouchsafe to all thy servants
What they ask of thee to gain,
What they gain from thee for ever
With the blessed to retain
And hereafter in thy glory
Evermore with thee to reign.

The bishop anoints this cross with chrism and says

B.   O God, the Rock of Ages, the strength of all who put their trust in you, we pray you will graciously regard our work and fill this house with your almighty power, that those who worship here may be girded with strength for your holy service.

Wherefore do we ✝ consecrate and✝ hallow this temple to the glory of God, to the perfecting of humanity and in honor of his glorious work ... (saint, or martyr, the holy St. ...). In the name of the ✝ Father and of the ✝ Son and of the ✝ Holy Spirit. Amen.

The eighth verse of the hymn is sung as the procession enters the chancel

Laud and honor to the Father,
Laud and honor to the Son,
Laud and honor to the Spirit,
Ever three and ever one,
Consubstantial, co-eternal,
While unending ages run.

The celebration resumes as usual

THE COLLECT

O CHRIST our Master, we pray that you will accept and ever to hallow this temple which we have now dedicated to your holy name; may the incense of praise and thanksgiving rise ever within its walls and may the lives of those who worship here be truly in accordance with your most holy will, who lives and reigns with the Father in the unity of the Holy Spirit, God throughout all ages of ages. R. Amen.

The collect of the day and such other collects as are usual follow here

APPROPRIATE READINGS

Choices to select from if following the Roman Catholic pattern for the ceremony

First Reading:

1.   Genesis 28:11-18
2.   First Kings 8:22-23, 27-30
3.   Second Chronicles 5:6-10, 13-6:2
4.   First Maccabees 4:52-59 (for the consecration of an altar)
5.   Isaiah 56:1, 6-7
6.   Ezekiel 43:1-2, 4-7

Responsorial Psalm:

1.   First Chronicles 29:10, 11, 11-12, 12
2.   Psalms 84:3, 4, 5-6, 8, 11
3.   Psalms 95:1-2, 3-5, 6-7
4.   Psalms 127:1-2, 3-4, 4-5, 8-9

Second Reading:

1. First Corinthians 3:9-13, 16-17
2. Ephesians 2:19-22
3. Hebrews 12:18-19, 22-24
4. First Peter 2:4-9

Gospel:

1. Matthew 5:23-24
2. Luke 19:1-10
3. John 2:13-22
4. John 4:19-24

THE EPISTLE

If following the Liberal Catholic Church pattern

The portion of scripture appointed for the epistle is taken from the twenty-first chapter of the Revelation of St. John the Divine, beginning at the second verse.

AND I John saw the holy city, new Jerusalem, coming down from God out of heaven, prepared as a bride adorned for her husband. And I heard a great voice out of heaven saying: Behold, the tabernacle of God is with men and he will dwell with them and they shall be his people and God himself shall be with them and be their God. And God shall wipe away all tears from their eyes; and there shall be no more death, neither sorrow, nor crying, neither shall there be any more pain: for the former things are passed away. And he that sat upon the throne said: Behold, I make all things new.

This is the word of the Lord
R. Thanks be to God

THE GOSPEL

If following the Liberal Catholic Church pattern

The holy gospel is taken from the fourteenth chapter of the Gospel according to St. John, beginning at the sixth verse.

JESUS said: I am the way, the truth and the life; no one cometh unto the Father but by me. He that bath seen me bath seen the Father; for I am in the Father and the Father in me. I and my Father are one; as the Father bath loved me so have I loved. you; and this is my commandment, that ye love one another, as I have loved you. When the Comforter is come, whom I will send unto you from the Father, even the Spirit of truth, who proceedeth from the Father, he shall testify of me. And ye also shall bear witness, because ye have been with me from the beginning. By this shall all men know that ye are my disciples, if ye have love one to another.

At the end of the hymn Adeste Fideles, *following the consecration, the Host is placed within the monstrance by the deacon*

THE PROCESSION OF THE BLESSED SACRAMENT

The people kneel.

The procession forms (the bishop or a priest carrying the monstrance, over which a canopy should be held) and moves through the body of the church as the litany is sung alternately. If it be convenient a cantor appointed by the bishop may sing the first, third, fifth and other verses bearing odd numbers, the even verses being sung by the choir and the people. In small churches the litany may be shortened

THE LITANY

God the Father, seen of
none,
God the co-eternal
Son,
God the Spirit-Three in
One,
Hear us, Holy Trinity.

*

Son of God and Prince
of light,
Throned in glory,
robed in might,
Morning star, serene
and bright,
Christ our Lord, we
hail thee.

*

Captain of the hosts of
light,
Overcoming sin's dark
blight,
Ever-glowing splendor
bright,
Son of God, we hail
thee.

*

Thou, before whose
purging ray
Mists of evil fade
away;
Orb of everlasting day,
Son of God, we hail
thee.

Thou, whose wisdom
all things planned,
Held by whose
almighty hand
All things in their
order stand,
We, thy church, adore
thee.

*

Thou, whose life and
strength pervade,
Whatsoever thou hast
made,
All-preserver, strong to
aid,
We, thy church, adore
thee.

*

Priest and victim,
whom of old
Type and prophecy
foretold,
Thee incarnate we
behold:
Son of God, we hail
thee.

*

Purged in vision
through thy grace,
We by faith may see
thy face.
Feel thee near in every
place,
Christ our Lord, we
hail thee.

Ruth divine that givest
heed
Unto every cry of
need,
Healing balm to hearts
that bleed,
Help us, holy Master.
*

Healer of the souls
distressed,
Happiness of all the
blest,
Peace of those who
long for rest;
We, thy church, adore
thee.
*

Sweet physician,
skilled to heal
Every pang the soul
can feel,
Thou that hearest each
appeal;
Help us, holy Master.
*

lest by thought or
action base,
Ignorant, we slight thy
grace,
I.lest we hide from us
thy face,
Help us, holy Master.

That our hearts may
win release,
That our hands from ill
may cease,
That our souls may
know thy peace,
Help us, holy Master.
*

That, from selfish lusts
made free,
Each, at length, clear-
eyed may see-
See and tread the path
to thee,
Help us, holy Master.
*

Till, our pilgrimage
complete,
Rest shall come and
comfort sweet,
Friend of pilgrims, at
thy feet,
Son of God, we hail
thee.
*

God the Father, seen of
none,
God the co-eternal
Son,
God the Spirit-Three in
One,
We are thine, O
Trinity.

After the procession returns to the chancel, the Holy Eucharist is continued to the end

When it is desirable to use a church before the bishop can conveniently attend to consecrate it, the priest should use the service for the Blessing of an Oratory, omitting the dedication

FESTIVAL

The anniversary of the consecration of a church should always be observed as its dedication festival. On that occasion the procession enters the chancel by the short way, and the asperges is recited as usual. Then the procession of consecration is repeated and the hymn Blessed city sung as prescribed in the service for the consecration of a church, the priest reciting at each cross the appropriate prayer, but in each case omitting the sentence, "Wherefore do we consecrate," and substituting for it the ending, "through Christ our Lord." The procession of the Blessed Sacrament takes place as in the service for the consecration of a church and the collect, epistle and gospel are those of that service.

THE USE OF HOLY OILS

Holy Oils are a sacramental modality, the use of which extends across the entire span of the sacred tradition from our own time, through the periods of Bible History, the earliest day when the Inner Mysteries became established on the Earth. We do not contend for them, since to the experienced Steward of the Mysteries, their efficacy is beyond question. It is an obvious fact that God has and is employing them as a means by which to release His Grace.

On Maundy Thursday *(no other day being permitted)* the Holy Oils are blessed in special Office, using only the finest quality of olive oil. The Bishop gathers with the Clergy at the appointed time and place, and following the Oblation of the Body and Blood of our Lord proceeds to bless the oils according to an ancient Rite.

Oil for the Sick

This Holy Oil is also called Oleum Infirmum, as the name implies. It is used for the anointing of those sick in body, mind, or spirit, as a channel to be used by God to effect a restoration of health.

For many centuries wide sections of the Church restricted the Sacrament of Unction in its use as a Final Unction. But at this time we see a revival of it as a healing instrument. Across the entire spectrum of Christianity, from the Church of Rome to Protestant Churches, and even metaphysical groups, it is used with beneficent results.

Oil of Catechumens

This Holy Oil is used for the anointing of objects that are being blessed by a Priest. The use of this oil is also a part of the Holy Rite of Baptism, as well as in the Ordination of Priests. In the case of persons that are anointed it serves the purpose of cleansing and safeguarding of those receiving the anointing. The purpose of anointing objects is to cleanse them as an effective channel for protection of the one using the object and to provide a channel for that person by which God's greater support and protection is provided.

Oil of Chrism

Also known as Myron, is used at Baptisms. In anointing the candidates with it, the Priest intends for the candidates to be more closely related to the Lord Christ and to help them to move more effectively in and out of their Christian obligation, in entering and completing the study and mastery of the Holy Mysteries.

In Confirmation, the Bishop, or authorized priest, invokes the Holy Spirit and employs the Chrism as a vehicle by which salvation and liberation is effectuated and the Holy Spirit given greater access to manifest in the life of the Confirmands.

At their ordination, Priests are anointed with Chrism.

At their Consecration, Bishops are anointed with copious amounts of Chrism, signifying that for the discharge of this Office an excess of the Spirit power is needed. It might also mean that none but the Bishop himself is to blame if in the performance of his duties he falls to perform acceptably.

In the blessing of Chrism, the Bishop not only uses the finest Olive Oil, but adds Balsam, which has also been specially blessed.

CONSECRATION OF HOLY OILS ON MAUNDY THURSDAY

The bishop celebrates in full pontifical robes. The oils and balsam for consecration are brought in at the offertory in solemn procession, by the deacon and subdeacon if possible

It is permitted to vary the order of the consecration of the holy oils

After the hymn Adeste Fideles *has been sung during the procession of the Blessed Sacrament, the bishop is seated at a table placed before the altar* in piano. *The bishop exorcises the oil and balsam as follows*

THE EXORCISM

Bishop. **In the name of God, I exorcise all influences of evil, that they may be cast out from this oil and balsam which we are about to dedicate to his service, in the power of the ✝ Father and of the ✝ Son and of the Holy ✝ Spirit. R. Amen.**

The vessels are now removed to the credence table, except that containing the oil for the sick

THE CONSECRATION OF THE OIL FOR THE SICK

The bishop rises and blesses this oil as follows

B. **In the name of our Lord Christ and invoking the assistance of the holy Archangel Raphael, I ✝ consecrate and ✝ hallow this oil for the healing of** the sick; may the blessing of the Great Physician rest thereupon, that it may give refreshment and peace alike to soul and body. Amen.

The newly consecrated oil is carried in procession to the sacristy

CONSECRATION OF THE OIL OF CATECHUMENS

The bishop blesses this oil as follows

B. **In the name of our Lord Christ, I ✝ consecrate and hallow this oil that it may serve for the cleansing and safeguarding of those who receive the holy rite of baptism or consecration to the order of the priesthood. R. Amen.**

The newly consecrated oil is carried in procession to the sacristy

THE CONSECRATION OF THE HOLY CHRISM

The bishop blesses the balsam and oil respectively as follows

The Consecration of the Balsam

B. **In the name of our Lord Christ, I ✝ consecrate and hallow this balsam that everything touched therewith may burn with his purity, before whose splendor the angels veil their faces. R. Amen.**

The Consecration of the Oil

B. **In the name of our Lord Christ, I ✝ consecrate and hallow this oil, now set apart for the making of holy chrism, that it may bestow upon those who receive it the fullness of spiritual strength. R. Amen.**

The balsam and oil are now mixed and the bishop, extending both hands over the oil, continues

B. **Let us pray.**

B. **O Lord Christ, the fountain of all goodness, who does pour down your gifts abundantly upon human beings and, for their strengthening, does hallow and set apart these earthly things as a channel of your marvelous power, send forth, we pray, your ✝ blessing upon this holy chrism, that whatever persons or things are anointed with it may receive the fullness of spiritual consecration. Let your heavenly blessing descend upon those who are signed by this chrism with the sign of your holy service that, guarding well their spiritual heritage, they may shed around them the fragrance of a godly life, O you, great shepherd and ruler of the souls of men, to whom be honor and glory for evermore. R. Amen.**

The bishop breathes three times in the form of a cross over the chrism. Each priest present also breathes over it in the form of a cross and it is then carried in procession to the sacristy. The bishop proceeds with the mass

AN ANTHOLOGY OF COMMON PRAYERS

Act of Faith

O my God, I firmly believe that you are one God in three divine Persons, Father, Son, and Holy Spirit; I believe that your divine Son became man and died for our sins, and that he will come to judge the living and the dead. I believe these and all the truths which the Holy Catholic Church teaches, because you revealed them, who can neither deceive nor be deceived.

Act of Hope

O my God, relying on your infinite goodness and promises, I hope to obtain pardon of my sins, the help of your grace, and life everlasting, through the merits of Jesus Christ, my Lord and Redeemer.

Act of Love

O my God, I love you above all things, with my whole heart and soul, because you are all good and worthy of all my love. I love my neighbor as myself for the love of you. I forgive all who have injured me and I ask pardon of all whom I have injured.

Glory be…

Glory be to the Father, and to the Son, and to the Holy Spirit … As it was in the beginning, is now, and will be for ever. AMEN.

Our Father

Our Father, who art in heaven, hallowed be thy name; thy kingdom come thy will be done, on earth as it is in heaven.

Give us this day our daily bread, and forgive us our trespasses as we forgive those who trespass against us, and lead us not into temptation, but deliver us from evil.

(For the kingdom, the power, and the glory are yours, now and for ever.)
AMEN.

Hail Mary

Hail Mary, full of grace. The Lord is with Thee. Blessed art thou among women, and blessed is the fruit of thy womb, Jesus. Holy Mary, Mother of God, pray for us sinners, now and at the hour of our death. AMEN.

O My Jesus

O my Jesus, forgive us our sins, save us from the fires of hell, lead all souls to Heaven, especially those who have the most need of your mercy. AMEN.

Morning Prayer

In the name of our Lord Jesus Christ I will begin this day. I thank you, Lord, for having preserved me during the night. I will do my   best to make all I do today pleasing to You and in accordance with Your will. My dear mother Mary, watch over me this

360

day. My Guardian Angel, take care of me. St. Joseph and all you saints of God, pray for me... (followed by Daily Offering)

Daily Offering

O Jesus, through the immaculate heart of Mary, I offer you my prayers, works, joys and sufferings of this day in union with the holy sacrifice of the Mass throughout the world. I offer them for all the intentions of your sacred heart: the salvation of souls, reparation for sin, the reunion of all Christians. I offer them for the intentions of our bishops and of all the apostles of prayer.

Evening Prayer

O my God, at the end of this day I thank You most heartily for all the graces I have received from You. I am sorry that I have not made a better use of them. I am sorry for all the sins I have committed against You. Forgive me, O my God, and graciously protect me this night. Blessed Virgin Mary, my dear heavenly mother, take me under your protection. St. Joseph, my dear   Guardian Angel, and all you saints of God, pray for me. Sweet Jesus, have pity on all poor sinners, and save them from hell. Have mercy on the suffering   souls in purgatory... (followed by an Act of Contrition)

Act of Contrition

O my God, I am heartily sorry for having offended You and I detest all my sins, because I dread the loss of heaven and the pains of hell, but most of all because they offend you, my God, who are all good

361

and deserving of all my love. I firmly resolve, with
the help of your grace, to confess my sins, to do
penance and to amend my life.

Prayer Before Meals

Bless us Oh Lord, and these thy gifts, which we are
about to receive, from thy bounty, through Christ,
Our Lord. AMEN.

Anima Christi

Soul of Christ, make me holy. Body of Christ, save
me. Blood of Christ, fill me with love. Water from
Christ's side, wash me. Passion of Christ, strengthen
me. Good Jesus, hear me. Within your wounds, hide
me. Never let me be parted from you. From the evil
enemy, protect me. At the hour of my death, call me.
And tell me to come to you. That with your saints I
may praise you. Through all eternity. AMEN.

Guardian Angel Prayer (Old)

O Holy Angel, attendant of my wretched soul and of
mine afflicted life, forsake me not, a sinner, neither
depart from me for mine inconstancy. Give no place
to the evil demon to subdue me with the oppression of
this mortal body; but take me by my wretched and
outstretched hand, and lead me in the way of
salvation. Yea, O holy Angel of God, the guardian
and protector of my hapless soul and body, forgive
me all things whatsoever wherewith I have troubled
thee, all the days of my life, and if I have sinned in
anything this day. Shelter me in this present night,
and keep me from every affront of the enemy, lest I
anger God by any sin; and intercede with the Lord in

my behalf, that He might strengthen me in the fear of Him, and make me a worthy servant of His goodness. AMEN.

Prayer to Our Lady

Remember, O most loving Virgin Mary, that never was it known that anyone who fled to your protection, implored your help, or sought your intercession was left unaided. Inspired with this confidence, we turn to you, O Virgins of virgins, our Mother. To you we come, before you we stand, sinful and sorrowful. O Mother of the Word Incarnate, do not despise our petitions, but in your mercy hear us and answer us. AMEN.

Prayer to the Holy Spirit

Breathe into me Holy Spirit, That all my thoughts may be holy. Move in me, Holy Spirit, that my work, too, may be holy. Attract my heart, Holy Spirit, that I may love only what is holy. Strengthen me, Holy Spirit, that I may defend all that is holy. Protect me, Holy Spirit, that I always may be holy. AMEN.

Another Prayer to the Holy Spirit

Spirit of wisdom and understanding, enlighten our minds to perceive the mysteries of the universe in relation to eternity. Spirit of right judgment and courage, guide us and make us firm in our baptismal decision to follow Jesus' way of love. Spirit of knowledge and reverence, help us to see the lasting value of justice and mercy in our everyday dealings with one another. May we respect life as we work to solve problems of family and nation, economy and ecology. Spirit of God, spark our faith, hope and love into new action each day. Fill our lives with wonder and awe in your presence which penetrates all creation. AMEN.

Saint Patrick's Breastplate

I bind unto myself today the strong Name of the Trinity, by invocation of the same, the Three in One and One in three.

I bind this day to me for ever, by power of faith, Christ's incarnation; His baptism in the Jordan River; His death on cross for my salvation; His bursting from the spiced tomb; His riding up the heavenly way; His coming on the day of doom; I bind unto myself today.

I bind unto myself the power of the great love of the Cherubim; the sweet "Well done" in judgment hour; the service of the Seraphim, Confessors' faith, Apostles' word, the Patriarchs' prayers, the Prophets' scrolls; all good deeds done unto the Lord, and purity of simple souls.

I bind unto myself today the virtues of the starlit heaven, the glorious sun's life-giving ray, the whiteness of the moon at even, the flashing of the lightning free, the whirling wind's tempestuous shocks, the stable earth, the deep salt sea, around the old eternal rocks.

I bind unto myself today the power of God to hold and lead, his eye to watch, his might to stay, his ear to hearken to my need. The wisdom of my God to teach, his hand to guide, his shield to ward; the Word of

God to give me speech, his heavenly host to be my guard.

Against the demon snares of sin, the vice that gives temptation force, the natural lusts that war with me, the hostile ones that mar my course; or few or many, far or nigh, in every place, and in all hours, against their fierce hostility, I bind to me these holy powers.

Against all Satan's spells and wiles, against false words of heresy, against the knowledge that defiles, against the heart's idolatry, against the wizard's evil craft, against the death wound and the burning, the choking wave and poisoned shaft, protect me Christ, till your returning.

Christ be with me, Christ within me, Christ behind me, Christ before me, Christ beside me, Christ to win me, Christ to comfort and restore me, Christ beneath me, Christ above me, Christ in quiet, Christ in danger, Christ in hearts of all that love me, Christ in mouth of friend and stranger.

I bind unto myself the Name, the strong Name of the Trinity; by invocation of the same: The Three in One, and One in Three, of whom all nature has creation: Eternal Father, Spirit, Word, praise to the Lord of my salvation, salvation is of Christ the Lord. AMEN.

Prayer of Peace of St. Francis of Assisi

Lord make me an instrument of your peace. Where there is hatred, let me sow love. Where there is injury, pardon. Where there is doubt, faith. Where there is despair, hope. Where there is darkness, light. And where there is sadness, joy.

O, Divine Master, grant that I may not so much seek to be consoled as to console, to be understood, as to understand, to be loved, as to love; For it is in giving that we receive, it is in pardoning that we are pardoned, and it is in dying that we are born to eternal life.

A Prayer of St. Thomas Aquinas on Receiving the Eucharist

LORD, Father all-powerful, and ever-living God, I thank Thee, for even though I am a sinner, Thy unprofitable servant, not because of my worth, but in the kindness of Thy mercy, Thou hast fed me with the precious Body and Blood of Thy Son, our Lord Jesus Christ.

I pray that this holy communion may not bring me condemnation and punishment but forgiveness and salvation. May it be a of faith and a shield of good will. May it purify me from evil ways and put an end to my evil passions. May it bring me charity and patience, humility and , and growth in power to do good. May it be my strong defense against all my enemies, visible and invisible, and the perfect calming of all my evil impulses, bodily and spiritual. May it unite me more closely to Thee, the one true God and lead me safely through death to everlasting happiness with Thee. And I pray that Thou wiliest lead me, a sinner to the banquet where Thou with Thy Son and Holy Spirit, are true and perfect light, total fulfillment, everlasting joy, gladness without end, and perfect happiness to Thy saints. Grant this through Christ our Lord. AMEN.

ANYWAY by Mother Teresa of Calcutta

People are unreasonable, illogical, and self-centered ... Love them anyway. If you do good, people will accuse you of ulterior motives ... Do good anyway. If you are successful, you win false friends and true enemies ... Succeed anyway. The good you do today will be forgotten tomorrow ... Do good anyway. Honesty and frankness make you vulnerable. ... Be honest and frank anyway. People favor underdogs but follow only top dogs ... Fight for some underdogs anyway. What you spend years building may be destroyed overnight ... Build anyway. People really need help but may attack you if you help them ... Help people anyway. Give the world the best you have, and you'll get kicked in the teeth ... Give the world the best you've got anyway.

The Rosary

The Fifteen Promises of Mary to Christians Who Recite the Rosary Given to St. Dominic and Blessed Alan.

1. Whoever shall faithfully serve me by the recitation of the rosary, shall receive signal graces.

2. I promise my special protection and the greatest graces to all those who shall recite the rosary.

3. The rosary shall be a powerful armor against hell, it will destroy vice, decrease sin, and defeat heresies.

4. It will cause virtue and good works to flourish; it will obtain for souls the abundant mercy of God; it will withdraw the hearts of men from the love of the world and its vanities, and will lift them to the desire of eternal things. Oh, that souls would sanctify themselves by this means.

5. The soul which recommends itself to me by the recitation of the rosary, shall not perish.

6. Whoever shall recite the rosary devoutly, applying himself to the consideration of its sacred mysteries shall never be conquered by misfortune. God will not chastise him in His justice, he shall not perish by an unprovided death; if he be just he shall remain in the grace of God, and become worthy of eternal life.

7.   Whoever shall have a true devotion for the rosary shall not die without the sacraments of the Church.

8.   Those who are faithful to recite the rosary shall have during their life and at their death the light of God and the plenitude of His graces; at the moment of death they shall participate in the merits of the saints in paradise.

9.   I shall deliver from purgatory those who have been devoted to the rosary.

10.   The faithful children of the rosary shall merit a high degree of glory in heaven.

11.   You shall obtain all you ask of me by the recitation of the rosary.

12.   All those who propagate the holy rosary shall be aided by me in their necessities.

13.   I have obtained from my Divine Son that all the advocates of the rosary shall have for intercessors the entire celestial court during their life and at the hour of death.

14.   All who recite the rosary are my sons, and brothers of my only son Jesus Christ.

15.   Devotion of my rosary is a great sign of predestination.

The Prayers of the Rosary

† Sign of the Cross. In the name of the Father, and of the Son, and of the Holy Spirit. AMEN.

In the western tradition, said while making the sign of the Cross by moving the right hand from the forehead to the chest, to the left shoulder, then to the right shoulder. In the eastern tradition this is done with the first two fingers and thumb together, from right to left.

The Apostles' Creed

- Our Father

- Hail Mary
- Hail Mary
- Hail Mary

- Meditation on first mystery

◊ (Medal)

Our Father

- Hail Mary
- Hail Mary
- Hail Mary
- Hail Mary
- Hail Mary
- Hail Mary
- Hail Mary
- Hail Mary
- Hail Mary
- Hail Mary

Glory be
Oh my Jesus

- Meditation on second mystery

Our Father

- Hail Mary
- Hail Mary
- Hail Mary
- Hail Mary
- Hail Mary
- Hail Mary
- Hail Mary
- Hail Mary
- Hail Mary
- Hail Mary

Glory be
Oh my Jesus

- Meditation on third mystery

Our Father

- Hail Mary
- Hail Mary
- Hail Mary
- Hail Mary
- Hail Mary
- Hail Mary
- Hail Mary
- Hail Mary
- Hail Mary
- Hail Mary

Glory be
Oh my Jesus

- Meditation on fourth mystery

Our Father

- Hail Mary
- Hail Mary
- Hail Mary
- Hail Mary
- Hail Mary
- Hail Mary
- Hail Mary
- Hail Mary
- Hail Mary
- Hail Mary

Glory be
Oh my Jesus

- Meditation on fifth mystery

Our Father

- Hail Mary
- Hail Mary
- Hail Mary
- Hail Mary
- Hail Mary
- Hail Mary
- Hail Mary
- Hail Mary
- Hail Mary
- Hail Mary

Glory be
Oh my Jesus

◊ Concluding prayers: Hail, Holy Queen

The Prayers Said with the Rosary

The Apostles' Creed

I believe in God, the Father almighty, creator of heaven and earth.

I believe in Jesus Christ, his only Son, our Lord. He was conceived by the power of the Holy Spirit and born of the Virgin Mary. He suffered under Pontius Pilate, was crucified, died, and was buried. He descended to the dead. On the third day he rose again. He ascended into heaven, and is seated at the right hand of the Father. He will come again to judge the living and the dead.

I believe in the Holy Spirit, the holy catholic Church, the communion of saints, the forgiveness of sins, the resurrection of the body, and the life everlasting.

AMEN.

Our Father

Our Father, who art in heaven, hallowed be thy name thy kingdom come thy will be done on earth as it is in heaven.

Give us this day our daily bread and forgive us our trespasses as we forgive those who trespass against us and lead us not into temptation, but deliver us from evil.

(For the kingdom, the power, and the glory are yours, now and for ever.)

AMEN.

Hail Mary

Hail Mary, full of grace. The Lord is with Thee. Blessed art thou among women, and blessed is the fruit of thy womb, Jesus.

Holy Mary, Mother of God, pray for us sinners, now and at the hour of our death.

AMEN.

Glory be (Prayer of Praise)

Glory be to the Father, and to the Son, and to the Holy Spirit

As it was in the beginning, is now, and will be for ever.

AMEN.

O My Jesus (Requested by the Blessed Virgin Mary at Fatima)

O my Jesus, forgive us our sins, save us from the fires of hell, lead all souls to Heaven, especially those who have the most need of your mercy.

AMEN.

Hail, Holy Queen

Hail, holy queen, mother of mercy, our life, our sweetness, and our hope.

To you we cry, poor banished children of Eve; to you we send up our sighs, mourning and weeping in this valley of tears. Turn then, O most gracious advocate, your eyes of mercy toward us, and after this our exile, show unto us the blessed fruit of your womb, Jesus. O clement, O loving, O sweet virgin Mary.

Pray for us, O holy Mother of God.

Response:

That we may be made worthy of the promises of Christ, Let us pray; O God, whose only begotten Son, by his life, death, and resurrection, has purchased for us the rewards of eternal life, grant, we beseech you, that meditating upon these mysteries of the most holy rosary of the Blessed Virgin Mary, we may imitate what they contain and obtain what they promise.

Through the same, Christ our Lord.

AMEN.

THE CYCLE OF THE ROSARY

- The Joyful Mysteries are usually said on Mondays.

- The Sorrowful Mysteries are usually said on Tuesdays and Fridays.

- The Glorious Mysteries are usually said on Wednesdays and Saturdays.

- The Luminous Mysteries are usually said on Wednesdays and Saturdays.

- The Mystery for Sunday varies with the seasons of the liturgical year. The Joyful Mysteries are on Sundays during the seasons of Advent, Christmas, and the first period of Ordinary time.

- Ash Wednesday marks the end of the first period of Ordinary time and the beginning of the season of Lent. During the season of Lent, the Sorrowful Mysteries are said on Sundays.

- The Easter season, which starts Easter Sunday, is the next season of the liturgical year. During the Easter season, and the second period of Ordinary time, which starts on Pentecost Sunday, the Glorious Mysteries are said on Sundays. The second period of Ordinary time ends with the first Sunday of Advent, when the Joyful Mysteries are said again.

THE MYSTERIES OF THE ROSARY

The Joyful Mysteries

1.   The Annunciation to Mary: The Messenger of God Announces to Mary that she is to be the Mother of God.

Theme: Humility.

Then the angel said to her, "Do not be afraid, Mary, for you have found favor with God. Behold, you will conceive in your womb and bear a son, and you shall name him Jesus. He will be great and will be called Son of the Most High, and the Lord God will give him the throne of David his father, and he will rule over the house of Jacob forever, and of his kingdom there will be no end." Luke 1:30-33

2.   The Visitation of Mary: Mary visits and helps her cousin Elizabeth.

Theme: Love of Neighbor.

When Elizabeth heard Mary's greeting, the infant leaped in her womb, and Elizabeth, filled with the holy Spirit, cried out in a loud voice and said, "Most blessed are you among women, and blessed is the fruit of your womb." Luke 1:41-42

3.   The Nativity of Our Lord: Mary gives birth to Jesus in a stable in Bethlehem.

Theme: Spirit of Poverty.

The angel said to them, "Do not be afraid; for behold, I proclaim to you good news of great joy that will be for all people. For today, in the city of David a savior has been born for you who is Messiah and Lord" Luke 2:10-11

4.   The Presentation of the Child Jesus in the Temple: Jesus is presented in the Temple.

Theme: Obedience to God's Will

"Now, Master, you may let your servant go in peace, according to your word, for my eyes have seen your salvation, which you prepared in sight of all the peoples, a light for revelation to the Gentiles, and glory for your people Israel." Luke 2:29-32

5.   The Finding of Our Lord in the Temple.

Theme: Fidelity to Vocation, Joy in finding Jesus.

When his parents saw him, they were astonished, and his mother said to him, "Son, why have you done this to us? Your father and I have been looking for you with great anxiety." And he said to them, "Why were you looking for me? Did you not know that I must be in my Father's house?" But they did not understand what he said to them. He went down with them and came to Nazareth, and was obedient to them; and his mother kept all these things in her heart. And Jesus advanced [in] wisdom and age and favor before God and man. Luke 2:48-52

The Sorrowful Mysteries

1.   The Agony in the Garden: Jesus undergoes his agony in the Garden of Gethsemane.

Theme: Spirit of Prayer, Sorrow for Sin

Then he said to them, "My soul is sorrowful even to death. Remain here and keep watch with me." He advanced a little and fell prostrate in prayer, saying, "My Father, if it is possible, let this cup pass from me; yet, not as I will, but as you will." Matthew 26:38-39

2.   The Scourging at the Pillar: Jesus is scourged at the pillar.

Theme: Modesty and Purity

Then Pilate took Jesus and had him scourged. John 19:1

3.   The Crowning with Thorns: Jesus is crowned with thorns.

Theme: Courage

The soldiers led him away inside the palace, that is, the praetorium, and assembled the whole cohort. They clothed him in purple and, weaving a crown of thorns, placed it on him. Mark 15:16-17

4.   The Carrying of the Cross: Jesus carries the cross to Calvary.

Theme: Patience in Suffering

[A]nd carrying the cross himself he went out to what is called the Place of the Skull, in Hebrew, Golgotha. John 19:18

5. The Crucifixion and Death of Our Lord on the Cross: Jesus dies on the cross for our sins.

Theme: Self-denial, Perseverance

After this, aware that everything was now finished, in order that the scripture might be fulfilled, Jesus said, "I thirst." There was a vessel filled with common wine. So they put a sponge soaked in wine on a sprig of hyssop and put it up to his mouth. When Jesus had taken the wine, he said, "It is finished." And bowing his head, he handed over the spirit. John 19:28-30

The Glorious Mysteries

1. The Resurrection of Our Lord: Jesus rises from the dead.

Theme: Faith

He said to them, "Do not be amazed! You seek Jesus of Nazareth, the crucified. He has been raised; he is not here. Behold, the place where they laid him. But go and tell his disciples and Peter, 'He is going before you to Galilee; there you will see him, as he told you.'" Mark 16:6-8

2. The Ascension of Our Lord: Jesus ascends into heaven. Hope

While they were looking intently at the sky as he was going, suddenly two men dressed in white garments stood beside them. They said, "Men of Galilee, why are you standing there looking at the sky? This Jesus who has been taken up from you into heaven will return in the same way as you have seen him going into heaven." Acts 1:10-11

3.	The Descent of the Holy Spirit upon the Apostles: The Holy Spirit comes to the apostles and the Blessed Mother.

Theme: Wisdom, Love of God, Zeal, Fortitude

When the time for Pentecost was fulfilled, they were all in one place together. And suddenly there came from the sky a noise like a strong driving wind, and it filled the entire house in which they were. Then there appeared to them tongues as of fire, which parted and came to rest on each one of them. Acts 2:1-4

4.	The Assumption of the Blessed Virgin Mary into Heaven: The Mother of Jesus is taken into heaven.

Theme: Eternal Happiness, Grace of a

Happy Death

As an apple tree among the trees of the woods, so is my lover among men. I delight to rest in his shadow, and his fruit is sweet to my mouth. He brings me into the banquet hall and his emblem over me is love. Strengthen me with raisin cakes, refresh me with apples, for I am faint with love. His left hand is under my head and his right arm embraces me. Song of Songs 2:3-6

5.	The Coronation of Our Lady as Queen of Heaven and Earth: Mary is crowned queen of heaven and earth.

Theme: Devotion to Mary and Final Perseverance, Trust in Mary's Intercession

And Mary said, "My soul proclaims the greatness of the Lord; my spirit rejoices in God my savior. For he has looked upon his handmaid's lowliness; behold, from now on will all ages call me blessed." Luke 1:46-4

The Luminous Mysteries

1.   The Baptism of Our Lord in the Jordan

Lesson: Openness to the Holy Spirit

Then Jesus came from Galilee to John at the Jordan to be baptized by him. John tried to prevent him, saying, "I need to be baptized by you, and yet you are coming to me?" Jesus said to him in reply, "Allow it now, for thus it is fitting for us to fulfill all righteousness." Then he allowed him. After Jesus was baptized, he came up from the water and behold, the heavens were opened [for him], and he saw the Spirit of God descending like a dove [and] coming upon him. 17 And a voice came from the heavens, saying, "This is my beloved Son, with whom I am well pleased." - Matthew 3:13-17

2.   The Self-Manifestation of Our Lord at the wedding of Cana

Lesson: To Jesus through Mary

On the third day there was a wedding in Cana in Galilee, and the mother of Jesus was there. 2 Jesus and his disciples were also invited to the wedding. 3 When the wine ran short, the mother of Jesus said to him, "They have no wine." [And] Jesus said to her, "Woman, how does your concern affect me? My hour has not yet come." His mother said to the servers, "Do whatever he tells you." Now there were six stone water jars there for Jewish ceremonial washings, each holding twenty to thirty gallons. Jesus told them, "Fill the jars with water." So they filled them to the brim. Then he told them, "Draw some out now and take it to the headwaiter." So they took it. And when the headwaiter tasted the water that had become wine, without knowing where it came from (although the servers who had drawn the water knew), the headwaiter called the bridegroom and said to him, "Everyone serves good wine first, and then when people have drunk freely, an inferior one; but you have kept the good wine until now." Jesus did this as the beginning of his signs in Cana in Galilee and so revealed his glory, and his disciples began to believe in him. - John 2:1-11

3.   The Proclamation of the Kingdom of God, with the Call to Conversion

Lessons: Repentance and Trust in God

After John had been arrested, Jesus came to Galilee proclaiming the gospel of God: "This is the time of fulfillment. The kingdom of God is at hand. Repent, and believe in the gospel." - Mark 1:14-15

4.   The Transfiguration

Lessons: Desire for Holiness

While he was praying his face changed in appearance and his clothing became dazzling white. - Luke 9:29

5.   The Institution of the Eucharist

Lessons: Adoration

Then he took the bread, said the blessing, broke it, and gave it to them, saying, "This is my body, which will be given for you; do this in memory of me." 20 And likewise the cup after they had eaten, saying, "This cup is the new covenant in my blood, which will be shed for you." - Luke 22:19-20

References

Handbook for Today's Catholic, copyright © 1994, Liguori Publications

Pray The Rosary Daily, copyright © 1991, Marian Helpers

How to Say the Rosary, copyright © 1991, TAN Books & Publishers, Inc.

The New American Bible for Catholics, copyright © 1970, the Confraternity of Christian Doctrine.

INTRODUCTION TO THE JESUS PRAYER

by H.R.H. Princess Ileana of Romania

Reprinted with permission of Forward Movement Publications, 412 Sycamore St. Cincinnati, Ohio.

Lord Jesus Christ, Son of God, have mercy upon me, a sinner.

I have often read the Jesus Prayer in prayer books and heard it in church, but my attention was drawn to it first some years ago in Rumania. There in a small Monastery of Smbata, tucked away at the foot of the Carpathians in the heart of the deep forest, its little white church reflected in a crystal clear mountain pond, I met a monk who practiced the "prayer of the heart". Profound peace and silence reigned at Smbata in those days; it was a place of rest and strength.-I pray God it still is.

I have wandered far since I last saw Smbata, and all the while the Jesus Prayer lay as a precious gift buried in my heart. It remained inactive until a few years ago, when I read *The Way of a Pilgrim.** Since then I have been seeking to practice it continually. At times I lapse; nonetheless, the prayer has opened unbelievable vistas within my heart and soul.

The Jesus Prayer, or the Prayer of the Heart, centers on the Holy Name itself. It may be said in its entirety: "Lord Jesus Christ, Son of God, have mercy upon me, a sinner"; it may be changed to "us sinners" or to other persons named, or it may be shortened. The power lies in the name of Jesus; thus "Jesus" alone, may fulfill the whole need of the one who prays.

384

The Prayer goes back to the New Testament and has had a long, traditional use. The method of contemplation based upon the Holy Name is attributed to St. Simeon, called the New Theologian (949-1022). When he was 14 years old, St. Simeon had a vision of heavenly light in which he seemed to be separated from his body. Amazed, and overcome with an overpowering joy, he felt a consuming humility, and cried, borrowing the Publican's prayer (Luke 18:13), "Lord Jesus, have mercy upon me." Long after the vision had disappeared, the great joy returned to St. Simeon each time he repeated the prayer; and he taught his disciples to worship likewise. The prayer evolved into its expanded form: "Lord Jesus Christ, Son of God, have mercy upon me, a sinner." In this guise it has come down to us frown generation to generation of pious monks and laymen.

The invocation of the Holy Name is not peculiar to the Orthodox Church but is used by Roman Catholics, Anglicans, and Protestants, though to a lesser degree. On Mount Sinai and Athos the monks worked out a whole system of contemplation based upon this simple prayer, practiced in complete silence. These monks came to be known as Quietists (in Greek: "Hesychasts").

St. Gregory Palamas (1296-1359), the last of the great Church Fathers, became the exponent of the Hesychasts. He won, after a long drawn out battle, an irrefutable place for the Jesus Prayer and the Quietists within the Church. In the 18th century when tsardom hampered monasticism in Russia, and the Turks crushed Orthodoxy in Greece, the Neamtzu monastery in Moldavia (Rumania) became one of the great centers for the Jesus Prayer.

The Prayer is held to be so outstandingly spiritual because it is focused wholly on Jesus: all thoughts, striving, hope, faith and love are outpoured in devotion to God the Son. It fulfills two basic injunctions of the New Testament. In one, Jesus said: I say unto you, Whatsoever ye shall ask the Father; in my name, he will give it you. Hitherto have ye asked nothing in my name: ask, and ye shall receive, that your joy may be full." (John 16:23, 24). In the other precept we find St. Paul's injunction to pray without ceasing,

(I. Thess. 5:17). Further, it follows Jesus' instructions upon how to pray (which He gave at the same time He taught His followers the Lord's Prayer). When thou prayest, enter into thy closet, and when thou hast shut thy door, pray to thy Father which is in secret; and thy Father which seeth in secret shall reward thee openly. (Math 6:6).

And Jesus taught that all impetus, good and bad, originates in men's hearts. "A good man out of the good treasure of his heart bringeth forth that which is good; and an evil man out of the evil treasure of his heart bringeth forth that which is evil: for of the abundance of the heart his mouth speaketh" (Luke 6:45).

Upon these and many other precepts of the New Testament as well as the Old, the Holy Fathers, even before St. Simeon, based their fervent and simple prayer. They developed a method of contemplation in which unceasing prayer became as natural as breathing, following the rhythmic cadence of the heart beat.

All roads that lead to God are beset with pitfalls

because the enemy (Satan) ever lies in wait to trip us up. He naturally attacks most assiduously when we are bent on finding our way to salvation, for that is what he most strives to hinder. In mystical prayer the temptations we encounter exceed all others in danger; because our thoughts are on a higher level, the allurements are proportionally subtler. Someone said that "mysticism started in mist and ended in schism"; this cynical remark, spoken by an unbeliever, has a certain truth in it. Mysticism is of real spiritual value only when it is practiced with absolute sobriety.

At one time a controversy arose concerning certain Quietists who fell into excessive acts of piety and fasting because they lost the sense of moderation upon which our Church lays so great a value. We need not dwell upon misuses of the Jesus Prayer, except to realize that all exaggerations are harmful and that we should at all times use self-restraint. "Practice of the Jesus Prayer is the traditional fulfillment of the injunction of the Apostle Paul to 'pray always:' it has nothing to do with the mysticism which is the heritage of pagan ancestry."*

The Orthodox Church is full of deep mystic life which she guards and encompasses with the strength of her traditional rules; thus her mystics seldom go astray. "The 'ascetical life' is a life in which 'acquired' virtues, i.e., virtues resulting from a personal effort, only accompanied by that general grace which God grants to every good will, prevail. The 'mystical life' is a life in which the gifts of the Holy Spirit are predominant over human efforts, and in which 'infused' virtues are predominant over the 'acquired' ones; the soul has become more passive than active. Let us use a classical comparison. Between the ascetic life, that is, the life in which human action predominates, and the mystical life, that is, the life in which God's action predominates, there is the same difference as between rowing a boat and sailing it; the oar is the ascetic effort, the sail is the mystical passivity which is unfurled to catch the divine wind"* The Jesus Prayer is the core of mystical prayer, and it can be used by anyone, at any time. There is nothing mysterious about this (let us not confuse "mysterious" with "mystic"). We start by following the precepts and examples frequently given by our Lord. First, go aside into a quiet place: Come ye yourselves apart into a desert place, and rest awhile" (Mark 6:31); "Study to be quiet" (I. Thess. 4:11); then pray in secret--alone and in silence.

The phrases "to pray in secret alone and in silence" need, I feel, a little expanding. "Secret" should be understood as it is used in the Bible: for instance, Jesus tells us to do our charity secretly--not letting the left hand know what the right one does. We should not parade our devotions, nor boast about them. "Alone" means to separate ourselves from our immediate surroundings and disturbing influences. As a matter of fact, never are we in so much company as when we pray " . . . seeing we also are compassed about with so great a cloud of witnesses . . ." (Hebrews 12:1). The witnesses are all those who pray: Angels, Archangels, saints and sinners, the living and the dead. It is in prayer, especially the Jesus Prayer, that we become keenly aware of belonging to the living body of Christ. In "silence" implies that we do not speak our prayer audibly. We do not even meditate on the words; we use them only to reach beyond them to the essence itself.

In our busy lives this is not easy, yet it can be done--we can each of us find a few minutes in which to use a prayer consisting of only a few words, or even only one. This prayer should be repeated quietly, unhurriedly, thoughtfully. Each thought should be concentrated on Jesus, forgetting all else, both joys and sorrows. Any stray thought, however good or pious, can become an obstacle. When you embrace a dear one you do not stop to meditate how and why you love--you just love wholeheartedly. It is the same when spiritually we grasp Jesus the Christ to our heart. If we pay heed to the depth and quality of our love, it means that we are preoccupied with our own reactions, rather than giving ourselves unreservedly to Jesus--holding nothing back. *Think* the prayer as you breathe in and out; calm both mind and body, using as rhythm the heartbeat. Do not search for words, but go on repeating the Prayer, or Jesus' name alone, in love and adoration. That is ALL! Strange--in this little there is more than all!

It is good to have regular hours for prayer and to retire whenever possible to the same room or place, possibly before an icon. The icon is loaded with the objective presence of the One depicted, and thus greatly assists our invocation. Orthodox monks and nuns find that to use a rosary (prayer rope) helps to keep the attention fixed. Or you may find it best quietly to close your eyes--focusing them inward.

The Jesus Prayer can be used for worship and petition; as intercession, invocation, adoration, and as thanksgiving. It is a means by which we lay all that is in our hearts, both for God and man, at the feet of Jesus. It is a means of communion with God and with all those who pray. The fact that we can train our hearts to go on praying even when we sleep, keeps us uninterruptedly within the community of prayer. This is no fanciful statement; many have experienced this life-giving fact. We cannot, of course, attain this continuity of prayer all at once, but it is achievable; for all that is worthwhile we must ". . . run with patience the race that is set before us . . ." (Hebrews 12:1).

I had a most striking proof of uninterrupted communion with all those who pray when I lately underwent surgery. I lay long under anesthesia. "Jesus" had been my last conscious thought, and the first word on my lips as I awoke. It was marvelous beyond words to find that although I knew nothing of what was happening to my body I never lost cognizance of being prayed-for and of praying myself. After such an experience one no longer wonders that there are great souls who devote their lives exclusively to prayer.

Prayer has always been of very real importance to me, and the habit formed in early childhood of morning and evening prayer has never left me; but in the practice of the Jesus Prayer I am but a beginner. I would, nonetheless, like to awaken interest in this prayer because, even if I have only touched the hem of a heavenly garment, I have touched it--and the joy is so great I would share it with others. It is not every man's way of prayer; you may not find in it the same joy that I find, for your way may be quite a different one--yet equally bountiful.

In fear and joy, in loneliness and companionship, it is ever with me. Not only in the silence of daily devotions, but at all times and in all places. It transforms, for me, frowns into smiles; it beautifies, as if a film had been washed off an old picture so that the colors appear clear and bright, like nature on a warm spring day after a shower. Even despair has become attenuated and repentance has achieved its purpose.

When I arise in the morning, it starts me joyfully upon a new day. When I travel by air, land, or sea, it sings within my breast When I stand upon a platform and face my listeners, it beats encouragement. When I gather my children around me, it murmurs a blessing. And at the end of a weary day, when I lay me down to rest, I give my heart over to Jesus: "(Lord) into thy hands I commend my spirit". I sleep--but my heart as it beats prays on: "JESUS."

STATIONS OF THE CROSS

AN ACT OF CONTRITION

O my God, my Redeemer, behold me here at Thy feet. From the bottom of my heart I am sorry for all my sins, because by them I have offended Thee, Who art infinitely good. I will die rather than offend thee again.

FIRST STATION: Jesus is condemned to Death

V. We adore Thee, O Christ, and bless Thee.
R. Because by Thy holy cross Thou hast redeemed the world.

My Jesus, often have I signed The death warrant by my sins; save me by Thy death from that eternal death which I have so often deserved.

Our Father.... Hail Mary.... Glory be....

V.   Jesus Christ Crucified.
R.   Have mercy on Us.
V.   May the souls of the faithful departed, through the mercy of God, Rest in peace.
R.   Amen.

SECOND STATION: Jesus bears His Cross

V.   We adore Thee, O Christ, and bless Thee.
R.   Because by Thy holy cross Thou hast redeemed the world.

My Jesus, Who by Thine own will didst take on Thee the most heavy cross I made for Thee by my sins, oh, make me feel their heavy weight, and weep for them ever while I live.

Our Father.... Hail Mary.... Glory be....

V.   Jesus Christ Crucified.

R.   Have mercy on Us.

V.   May the souls of the faithful departed, through the mercy of God, Rest in peace.

R.   Amen.

THIRD STATION: Jesus falls the First time Beneath the Cross

V.   We adore Thee, O Christ, and bless Thee.

R.   Because by Thy holy cross Thou hast redeemed the world.

My Jesus, the heavy burden of my sins is on Thee, and bears Thee down beneath the cross. I loathe them, I detest them; I call on Thee to pardon them; my Thy grace aid me never more to commit them.

Our Father.... Hail Mary.... Glory be....

V.   Jesus Christ Crucified.

R.   Have mercy on Us.

V.   May the souls of the faithful departed, through the mercy of God, Rest in peace.

R.   Amen.

FOURTH STATION: Jesus Meets His Holy Mother

V.   We adore Thee, O Christ, and bless Thee.

R.   Because by Thy holy cross Thou hast redeemed the world.Jesus most suffering, Mary Mother most sorrowful, if, by my sins, I caused you pain and anguish in the past, by God's assisting grace it shall be so no more; rather be you my love henceforth till death.

Our Father.... Hail Mary.... Glory be....

V.   Jesus Christ Crucified.

R.   Have mercy on Us.

V.   May the souls of the faithful departed, through the mercy of God, Rest in peace.

R.   Amen.

FIFTH STATION: Simon of Cyrene helps Jesus to carry the cross.

V.   We adore Thee, O Christ, and bless Thee.

R.   Because by Thy holy cross, Thou hast redeemed the world.

My Jesus, blest, thrice blest was he who aided Thee to bear the cross.

Blest too shall I be if I aid Thee to bear the cross, by patiently bowing my neck to the crosses Thou shalt send me during life. My Jesus, give me grace to do so

Our Father.... Hail Mary.... Glory be....

V.   Jesus Christ Crucified.

R.   Have mercy on Us.

V.   May the souls of the faithful departed, through the mercy of God, Rest in peace.

R.   Amen.

SIXTH STATION: Jesus and Veronica

V.   We adore Thee, O Christ, and bless Thee.

R.   Because by Thy holy cross, Thou hast redeemed the world.

My tender Jesus, Who didst deign to print Thy sacred face upon the cloth with which Veronica wiped the sweat from off Thy brow, print in my soul deep, I pray Thee, the lasting memory of Thy bitter pains.

Our Father.... Hail Mary.... Glory be....

V. Jesus Christ Crucified.
R. Have mercy on Us.
V. May the souls of the faithful departed, through the mercy of God, Rest in peace. R. Amen.

SEVENTH STATION: Jesus Fall a Second Time

V. We adore Thee, O Christ, and bless Thee.
R. Because by Thy holy cross, Thou hast redeemed the world.

My Jesus, often have I sinned and often, by sin, beaten Thee to the ground beneath the cross. Help me to use the efficacious means of grace that I may never fall again.

Our Father.... Hail Mary.... Glory be....

V. Jesus Christ Crucified.
R. Have Mercy on Us.
V. May the souls of the faithful departed, through the mercy of God, Rest in peace.
R. Amen.

EIGHTH STATION: Jesus comforts the women of Jerusalem

V. We adore Thee, O Christ, and bless Thee.
R. Because by Thy holy cross Thou hast redeemed the world.

My Jesus, Who didst comfort the pious women of Jerusalem who wept to see Thee bruised and torn, comfort my soul with Thy tender pity, for in Thy pity lies my trust. May my heart ever answer Thine.

Our Father.... Hail Mary.... Glory be....

V.   Jesus Christ Crucified.

R.   Have Mercy on Us.

V.   May the souls of the faithful departed, through the mercy of God, Rest in peace.

R.   Amen.

NINTH STATION: Jesus falls a third time

V.   We adore Thee, O Christ, and bless Thee.

R.   Because by Thy holy cross Thou hast redeemed the world.

My Jesus, by all the bitter woes Thou didst endure when for the third time the heavy cross bowed Thee to the earth, never, I beseech Thee, let me fall again into sin. Ah, my Jesus, rather let me die than ever offend Thee again.

Our Father.... Hail Mary.... Glory be....

V.   Jesus Christ Crucified.

R.   Have mercy on Us.

V.   May the souls of the faithful departed, through the mercy of God, Rest in Peace.

R.   Amen.

TENTH STATION: Jesus is stripped of His garments and given gall to drink

V.   We adore Thee, O Christ, and bless Thee.

R.   Because by Thy holy cross Thou hast redeemed the world.

My Jesus, stripped of Thy garments and drenched with gall, strip me of love for things of earth, and make me loathe all that savors of the world and sin.

Our Father.... Hail Mary.... Glory be....

V. Jesus Christ Crucified.

R. Have mercy on Us.

V. May the souls of the faithful departed, through the mercy of God, Rest in peace.

R. Amen.

ELEVENTH STATION: Jesus is nailed to the Cross

V. We adore Thee, O Christ, and bless Thee.

R. Because by Thy holy cross Thou hast redeemed the world.

My Jesus, by Thine agony when the cruel nails pierced Thy tender hands and feet and fixed them to the cross, make me crucify my flesh by Christian penance.

Our Father.... Hail Mary.... Glory be....

V. Jesus Christ Crucified.

R. Have mercy on Us.

V. May the souls of the faithful departed, through the mercy of God, Rest in peace.

R. Amen.

TWELFTH STATION: Jesus Dies

V. We adore Thee, O Christ, and bless Thee.

R. Because by Thy holy cross Thou hast redeemed the world.

My Jesus, three hours didst Thou hang in agony, and then die for me; let me die before I sin, and if I live, live for Thy love and faithful service.

Our Father.... Hail Mary.... Glory be....

V. Jesus Christ Crucified.

R. Have mercy on Us.

V.   May the souls of the faithful departed, through the mercy of God, Rest in peace.

R.   Amen.

THIRTEENTH STATION: Jesus is taken from the cross and laid in Mary's arms

V.   We adore Thee, O Christ, and bless Thee.

R.   Because by Thy holy cross Thou hast redeemed the world.

O Mary, Mother most sorrowful, the sword of grief pierced thy soul when thou didst see Jesus lying lifeless on thy bosom; obtain for me hatred of sin because sin slew thy Son and wounded thine own heart, and grace to live a Christian life and save my soul.

Our Father.... Hail Mary.... Glory be....

V.   Jesus Christ Crucified.

R.   Have mercy on Us.

V.   May the souls of the faithful departed, through the mercy of God, Rest in peace.

R.   Amen.

FOURTEENTH STATION: Jesus is laid in the tomb

V.   We adore Thee, O Christ, and bless Thee.

R.   Because by Thy holy cross Thou hast redeemed the world.

My Jesus, beside Thy body in the tomb I, too, would lie dead; but if I live, let it be for Thee, so as one day to enjoy with Thee in heaven the fruits of Thy passion and Thy bitter death.

Our Father.... Hail Mary.... Glory be....

V.   Jesus Christ Crucified.

R.   Have mercy on Us.

V.   May the souls of the faithful departed, through the mercy of God, Rest in peace.

R.   Amen.

LET US PRAY

O God, Who by the precious blood of Thine only-begotten Son didst sanctify the standard of the cross; grant we beseech Thee, that we who rejoice in the glory of the same holy cross may feel everywhere the gladness of Thy sovereign protection. Through the same Christ our Lord... Amen ....

ABOUT ASCENSION

The Ascension Alliance and Community of Ascensionists is a religious jurisdiction and congregation; an Independent Catholic organization; part of the one Mystical Body of Christ; a Church; an umbrella religious organization; and expression of God's mystical movement of Spirit. We draw our lines of apostolic succession from the historic churches of the West and East, although we are not a part of the Roman Catholic or Eastern Orthodox churches. We derive our chief western line through the Old Catholic (and Liberal Catholic) churches of Europe, which separated from the see at Rome in the early 1700s. Our principal eastern line comes from the ancient churches of India, which are believed to have been established by the Apostle Thomas in the year 52, C.E., and which were served by Assyrian and Syrian Orthodox bishops for generations. We like to think of ourselves as born of a "free" Catholic vision and a much larger stirring of Spirit, which beckons us to transcend old ways that no longer work, ascend to higher levels of consciousness, and be transformed. In addition, we are dedicated to helping other seekers who wish to do the same.

**We Joyfully Celebrate the Sacraments
in Communities Worldwide**

**Mailing Address:
P.O. Box 167, Vaughn, WA 98394**

Website: ascensionalliance.org

www.ingramcontent.com/pod-product-compliance
Lightning Source LLC
Chambersburg PA
CBHW060236100426
42742CB00011B/1552